P9-CJQ-241

INSTANT EMPIRE

INSTANT EMPIRE

SADDAM HUSSEIN'S

★ ★ ★

AMBITION FOR IRAQ

BY

SIMON HENDERSON

Mercury House, Incorporated
San Francisco

Riverside Community College
Library

MAY   '92   4800 Magnolia Avenue
Riverside, California 92506

DS79.66.H87 H46 1991
Henderson, Simon, 1950–
Instant empire : Saddam
Hussein's ambition for Iraq

Copyright © 1991 by Simon Henderson

Published in the United States by
Mercury House
San Francisco, California

All rights reserved, including, without limitation, the right of publisher to sell directly to end users of this and other Mercury House books. No part of this book may be reproduced in any form or by any electronic or mechanical means, including information storage and retrieval systems, without permission in writing from the publisher, except by a reviewer who may quote brief passages in a review.

Mercury House and colophon are registered trademarks
of Mercury House, Incorporated

Printed on acid-free paper
Manufactured in the United States of America

Library of Congress Cataloging-in-Publication Data

Henderson, Simon, 1950–
  Instant empire : Saddam Hussein's ambition for Iraq / by Simon Henderson.
    p. cm.
  ISBN 1–56279–006–4 (cloth) : $21.95. — ISBN 1–56279–007–2 (paper) :
$14.95
    1. Husayn, Saddam. 2. Presidents—Iraq—Biography. 3. Iraq—Politics and
government. I. Title.
DS79.66.H87H46   1991
956.704'3'092—dc20   90–23187
                                                              CIP

To Dina

★ ★ ★

Contents

★ ★ ★
Preface

Instant Empire is the culmination of seven years of personal interest in the politics of Iraq. Starting from a base of almost total ignorance, I steadily built my knowledge of the country's economy, political structure, and military power. In the last four years I have become particularly interested in the personality of President Saddam Hussein.

The final draft of the book was completed a few days before January 16, 1991, when the US-led coalition forces started their effort to push Iraq from Kuwait, an event that caused the final chapter to be rewritten. Otherwise, despite its title, this is not an instant book, but rather my attempt to show how Saddam grew to become a menace, and how many misunderstood him.

Articles that I have written on Iraq have appeared in the *Financial Times* of London; *Mideast Markets,* the specialist newsletter owned by the Financial Times until May 1990; and the quarterly economic reviews of Iraq published by the Economist Intelligence Unit of London. (I was the editor of *Mideast Markets* from 1981 until its sale, and the author of the *Economist Iraq* quarterly from mid-1987 until early 1990.)

During my time as a journalist specializing in the Middle East, I have traveled widely in the area, including five of the countries bordering Iraq: Turkey, Syria, Jordan, Kuwait, and Iran. My first and only visit to Iraq was in July 1986, during which the atmosphere of suspicion and the official encouragement of fear were all too apparent. Deciding afterward to concentrate my research on Saddam himself, I also concluded that it would be prudent not to return to Iraq while he remained in power.

I am grateful to the many people over the years who have helped me to develop my understanding of Iraq. Many gave generously of their time and knowledge during the writing of this book. A good number — about twenty — spoke on the condition that they not be identified. These requests for anonymity were made for a variety of reasons: some of these people hold positions in governments that prohibit them from speaking to journalists; some fear retribution by Saddam's agents; and some want to continue traveling to Iraq to do business. The motive of everyone who spoke to me was simple — that the book be good, and accurate. Although some of these people supported Saddam, none tried to influence me to write anything contrary to what I felt was the most accurate version of events.

Of those people who are willing to be acknowledged publicly, I am particularly grateful to Ofra Bengio, the Iraq expert at the Dayan Center at Tel Aviv University, who opened my eyes to the range of open source material on the country, and to Jonathan Crusoe, the Iraq writer at the *Middle East Economic Digest* magazine of London, whose memory of Iraq's business dealings is unsurpassed. Other people with whom I have enjoyed discussing Iraq include Christine Moss Helms, a writer and consultant in Washington, DC; Phebe Marr of the National Defense University in Washington, DC; and Amatzia Baram of Haifa University. On matters of weapons proliferation I must thank Leonard Spector of the Carnegie Endowment for Peace in Washington, DC; Randy Rydell, a staff aide to Senator John Glenn; Warren Donnelly of the Congressional Research Service; Gary Milhollin of the Wisconsin Project on Nuclear Proliferation in Washington, DC; and Seth Carus of the Washington Institute for Near East Policy. Peter Galbraith, a staff member of the Senate Foreign Relations Committee, has been generous in sharing his experiences of Iraq with me, and his appreciation of the ups and downs of US-Iraq ties.

In Europe, aside from colleagues at the *Financial Times,* I am grateful to Philip Robins, the head of the Middle East program at the Royal Institute for International Affairs, at Chatham House in London. I have enjoyed a friendly rivalry with Alan George, a freelance writer on superweapons, who shares my disdain of inaccurate articles by others. He contributed some of his knowledge so that the superweapons chapters of this book would be accurate, without insisting on knowing the fresh information that is in them. At the Economist Intelligence Unit, I would like to thank Naomi Sakr, a director, and Sylvia Poelling, the Middle East editor.

Of television journalists with whom I have shared bits of information in order to piece together the larger story, I would like to mention Charles Furneaux and John Ware of the BBC Panorama program, Ian Williams of ITN Channel 4 News, and John Cooley of the London office of ABC News. Many of my scoops on Iraqi weapon projects over the years have come from working with Egmont R. Koch, a German television journalist and writer, whose trust and friendship I value highly.

Jacky Williams enthusiastically helped me find the photographs that I wanted for the book, and dealt with the arduous task of obtaining permissions to use them.

I am particularly grateful to Asher Susser, the head of the Dayan Center for Middle East and African Studies at Tel Aviv University, Israel, for his hospitality and that of his colleagues while I was on sabbatical leave from the *Financial Times* as a Dayan Fellow in January and February 1990. Of his many colleagues to whom I am grateful, I would like to mention Yossi Kostiner and Uriel Dann. I found the center to be a haven of stringent academic research, the standards of which I know that I will not reach.

I am also grateful to my literary agent, Andrew Lownie, for helping in the initial thinking for this book, and to William Brinton, the publisher, and Thomas Christensen, the executive editor of Mercury House, for their faith in me. Amy Einsohn was a hardworking copyeditor, Adrienne Morgan did the fine maps and drawings (except the supergun, which I drew), and Zipporah Collins saw the whole book through its production with scrupulous attention and good humor.

None of this book would have been possible without the encouragement, support, and assistance of my wife, Dina, to whom it is dedicated.

Simon Henderson
London
January 1991

★ ★ ★

Note on Transliteration,
Style, and Sources

There is no universally agreed-upon system for rendering Arabic
words in English. In this book, spelling and forms commonly used
in newspapers are adopted as a convenience for nonspecialist
readers. Similarly, proper names are given forms likely to be most
familiar to Western readers. In the case of Saddam Hussein, it is not
a sign of disrespect or informality to refer to him as Saddam —
indeed, he himself prefers to be called by his given name alone.

Because of the oppressive nature of Saddam Hussein's Iraq, it is
difficult to verify various types of information. In some instances we
may never be certain what happened. With the truth not readily
ascertainable, there is a tendency to see a dark explanation for every
event; for example, people seldom seem to die "naturally" but
rather "mysteriously." In this book, I offer the most credible
interpretation, along with some caveats denoting uncertainty.
Sometimes I have revised and recast what I originally reported in
articles over the past seven years.

★ ★ ★

CHAPTER

1

A Cradle of Ancient Civilization

The independent nation of Iraq was not established until 1932, but a large urban population was living on the land between the Tigris and Euphrates rivers as early as 3000 BC. The five milleniums of Iraq's history are rightly a source of much pride to Saddam Hussein, though, as we shall see, there were long periods of foreign domination and humiliation as well. The lessons of history and reference to its greatest heroes and martyrs permeate Saddam's political speeches; if we are to understand Saddam, we must try to understand his version of Iraqi history, its splendors and its failures.

Mesopotamia (Greek for "the land between two rivers") is the name classical Western historians have given to the area surrounding the Tigris and Euphrates rivers. In Arabic, the region was called Rafidain (also meaning "land of two rivers"), a term still commonly used in Iraq. To the east and west of the river plain are hundreds of miles of desert, but the two rivers supported enough agriculture to feed vast populations. Among the earliest Mesopotamian cities were

Ur (home of the Old Testament patriarch Abraham) and Lagash, to the south, which was populated by the Sumerians. Each city was believed to be under the protection of its own god, for whom a ziggurat—a huge terraced temple—was built. One of the biggest ziggurats was at Ur, the remains of which survive today.

Situated on waterways close to the Persian Gulf, the prosperity of Mesopotamia's cities reflected their military prowess and their position on trading routes. The rivers provided means of transport from the Gulf almost as far as the Mediterranean, the so-called Fertile Crescent. Spices from India and fish from the Gulf could be sold in exchange for agricultural products, which were plentiful, particularly after periodic river flooding had been controlled by irrigation canals. The river banks were, and still are, lined by groves of date palms—dates are Iraq's largest export after oil. The idyllic ambiance on the riverbanks has led some people to propose Qurna, the town at the confluence of the Tigris and Euphrates rivers, as the site of the Garden of Eden; a wizened old tree there is known as "Adam's Tree."

The individual city-states of Mesopotamia struggled among themselves for local influence and were also continually threatened by peoples living in adjacent areas, who often saw the cities as ripe for plunder. Military ability became essential for survival and for expansion. Swords and arrows made from metal—particularly the newly discovered, more durable, and much harder bronze—represented one line of technological innovation. The development of the chariot and cavalry tactics also radically changed military strategy over the course of centuries. The Sumerians faded, to be replaced by Amorites, who moved into the area from what is now Syria. Several local dynasties emerged, of which the most important were Assyria, centered around Nineveh and Nimrod in the north on the river Tigris, and Babylon in the south on the river Euphrates. Babylon—the site of which is fifty miles south of modern Baghdad—became preeminent as a result of the statesmanship of Hammurabi, its king from 1792 to 1750 BC, and Babylon's empire at one point stretched deep into present-day Syria and southern

Turkey. Hammurabi also established one of the earliest codes of law.

By 1595 BC this Babylonian empire had collapsed. It was not until 625 BC that Babylon revived under King Nabopolassar, who allied with Medes from northern Persia and Scythians, nomads from northern Asia, to defeat the Assyrians to the north in several battles over the course of twenty years. The prestige of Babylon was further enhanced during the reign of Nebuchadnezzar (605 to 562 BC), a political administrator who extended his empire to Jerusalem, which he conquered in 507 BC. His troops destroyed Jerusalem's temple and brought a majority of the Jewish population back to Babylon. Nebuchadnezzar also directed great artistic and architectural projects, including the Hanging Gardens of Babylon. The city of Babylon at this time was said to have been surrounded by a wall 55 miles long, 340 feet high, and 85 feet thick, with 250 towers and 100 brass gates.

Saddam Hussein is particularly fascinated by Nebuchadnezzar, and he has ordered projects to rebuild Babylon. Archaeologists, however, are pained by Saddam's efforts, for state-ordered projects often halt the excavation of sites, and they worry that fragile ruins are being destroyed by huge earth-levelers and by Sudanese construction workers, brought in as laborers, who scavenge among the ancient ruins to build humble, temporary living quarters for themselves. To complete Saddam's self-glorification, specially inscribed bricks are placed every two yards, recording that they were "rebuilt in the era of the leader Saddam Hussein."

After Nebuchadnezzar, Babylon's days of glory were numbered. To the east, the emergence of the first Persian empire marked the start of a rivalry that continues to the present day. The Persians captured Babylon in 538 BC. Some two hundred years later the Persians were ousted by the Greeks, and again Babylon was dominated by foreigners. Saddam has compared this period to that of his childhood. The difference in his mind between the ancient Persians or Greeks and a modern consortium of imperialist powers and foreign oil companies is not substantial. While the ancient Greeks may be credited in Western culture for establishing modern learning, they had culled much from Babylonian mathematics and geometry, astronomy, medicine, and literature. In Iraq, thus, the ancient Greeks are more remembered for marching to and fro, trying to expand their empire: Alexander the Great died in Babylon, after returning from an expedition to the Indus valley in India.

Saddam's pride in this Babylonian heritage may be stronger than his appreciation of Iraq's Islamic heritage, which dates from the Arab Islamic conquest of then Persian-dominated Iraq in 632 AD. (For example, while names associated with the Prophet Mohammed and Islamic heroes are most popular in Arab countries today, Saddam's two sons—Udai and Qusai—were given names from the pre-Islamic era.) Until the coming of Islam the only Arabs in the area were nomadic tribes, but within a couple of centuries Arab domination was complete, although religious minorities survived. The Kurdish tribes in the north adopted Islam but retained their separate identity and language.

The advent of Islam gave the people of the region a unifying religion, based on a single god rather than many different gods, although the spread of Islam owed much to military force. For Islam the primacy of religion persists to this day. Other religions might be tolerated but are not equal. Perceived heresy, such as the Bahai sect in Iran and elsewhere in the Middle East, or the insult to the prophet in Salman Rushdie's *The Satanic Verses*, still risks draconian punishment. The call to *Jihad*, or holy war, evokes fervent passions. Tolerance for dissent in religious and personal views is not a value in the Islamic religion, although the Islam of the Middle East allows a distinction between public and private interpretations of spiritual matters.

Though Islam has been the source of a unified cultural tradition, it has also bequeathed a schismatic tension between rival sects, the Sunnis and the Shias. Of the two, the Shias are today the majority in Iraq, but some 85 percent of the world's Muslims are Sunnis. And though Iraq has a Shia majority, Saddam and most of his closest colleagues are Sunnis. The Iran-Iraq War was not just a conflict of

Persians versus Arabs but also of Shias versus Sunnis. Outbreaks of fighting between Sunni and Shia communities also occur in Lebanon, where they are just one component of the continual fighting along ethnic lines.

The origins of the Islamic split stem from the rivalry for leadership after Mohammed died in 632. In Arab society, leadership runs in the family as long as a suitable candidate is available. But it was Abu Bakr, a companion of Mohammed's, who assumed the role of caliph, ignoring the rival claims of Ali, Mohammed's cousin and son-in-law. (Ali had married Mohammed's daughter, Fatima.) To make matters worse, Abu Bakr was from a more minor clan. When Abu Bakr died two years later, he was succeeded by Omar, who in turn was succeeded by Othman. By this time, the advancing military conquest of the Islamic armies had slowed, and both war booty and tax revenue were declining. Economic uncertainties led to further tension in the Islamic empire, which now stretched from its origins in southwestern Arabia to include Egypt, Damascus (Syria), and the area south of present-day Iraq. When Othman was murdered in 656, Ali, still pressing for the leadership, seized his opportunity.

Supporters of Othman disputed Ali's leadership and demanded that Othman's murderers be brought to justice. Ali hoped to sidestep the issue, but after a military clash at the Plain of Siffin (on a bend of the Euphrates river), he was forced to go to arbitration before Islamic judges. The full judgment of the arbiters is lost to history, but Ali was removed from his position as caliph, and shortly afterward he was murdered by some of his former supporters. The caliphate was taken over by the Muawiya, who founded the Omaiyad dynasty and made their capital in Damascus.

But Ali's son Hussein took up the challenge to recover the leadership for his family. Plotting a revolt, his band of about two hundred men and women were surrounded at Kerbala. The rebels refused to surrender and were slaughtered by four thousand troops. Hussein and his brother Abbas were killed, and Hussein's head was cut off and presented to the Muawiya caliph. Hussein became the first Shia martyr, and the day of his death in 680, the tenth of the Muslim month of Muharram, is observed as a day of mourning by all Shias. The term *Shia* comes from the Arabic *Shia Ali,* meaning "followers of Ali," and the cornerstone of Shia belief is that Ali, the fourth caliph, was the first true caliph. The Sunnis, in contrast, recognize Abu Bakr, Omar, and Othman as the bona fide successors of Mohammed; the term *Sunni* comes from the Arabic *sunna,* meaning "tradition."

In the mid-eighth century, another branch of the family of Mohammed eventually gained the leadership of mainstream Islam. The Abbasids—the descendants of Abbas, an uncle of Mohammed's—had at first supported the Shias. After a bloody rebellion against the Omaiyads, the Abbasids claimed the caliphate and moved it to Baghdad. This historical struggle between the Damascus-based Omaiyads and the Baghdad-based Abbasids is the background of the modern rivalry between Syria and Iraq.

Despite these internal schisms, the first centuries of Islam were another golden era for the arts and sciences, rivaling the reign of Nebuchadnezzar. It was a renaissance, a *baath* in Arabic, the name chosen by the modern Baath party to recall this age of greatness. Under the caliphate of Omar, the port city at the head of the Gulf, Basra, was founded. Baghdad, on the Tigris River, was built in 762, with the seat of the caliphate moving temporarily to Samarra, further north on the river in 836, where the grand mosque was once the largest in the Muslim world. Nearby there is a huge minaret (tower), 160 feet high, with a famous spiral ramp curling up the outside. On returning to Baghdad the Abbasid caliphs patronized and encouraged medicine, chemistry, geometry, mathematics, astronomy, and poetry. For a time, Baghdad was the leading city in the world, and the writ of the caliphate stretched westward to Spain and eastward to India. During the caliphate of al-Mustansir the renowned Mustansiriya school was founded, then the most prominent university in the Islamic world. But the most famous of the Abbasid caliphs was probably Haroun al-Rashid, who reigned in the early ninth century, at the same time that Charlemagne ruled in Europe. Arabic culture and intellectual life flourished under Haroun al-Rashid and reached their peak during the reign of his successor, his son, Mamun.

Yet during Mamun's time, two hundred years after the establishment of the caliphate, Abbasid rule began to weaken, the administration and military relying on Turkish slaves, who won increasing influence in the court of the caliph. There were niggling attacks by rampaging tribes from central Asia, and the once-great irrigation system that controlled the flooding of the Tigris and the Euphrates fell into disrepair. Agricultural land was replaced by marsh and swamp, which persist to this day over vast tracts of southern Iraq.

In 1258 any residual glory of the Abbasid caliphate was finally ended by the arrival of the Mongol invaders under the leadership of Hülegü, a grandson of Genghis Khan. Murder and pillage ensued. Anything of value too large to be carried off was burned or smashed. Folklore holds that Hülegü ordered all the books in the Mustansiriya library thrown into the Tigris, which for days ran black from the ink. The Mustansiriya school was badly damaged, though not destroyed. (It has since been rebuilt in its original style.) Over the next few centuries Baghdad diminished from a city that was once home to 1.5 million people to a town a tenth that size. The Arabs returned to a nomadic existence. As the land trade route between Europe and Asia was replaced by sea routes, the local economy suffered severely—few taxes could be imposed on sea cargo. The territory of Iraq found itself the tramping ground of two new rival empires, the Ottomans in Turkey and the Safavid dynasty in Persia. As with the empires of old, conquest of territory ebbed and flowed, but by 1634 most of contemporary Iraq was ruled by the Ottomans, who reestablished an administered system of government in the towns and cities.

Soon, however, the Ottomans became less concerned with the outlying regions and focused their attention instead on Constantinople (present-day Istanbul) on the Bosporus Strait between the Black Sea and the Mediterranean. Within the territory of Iraq the Ottomans initiated a system of favoritism toward the minority Sunni Muslim population because they felt the majority Shias might be more loyal to neighboring Persia. Outside Baghdad and the other main towns a system of local dynasties and warlords held sway. Kurds in the north enforced local hegemony, while in the south, near the head of the Gulf, a local tribe largely ignored the central government. Other tribes moved in by nomadic drift from Arabia in the south.

Some stability and some steps toward modernization were achieved when Ottoman rule was transferred to Mamelukes— slaves from the Caucasus region of southern Russia who were bought or captured, converted to Islam and then trained as administrators. It was a thoroughly alien, non-Iraqi system of government, but one that allowed a degree of progress. In the 1840s, however, the Ottomans reexerted themselves and Mameluke rule ended. This time the Turks widened their administrative control, introduced education, and made efforts to settle the tribes. But although the Ottomans were Muslims, they were foreigners who spoke Turkish, not Arabic. By 1914 the Ottoman empire was already crumbling from the center. The so-called Young Turks held out the promise of change, introducing an elected parliament and thereby giving a nudge to Arab nationalism. But Turkey joined the side of Germany in World War I, rather than its traditional ally, Britain, opening the opportunity for yet another empire to make its mark on Iraq.

London already had exerted influence in the Gulf and in Persia as a way of protecting the flank of its greatest imperial treasure, India. In November 1914 British troops occupied first the Fao peninsula and then the port city of Basra. By 1916 the local British commanders had decided to push up the Tigris River, but the force was beaten back by the Turks to Kut, besieged, and forced to surrender after 140 days.

By the end of 1916, though, Britain was ready for another advance. T. E. Lawrence (Lawrence of Arabia), a British officer advising Arabs in western Arabia, was helping to orchestrate an

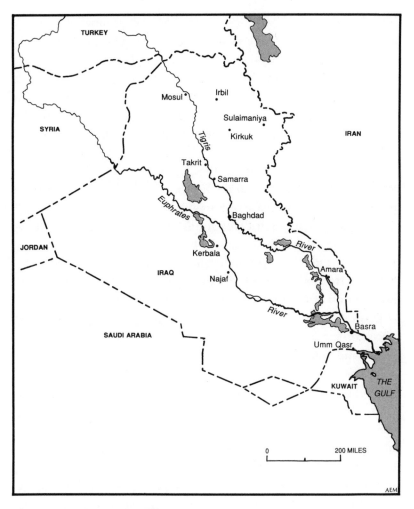

Major cities and geography of Iraq

Arab revolt against the Ottoman Turks. Both the leader of the revolt, Sherif Hussein of Mecca, and Britain's imperial rival, France, had recognized Britain's right to seize and control Basra and Baghdad. So British forces pushed again from the south — this time 600,000 strong — and by March 1917 had taken Basra. Within weeks, British troops had advanced to the north, taking Kirkuk. By the end of the war the British were just short of Mosul, occupying it a week after fighting should have ceased because an armistice had been signed. This incident is the basis for the Turkish view, which lingers today, that what became northern Iraq under the British mandate should in fact be part of Turkey. (A third view is that northern Iraq should be an independent Kurdish state, but the discovery of oil in the region ensured that Baghdad would never allow that.)

The British advance along the Tigris had missed other areas besides the Kurdish lands in the north, notably the Shia holy cities of Kerbala (the burial place of Hussein) and Najaf (the burial place of Ali), and the Euphrates area south of Baghdad. Although these regions were eventually gained, British writ of law did not always run well in them. But generally the British system of administration, or rather its Indian empire variety, was imposed, even down to introduction of the Indian rupee as the legal currency.

Iraq's status after World War I was initially decided at the Paris peace conference in 1919, when the victorious European powers, Britain and France, reneged on any commitments to Arab independence they may have made. The following year, at the San Remo peace conference in Italy, Britain was rewarded with a mandate to govern Iraq. (Britain also was given a mandate to rule the area known as Palestine, which included both banks of the River Jordan, and France won a mandate for Syria.) It was at about this time that the land was first called Iraq, meaning "cliff" in ancient Arabic, supposedly a reference to the rocky precipice west of the river valley.

In Iraq the imposition of the British mandate sparked immediate revolt by a curious combination of nationalists, Shia religious leaders, and tribal leaders, each acting from a variety of motives. Although the rebellion was put down, Britain sent Sir Percy Cox to Basra in October 1920 to set up a procedure for the establishment of an independent Arab government. (Cox is also credited with drawing many of the borders between countries in the area, including the disputed Iraq-Kuwait frontier, as we will see in chapter 2.) A council of state was set up representing the upper classes, the religious leaders, and the tribal sheikhs, but before the council could act the British changed their minds again, now deciding that a monarchy should be established in Iraq. In 1921 Faisal, the third son of Sherif Hussein of Mecca, was installed as king. Faisal was an Arab and a Muslim, but he was also a foreigner, born in a city more than eight hundred miles from Baghdad, on the other side of the Arabian peninsula. Moreover, he was already a failed king, having been thrown out of Damascus after just two years by a combination of Syrian resentment and French intrigue. By making him king, the British were doing him a favor and placing him in their debt. Faisal was lucky: in Arabia, his father was pushed out by Ibn Saud, the founder of the present Saudi kingdom, in 1923 and did not receive another kingdom.

Iraq had become a country, but it was controlled by the British and ruled by the foreigner London had selected. To many Iraqis, the monarchy was wholly unacceptable, another insult to Arab nationalism, another instance of foreign occupation. The struggle to overthrow the monarchy and free Iraq from colonial and postcolonial influences was the principal political theme during Saddam's youth, and foreign intervention in the region is no less abhorred today.

★ ★ ★

Iraq's Borders

Iraq has common frontiers with no fewer than six countries: Kuwait, Iran, Turkey, Syria, Jordan, and Saudi Arabia. For a country of its size — about the same as the state of California, or nearly twice the size of Britain — this is almost a record. Politically, it makes for complications, for Iraq has to maintain relations with six neighbors, knowing that to be at odds with one may be played to advantage with another. In the Middle East, this balancing act is alluded to in the adage "My enemy's enemy is my friend," and it gives rise to "checkerboard diplomacy," where the alternating black and white squares also represent friend and foe. Thus during the Iran-Iraq War the alliance between Iran and Syria greatly discomforted and isolated Iraq. After the war, in 1989, Iraq started a new game by entering into an alliance with North Yemen (in early 1990 North and South Yemen combined to form Yemen), to the annoyance of the state in between — Saudi Arabia.

In terms of international law, the sovereignty of Iraq can be traced back to an exchange of letters during World War I. The so-called McMahon correspondence in 1915 and 1916, between the British high commissioner in Cairo and Sherif Hussein in Mecca, discussed British support for an independent Arab state that would comprise much of present-day Syria, Iraq, Saudi Arabia, Israel, Lebanon, and Jordan, in return for Arab help in defeating the Turks. Britain insisted that the Arabs recognize that British interest "necessitated special administrative arrangements" in the then Turkish vilayets of Baghdad and Basra, the southern two-thirds of modern Iraq. (*Vilayet* is the term used in Ottoman Turkey to describe a large province.)

The McMahon correspondence led to the Sykes-Picot agreement, a secret accord between Britain, France, and Czarist Russia that pointedly did not include any Arab leader. (The agreement was published with unconcealed glee in 1917 by the new Bolshevik revolutionaries in the Soviet Union, who discovered it in the archives of the foreign ministry in Moscow and saw it for what it was—an example of imperialist self-interest over the interests of others.) The agreement, and an associated map that crudely partitioned the area, had been devised by Sir Mark Sykes for Britain and Charles François Georges-Picot for France. It divided the Arab world between France and Britain, with France having paramount influence over present-day Lebanon and Syria, while Britain was to take control of the areas represented by modern Israel, Jordan, and Iraq. The partition was executed after the defeat of Turkey and Germany, when the League of Nations awarded France and Britain mandates to govern these territories.

Some of the new borders respected those recognized under Ottoman rule, notably Iraq's longest border, the easterly one with Iran. But Sykes and Picot had chopped and changed other borders. Thus, even before the invasion of Kuwait in August 1990, the history of modern Iraq is largely a succession of border disputes. And, despite its longevity, the Iran-Iraq border has been the subject of fierce arguments that predate the Iran-Iraq War.

International borders were seldom defined with great precision until this century, when the idea of sovereign nation-states became commonplace. (Nor could borders be defined accurately with earlier mapmaking techniques.) The distinction between the Ottoman empire and Persia, as Iran used to be called, appeared obvious. Early in this century, for example, here, to one side, lived the Persians, and there, to the other side, in what was then Ottoman-ruled territory, lived the Arabs. However, Kurds lived on both sides of the border in the north, and Arabs were living in southern Persia. A rough border had been hammered out in the middle of the nineteenth century, mainly as a result of British imperialistic intrigue intended to check the Russian empire, which London thought might try to expand at the expense of the weak Ottoman and Persia empires. (Until the 1700s the eastern border of the Ottoman empire had extended deep into present-day northern and central Iran — roughly speaking, about halfway to Tehran, the capital. But the border of the Ottoman empire was pushed back over the years, in a series of Persian military thrusts.) But a chain of diplomatic delays postponed the demarcation of the border with Iran until 1914.

Though the diplomats consented, this demarcation was not popular with the Iranians. It was absurd, the Iranian Shia Moslems argued, for a border to separate them from their two great places of pilgrimage, Kerbala and Najaf, to the south of Baghdad. Also, Iran felt it had received the worst of the border settlement, even though the plan confirmed Iran's 1847 annexation of the port of Khorramshahr, on the eastern side of the Shatt al-Arab, which had previously been called Mohammarah (and still is on Iraqi maps). Indeed, after World War I, when Iran's new leader Reza Shah (the father of the shah overthrown by Ayatollah Khomeini in 1979) was asserting his authority, his forces were ruthless in putting down a local Arab leader, Sheikh Khazal, who wanted a degree of autonomy and preferred to look to Iraq for protection, rather than to Tehran. Reza Shah used the whole incident as a means of polishing his (Persian) nationalist credentials.

Despite Iraq's current complaints about the injustices of British imperialism, the backing of Britain helped a great deal in establishing borders that were advantageous to Iraq at the expense of other states. The contentious part of the Iran-Iraq border is along the Shatt al-Arab, as the confluence of the Tigris and Euphrates is called for the last 120 miles or so as they flow jointly into the Gulf. (Locally, the Gulf is called the "Persian Gulf" or the "Arabian Gulf," according to one's ethnic loyalties, although foreigners usually call it the "Persian Gulf" out of accepted usage or because Iran's section of the coastline vastly outdistances that of any other littoral state.)

With British backing, in 1937 (the year of Saddam Hussein's birth), Iraq negotiated a treaty with Iran whereby the border along the Shatt al-Arab was deemed to be at the low-water mark on the Iranian side. (The waterway is tidal up to and beyond the city of Basra.) This notion, already partly in place by virtue of the 1913 agreement with the Ottomans, slightly eased Iran's position, allowing for anchorage of the recently completed refinery at Abadan, half-way up the Shatt toward Basra. The treaty also allowed for free passage of ships of all nations. But in effect Iranian vessels could use the waterway only with Iraqi consent, if not outright permission, for these vessels were required to take on Iraqi pilots and pay transit fees to the port authorities in Basra. Iran blamed British imperialistic pressures for this unfairness and declared that the boundary should be the midpoint of the deep-water channel—the *thalweg*, from the German, meaning the deepest part of the valley—which meanders from one side of the river to the other. Tehran's argument was that such a principle was common international practice, which is debatable as a point of law but surely the most commonsensical and fairest solution.

The dispute remained in limbo until 1969, a year after the Baath party came to power in Iraq. The Iraqi government declared the waterway to be an integral part of its territory and threatened to close the waterway to Iranian shipping. (Baghdad also raised the propaganda temperature by reviving Arab claims to the southwestern Iranian province of Khuzestan, which it referred to as Arabistan.) Iran refused to recognize Iraq's claims and continued sending ships along the river.

By 1974 reconciliation talks between Iraq and Iran were finally under way in Algiers. Iraq was represented by its heir-apparent, the thirty-seven-year-old Saddam Hussein. For leverage in these negotiations and in years of earlier talks, Iran had sponsored Kurdish rebels to carry out a rebellion in Iraq's traditionally Kurdish areas. For their own reasons (curbing an Arab power and embarrassing an ally of Moscow's), Israel and the United States supported the Kurdish rebellion.

Iran and Iraq signed a new border treaty in 1975, recognizing and reaffirming the 1914 land borders. But resentments over concessions persisted, and Saddam wholly abrogated the treaty in 1980 by invading Iran.

Iraq's northern border with Turkey has also had its share of problems. It represents the boundary between Ottoman Turkey and the vilayet of Mosul (which together with the vilayet of Baghdad and the vilayet of Basra make up the territory of modern-day Iraq). The roots of the trouble, which persist to this day, are that Turkish troops were still in the vilayet of Mosul at the end of World War I, when Turkey and Britain signed an armistice agreement at Sèvres, in France. The victorious Allies hoped to partition Turkey, reserving a piece of its territory for an independent Kurdish state to be called Kurdistan. But the Allies backed down when Kemal Ataturk, the founder of modern Turkey, came to power, and the Allies were forced to renegotiate the peace treaty at Lausanne in 1923. At Lausanne, Britain played a useful role for the new republic of Iraq, helping it rebut Turkey's claim to the vilayet of Mosul. The issue was referred to the League of Nations, which in 1926 finally decided in favor of Iraq. In the meantime the Turks backed local troublemakers in an effort to make the area ungovernable, not a difficult task because Mosul's large Kurdish population did not want to be ruled by Turks or Arabs. As a sop, an Anglo-Turco-Iraqi treaty of July 1926 promised the Turks 10 percent of all oil revenues that accrued in the area, an undertaking on which Iraq defaulted. (If Ankara wanted to press this claim now, it would make Iraq's multibillion-dollar claims on Kuwait appear as chicken feed.)

Iraq's northwestern border with Syria also reflects Ottoman administrative partition, as well as the division of territory effected by Britain and France at the end of World War I. The border is a series of straight lines drawn between the spare and infrequent geographical features of the moonlike landscape. The border starts from the Turkish-Iraqi border at the point where the Tigris flows into Iraqi territory and, apart from three or four roads crossing it, the only other feature of any note in over three hundred miles is the Euphrates.

The quintessential postcolonial border is Iraq's western border with Jordan—a purely artificial straight line. Though the land for hundreds of miles on both sides is mere barren desert, Iraq and Jordan waited until March 1984 to sign a treaty that set the border just over a quarter of a mile eastward from the colonial line. The upshot was that Jordan gained—and Iraq lost—about twenty square miles of sand.

Iraq's border with Saudi Arabia is also long, though shorter than the frontier with Iran. The remoteness of the area, home to but a small nomadic population, makes it an uncontentious frontier nowadays, but in the 1920s there were frequent cross-border raids by tribes that would steal or kill one another's livestock. The British, considering themselves friends of both sides, organized a conference in 1922 to sort out the contending claims. The British high commissioner in Baghdad, Sir Percy Cox, attended the meeting and soon despaired of eliciting an agreement. With a red pencil he carefully drew a line on the map from the head of the Gulf to the border of what was then Transjordan and is now Jordan. In the process, Abdul Aziz al-Saud, or Ibn Saud, as he was known, gained a chunk of Kuwaiti territory while a large slice of Ibn Saud's territory went to Iraq. Kuwait, which had been unrepresented at the talks, burned with resentment at the perceived injustice of its territorial loss. Ten years later Ibn Saud went on to establish the present Saudi kingdom, though the border became quiet only after the new Saudi regime was able to exert control over its more rebellious tribes.

Both sides of the Saudi-Iraq border lack proper roads, and there are no oilfields in the immediate vicinity. And so this border has remained quiet, despite tensions between royalist Saudi Arabia and republican Iraq. The demarcation of the border was reendorsed by an agreement signed in Baghdad in April 1975.

A cartographical oddity of this border still shows up on many maps, although its status has changed from when it was established nearly seventy years ago. This is a diamond-shaped feature known as the Iraq–Saudi Arabia Neutral Zone, about a hundred miles from east to west, and forty-five miles from north to south, with its eastern point touching the westernmost corner of Kuwait. This zone was intended to accommodate the migrations of nomadic Arabs who traveled with their camels and other livestock, moving from place to place, depending on the availability of pasture. This zone was also a creation of the mind and red pencil of Sir Percy Cox, and a few months after the 1922 treaty the Saudis and Iraqis agreed not to control movement into the zone nor to build permanent dwellings or installations there. Hence the nomads were saved from modern border regulations and from that other feature of modern diplomacy—the closure of a border. The two countries reached a further agreement on the administration of the zone in 1938.

In July 1975, however, Iraq and Saudi Arabia decided to divide the Neutral Zone; the question of tribal grazing lands had become an anachronism by then. The new border was to be a line drawn from the western to eastern points of the diamond. Whether this agreement was formally enacted or not, it remains a source for potential dispute or an opportunity for diplomatic leverage, depending on one's perspective.

(There used to be a second neutral zone in the region, the Kuwait–Saudi Arabia Neutral Zone, a chunk of 2,200 square miles adjacent to the Gulf coast, to the south of Kuwait. The origins of this zone were different: it was designed to partition two areas of oil exploitation, with the oil revenues from the entire zone shared equally between the two states. In the north of the zone, the oilfield is on land; in the south, the wellheads are offshore. Historically oil production within the zone was not included in the production quotas of Kuwait or Saudi Arabia, both members of OPEC, the Organization of Petroleum Exporting Countries. For much of the Iran-Iraq War, Kuwait and Saudi Arabia gave the proceeds of the sales of so-called neutral zone crude to Iraq. Since 1988 the quotas have been absorbed into the quotas of both countries. Each country administers its half, and has effectively integrated it into its own state. But the difference over oil remains a potential issue of contention.)

The border between Iraq and Kuwait has been the subject of agreement and disagreement for many years. Despite the urging of Kuwait, which became louder after the cease-fire and effective end of the Iran-Iraq War in 1988, Iraq was always loathe to agree on a final demarcation. When Saddam invaded Kuwait in August 1990, he partially justified his action by stating his objection to the statements of past Iraqi regimes that had implied an acceptance of the colonial border. Curiously, but also infuriatingly, there were border posts but no agreed border.

The story of this border dispute began more than two hundred years ago, when the Ottoman empire extended to Basra and beyond, and the question everyone asked was, How far beyond? As early as the 1750s, the Sabah family had been appointed to handle the administrative affairs and contacts with the Ottoman Turks in Basra on behalf of the people living on the northwestern edge of the Gulf. In the mid-nineteenth century one of the rulers of the tribes then occupying the territory that is now Kuwait discussed arrangements for his continuing autonomy with the Turkish governor of Basra, because he considered the maintenance of good relations vital to his independence. Sheikh Abdullah bin Sabah agreed to pay the tribes money, known as a tribute, in return for Turkish suzerainty over the area. (The term *suzerainty* was used at the time although, confusingly, it means both "paramount authority" and "nominal sovereignty," which does not clarify arguments today about the relationship then.) The sheikh also accepted an Ottoman title, roughly translated as "commandant," in 1871. But in 1896 Abdullah was killed by his brother, Sheikh Mubarak, who, understandably afraid of Turkish retribution, looked to Britain for help. At the time the British were mainly concerned with securing links to the empire in India, rather than colonizing the Gulf. In return for British support, Sheikh Mubarak signed an agreement in 1899 whereby he pledged not to cede any of his territory to anyone except Britain, and not to have relations with a foreign government without British consent. From the British point of view the agreement had the advantage of preventing Britain's chief European rival, Germany, from extending the projected Berlin-to-Baghdad railway to a coastal terminal in Kuwait.

By 1904 Britain had appointed a political agent for Kuwait, and in 1909 Britain began talks with Turkey on defining Kuwait's status. (Some accounts say that these talks were concluded to Kuwait's satisfaction in 1913, but other reports say the situation had still not been clarified before Britain and Turkey went to war in 1914.) Oil, of course, was yet to be discovered in the Gulf, and the prosperity of Kuwait was based on its trading role, as well as fishing and diving for pearls. Indeed, this prosperity was such, in relative terms, that most of Kuwait's principal families wanted to engage in business and were not interested in ruling. (After the discovery of oil, and the extensive drilling following World War II, ruling became a vastly more prosperous endeavor, which provoked tensions between Kuwait's principal families and the now fabulously wealthy Al-Sabahs, descendants of the Ottoman liaisons.)

When Sheikh Mubarak died in 1915, Kuwait was an autonomous state but not independent from Britain or the Ottoman suzerainty. A hiccup to independence was heard during the rule of Sheikh Mubarak's second son, Salim, who succeeded his father in 1917. Salim supported the Turks in World War I, and so the British blockaded Kuwait. Salim was replaced by his nephew, Ahmed, in

1921. The Iraq-Kuwait border was effectively recognized by the new state of Iraq in an exchange of letters in 1923. (To an extent, whether the border was recognized in 1913 is academic, because the state of Iraq did not yet exist.)

Even though the border might have been recognized, it has never been properly demarcated, and this lack of definition has been a constant source of irritation to the Kuwaitis. The most significant border crisis occurred in 1961, a crisis manufactured to a large extent by Iraqi prime minister and commander-in-chief Abdul Karim Qassem, who had overthrown the monarchy three years earlier. By 1960 Qassem had lost much of the support that had gathered around him after the revolution, and he was ruling as demagogic dictator, with the support of the Communist party. The border incident started in June 1961, when Britain terminated the agreement of 1899 and Kuwait became fully independent. Instead of sending a congratulatory diplomatic message, Qassem sent an ambiguous one, and followed it up by declaring Kuwait an integral part of Iraq. Adding insult to injury, Qassem appointed the ruler of Kuwait as the local administrator and made him answerable to the local governor in the Iraqi city of Basra. Qassem said that he did not intend to use force, although Iraqi troops were rumored to have moved up to the border. But Qassem's bluff was rather transparent, since his troops were all in the north, fighting rebellious Kurds, and Britain quickly sent reinforcements to bolster Kuwait. Qassem's provocation was condemned by other Arab states, which also blamed Iraq for the consequent intrusion of British military forces in the area. The British forces were quickly replaced by Arab units, and Iraq was left with few cards to play. Qassem announced that Iraq would withdraw its cooperation from the Arab League, which had granted membership to the new state of Kuwait, and Iraq broke off diplomatic relations with countries that recognized Kuwait. But these moves won few points for Qassem at home, and he became increasingly isolated before he was overthrown in 1963. The new Arab nationalist regime of General Abdul Salem Aref, with the support of the Baath party, quickly mended fences and explicitly accepted the independence of Kuwait.

Contributing to the confusion over where the Iraq-Kuwait border lies has been the growth of the southernmost Iraq town of Umm Qasr, and its associated port, used both for commercial purposes and as the headquarters of the Iraqi navy. On most maps Umm Qasr is shown as being north of the border, but on tactical pilot charts, the maps openly on sale in the West and used by commercial and military pilots, the border is shown as running right through the shaded square signifying Umm Qasr. Classified aerial reconnaissance photographs, obtained by satellites and high-flying aircraft, also show that the border runs through the port and downtown area of the Iraqi town. Whether this Iraqi urban creep is the result of quiet local agreements or Iraqi muscle, we do not know. But Kuwait has not called attention to this embarrassing development, either to save face or to avoid the issue of Iraqi claims to at least part of Kuwaiti territory.

The possible origin of the encroachment of Umm Qasr on Kuwait was the 1973 border dispute, which has been relegated to a paragraph or two in the history books but at the time was quite a lively event. It started in March when Iraqi artillery opened a nighttime barrage on two isolated Kuwaiti border posts in the northeast of Kuwait, that is, the area close to Umm Qasr. Iraqi infantry seized the Al Samitah border post and blew up the build-ings there, but did not occupy the other installation. As a result of Arab mediation, the Iraqi forces were to have withdrawn, but they stayed put, establishing a cordon, though allowing Kuwaiti police through to man a temporary new police post, composed of several tents. The Iraqis also built a surfaced road to their positions, stopping construction for a while when the Kuwaitis protested. Publicly though, the story was that Iraqi forces had withdrawn completely.

The final part of Iraq's border is with the open sea, but there can be few countries with a seacoast whose coastline is so short. On one side there is the Shatt al-Arab waterway and the border with Iran.

On the other side is the Khor Abdullah waterway and the coastline of the Kuwaiti islands of Warbah and Bubiyan. The distance between the two midchannel lines that mark the border is a mere fifteen miles, although the edge of the Fao peninsula, the marshes and mudflats that represent the Iraqi coast, is about thirty-five miles long.

In any other part of the world the islands of Warbah and Bubiyan would be of little consequence. They contain only a couple of police buildings and no trees. At high tide the islands are mostly covered by water: the highest point on Bubiyan, the larger of the two, is little more than a few feet above sea level. Ownership of the islands by Kuwait was first confirmed in 1923 by Sir Percy Cox as part of his bid to define the borders of the new Iraqi state. The coast of the mainland, across the narrow channel, was once a favorite place for Kuwaitis and foreign workers to take their families picnicking. The island of Bubiyan itself remained out of bounds despite the construction in the early 1980s of a huge bridge joining it to the mainland. The bridge was entirely symbolic of the reach of Kuwaiti sovereignty in the face of continuing Iraqi pressure, and had little other value. In the words of the French engineer who built it: "If the Kuwaitis now let me tarmac over the whole of the island, there will be some point in having the bridge." The sarcastic remark, made in French at the opening ceremony while the whole of the Kuwaiti government looked on, was broadcast on local television that evening because no Kuwaiti of any importance understood French well enough to order it edited out.

Thus Iraq felt itself half-strangled, with its main port, Basra, more than fifty miles from the open sea along a contested waterway, and the entrance to the only alternative port, Umm Qasr, flanked by a second foreign country. To avoid dependence on oil tankers loading on the Gulf coast, Iraq was compelled to build oil export pipelines in many different directions. The dangers of such dependence were neatly illustrated in 1980, during the first weeks of the war with Iran, when Iranian commandos landed on the offshore loading platforms, which were built twenty miles out into the Gulf because of the shallow coastal water, and blew them up. These platforms were out of commission for the duration of the war, until the cease-fire in 1988, and then took many months to repair.

During the 1973 border crisis Kuwait let it be known that it was prepared to have an Iraqi crude oil export pipeline run across its territory to an export terminal south of Kuwait City, adjacent to the deeper waters off Kuwait's coast. But Kuwait was never prepared to countenance giving up or leasing any of its territory, including the islands of Warbah and Bubiyan, which were a continual focus of Iraq's attentions, nor would Kuwait have tolerated the Iraqis' idea of dredging a deep-water channel through to the Gulf waters from Umm Qasr, which would have cut off the northern coast of Warbah. The West fully supported Kuwait's position because Umm Qasr was believed to be serving as a supply port for Soviet naval vessels. Keeping the Soviets out of the Gulf was a rare point of agreement among the West, conservative Arab states such as Saudi Arabia and the Gulf sheikhdoms, and Iran under the Shah.

Another approach to Iraq's predicament was for Baghdad to maintain the best of relations with its Gulf coastal neighbors. Indeed, during the Iran-Iraq War supplies for Iraq flowed through Kuwait, where the Mina Abdullah harbor became virtually an Iraqi port. But dependence on Kuwaiti goodwill did not recommend itself as a long-term solution, and at least one analyst[1] has interpreted Iraq's invasion of Kuwaiti in August 1990 as principally motivated by the search for a deep-water port.

★ ★ ★

3

Religious and Ethnic Rivalries

At the time of the census held in Iraq in October 1987, there were said to be 16,278,000 people living there, including foreigners. This figure may be viewed with some skepticism, however, because it was announced within two days of the census day, and even the dictatorship in Iraq is not efficient enough to do its sums so quickly. (Based on past growth rates, an estimate for early 1991 is that about 19 million people live in Iraq.) What the census did not reveal was the size of the country's various ethnic and religious groups. Such information was not sought by the Iraqi government, nor does the government want such information revealed. In public, at least, President Saddam Hussein and Iraqi officials insist that there is one Iraqi nation and all its inhabitants are, simply, Iraqis.

Yet even Iraqi officials who parrot this argument implicitly cast doubt on it. For example, at the national day celebrations in 1989 held at the Iraqi ambassador's residence in London, a visiting senior official from the Iraqi foreign ministry was asked about Iraq's reasons for supporting the rebel Lebanese Christian leader, General Michel Aoun. He replied that Iraq saw an analogue in Lebanon: both countries had almost exactly the same range of ethnic groupings. (He was wrong in the detail: Iraq does not have any Druze, a community that spreads across Lebanon, Syria, and Israel.) So, he continued, Iraq wanted a united Lebanon because a splintered Lebanon might portend a splintered Iraq. At one level, this answer was merely a tidy piece of Iraqi self-justification, but it also suggests a continuing uncertainty about whether such mixtures of ethnic communities can effectively coalesce as a modern nation.

The range of Iraq's ethnic and religious communities is extensive, and the relative sizes are open to debate. Perhaps the most authoritative numbers are those provided by the Jaffee Center for Strategic Studies at Tel Aviv University in Israel. Its researchers say that the figures are pulled together from a variety of sources, and one assumes that they check their estimates against those of the various branches of the Israeli intelligence community.

According to *The Middle East Military Balance, 1988–1989,* published by the Jaffee Center, the ethnic composition of Iraq is:

Arabs	73.5 percent
Kurds	21.6 percent
Turkomans	2.4 percent
Persians	1.7 percent
Others	0.8 percent

And the religious makeup is:

Shia Muslims	53.5 percent
Sunni Muslims	41.5 percent
Chaldean Christians	3.6 percent
Others	1.4 percent

These figures indicate both dominance and diversity, depending on how they are interpreted. About 95 percent of Iraqis are Muslim, and nearly three-quarters are Arab. But the Sunni-Shia rivalry has been going strong for more than twelve hundred years, and their relative proportions ensure continuing inter-Islamic tensions. At the same time, the high proportion of non-Arabs—meaning, at its simplest, people who do not speak Arabic as a mother tongue—somewhat belies Saddam Hussein's claim to be a leader of the Arab world. (Few other Arab states have such a high proportion of non-Arab citizens, although in Sudan Arabs are in the numerical minority.)

Thus, looked at another way, the population figures depict a nation of religious minorities, each of which has historical reasons for expecting little tolerance from the majority. The Shias were brutally repressed in the 1920s, as were the Assyrian Christians during the 1930s, while several hundred Jews were killed during the riots of 1941, when the British drove out the pro-Nazi Rashid Ali regime. At any time, one senses, one group or another might make demands that the government redress decades of historical injustice to its members.

Of course, given Iraq's geography, which includes vast areas of both high mountains and inhospitable desert, the population is not by any means evenly distributed. The bulk of the population lives in proximity either to the river Euphrates or to the river Tigris. More than 4 million people live in the capital, Baghdad, and 1.5 million live in the country's second largest city, Basra. Other cities with a significant population are Mosul and Irbil in the Kurdish north, and the Shia holy city of Kerbala and the nearby industrial center of Al-Hillah, to the south of Baghdad.

The Shias and the Sunnis each have their own unofficial homeland. The majority group, the Shia Muslims, live in the great swath of territory stretching from Baghdad (which is effectively a Shia city), southeast along the two rivers to Basra. The Sunni Muslim heartland also starts in Baghdad, but stretches north, and to the east and west. The Kurds—most of whom are Sunnis, but some of whom are Shias (the Jewish Iraqi Kurds emigrated to Israel soon after statehood)—inhabit the northeast of the country. The towns of Irbil and Sulaimaniya are almost exclusively Kurdish, as Mosul and Kirkuk once were. But the central government did not want those oil-rich towns to be dominated by non-Arabs, and it has encouraged Sunni Arabs to migrate there.

Perhaps the most significant feature of the Iraqi Kurds, apart from not speaking Arabic, is that they form a transnational community with other Kurds living as minorities in the neighboring states of Iran, Syria, Turkey, and the Soviet Union. Together, there are perhaps between 8 and 10 million Kurds in these countries. The Iraqi group is the largest both in number and in population share in its home nation.

Throughout the region, Kurds live in mountainous areas and in the valleys in between, and mostly are engaged in agriculture of one form or another. Their economic independence and their linguistic isolation have historically made for a difficult relationship with central governments, in Iraq and in the other states. Hopes of achieving an independent Kurdish state were first encouraged by the demise of the Ottoman empire, but to no avail. The Kurds remain fiercely independent, their spirit yet to be totally vanquished by military force during a long history of repression. Over the years, some thousands of Iraqi Kurds have been forcibly transferred to camps in the southern desert areas near the border with Saudi Arabia—there can be no greater contrast with the hills of Kurdistan. But the exact location of these camps, and the fate of the Kurds sent there, is unclear. Kurds were also the target of aircraft bombing and poisonous gas attacks by the regime of Saddam Hussein in 1988.

The remaining Jewish population of Iraq now lives in Baghdad, and numbers an estimated 3,000. (The vast majority emigrated to Israel in the early 1950s.) They are treated with suspicion because of possible links to, or at least sympathy for, Israel. But the community's elders have professed pious loyalty to the regime of Saddam Hussein, even in an open letter to the Baghdad *Observer* daily newspaper after the invasion of Kuwait.

Christian groups are found in Basra, Baghdad, and to the northeast of Mosul. The range and variety of their Christianity is extraordinary, the result of historic diversity, enhanced by changes in borders over the years, rather than any state-acknowledged religious freedom. Recent Iraqi governments have, however, acknowledged the right of religious freedom, partly to reinforce the concept of a unified Iraqi nation, but also for ideological reasons. The creed of the ruling Baath party calls for both Arab nationalism and socialism, not for Islam per se. Indeed, the founder of Baathism was a Christian, Michel Aflaq (he died in 1989 and was buried in Baghdad); Tariq Aziz, Saddam's foreign minister and also a deputy prime minister, is also a Christian. The largest Christian group is the Chaldeans; smaller numbers of Iraqis are Syrian Catholics, Gregorians, Nestorians, Syrian Orthodox, Armenian Catholics, Roman Catholics, Greek Catholics, Greek Orthodox, and Protestants. At least some members of Saddam's regime were educated at a school in Baghdad that is run by a Christian order.

Until 1979 Iraq also had a substantial Iranian population, Persian-speaking Shia Muslims engaged mainly in commerce, some of whose families had lived in Iraq for several generations. But many Iraqis of Persian descent were expelled by Saddam after the Iranian revolution. Saddam feared that the Iranians would be a fifth column promoting the revolutionary ideas of Ayatollah Khomeini, and he wanted to show the new regime in Tehran that it had a tough neighbor. Those of Iranian ancestry who remained in Iraq live in the Shia Muslim cities of pilgrimage, Kerbala and Najaf.

A few of the minor ethnic groupings are so esoteric as to appear of no significance to the outsider, but they remain of concern to the government of Iraq. (Who can tell what group might be quietly plotting to revenge a real or imagined religious or ethnic grievance against the government?) In the north, to the west of Mosul, the Yazidis maintain almost closed communities. The Yazidi religion is a unusual mixture of Christianity and Islam, with elements also of paganism and fire-worship (Zoroastrianism). In the south are the Mandaeans, who number only several thousand but still maintain an independent existence; their religion has elements of Judaism. There is also a small Bahai community, as there is in Iran, although in Iran they have been aggressively persecuted since the revolution for believing that other prophets came after Mohammed.

Other significant ethic communities are the Turkomans, who number more than 2 percent, and much smaller groups of Armenians, Circassians, and Assyrians. The Turkomans are part of a disparate community stretching across the north of Asia from Turkey to China. The Iraqi Turkomans live in the north, alongside the Kurds, and like the Kurds, they have been persecuted because of their antagonistic attitude to central government. The Turkomans' fate, though, has been complicated by their traditional role as guardians at the bottom of Kurdish valleys, where they would stop the Kurds from raiding the main roads and towns. When Saddam ordered the destruction of Kurdish villages in the 1980s, as a way of improving the policing of the area, Turkoman settlements also suffered.

Iraq's Armenians are descendants of families who fled Ottoman oppression in the Armenian heartland of Turkey. The Circassians come from farther north, in what is now the Soviet Union; owing to their military tradition, they have found a sympathetic patron in Saddam Hussein, who has many Circassians in his bodyguard and presidential guard. The Assyrians are also Christians, their name reflecting their origin in the northwest of the country, rather than any direct biblical forebears.

The Marsh Arabs, also known as the Madan, are Shia Muslims who live in the marshes between the two rivers to the south of Baghdad and to the north of Basra. They live in huts, in small groups, making their livelihood from fishing and hunting, although over the last forty years they have become progressively urbanized.[1] The Marsh Arabs are worth considering not only because they upset Western notions about Arabs living only in desert areas, but also because, being both seminomads and Shias, they have maintained a sometimes difficult relationship with the central government. During the Iran-Iraq war and possibly since, the marshes became a haven for army deserters, who then launched attacks of banditry on some of the main north-south roads. The authorities reportedly flew in helicopter gunships to police the area, in a manner reminiscent of US efforts to control the rice paddies of Vietnam, and probably with no greater success.

Demographic reports also show that, like many developing countries, Iraq is very youthful, with about 60 percent of the population under the age of twenty. Economically, this puts pressure on the government to allocate funds for education to expand the economy so that there are enough new jobs to absorb all the students leaving school and college each year. Politically, though, the youthfulness of the population is a benefit to the government: none of these teenagers has known anything but Baathist rule in Iraq, and most cannot remember any national leader other than Saddam Hussein. Moreover, with such a large school-age population, the government can easily use the school system to inculcate vast support for the regime. The government also uses the schools to check up on parents: pupils are asked to report dissident remarks heard at home. (The experience of one Iraqi woman, now an exile, is typical: while living in Baghdad she had to be careful about everything she said to her children in case they innocently repeated her words at school.) Given the expansion of education facilities, and the urbanization of the tribes, this means of state control extends even to Kurds and Shias.

Casualties and fatalities during the eight-year Iran-Iraq War — as many as 100,000 Iraqis lost their lives, and several times that number were wounded — only marginally slowed Iraq's population growth. The rate of growth is calculated at 3.3 percent, one of the highest in the world, but considered low by ambitious Iraqi government planners. Between 1957 and 1991, Iraq's population almost trebled (from 6.3 million to 18 million), and it is expected to reach 22 million by the year 2000. (Given Saddam Hussein's appreciation for history, he has probably noticed that 22 million is also the estimated population for the period of the height of Arab civilization, from 700 to 1100, before the region was devastated by the Mongol invaders, and then Ottoman neglect.) Rapid population growth always brings with it unpredictable social pressures, and in

Iraq's case differences in birthrates between the various ethnic and religious communities could cause instability. Though information is not available, intuition suggests that the birthrates in Shia and Kurdish communities are higher than that of the loyal Sunnis because of the former's poorer economic circumstances.

Various changes in Iraqi society over the last hundred years can be explained by reference to two different trends: repeated waves of migration to the towns and cities, and the impact of foreign ideologies. The migrations began during the reign of the Ottoman Turks, when Sunni Muslims were encouraged to come into the towns and serve as the local backbone of the central administration, a crucial role that they retain to this day. (Saddam's regime is dominated by Sunnis like himself.) The British, after World War I, built on this system but also gave preference in the new nation's nascent armed forces to minority groups. Throughout the empire, Britain everywhere found such groups, the so-called warrior castes, who could be trained as soldiers to back up British rule. In Iraq, Britain chose Christian groups, some of whose descendants are perpetuating this tradition. During the 1920s Iraqi towns also received an influx of tribal peoples from the Red Sea coast of Arabia who came to bolster their kinsman, the new king, Faisal I. These immigrants were rapidly assimilated, forming an integral part of the Iraqi Sunni community.

A third migration occurred after the failure of the ill-thought-out agrarian reforms of Qassem in 1958. Many farmers had no choice but to move into the towns to look for work. Yet another migration to the towns followed the rise in oil prices in the 1970s, which led to construction booms and the rapid expansion of urban-based businesses.

Arab nationalism also diminished tribal bonds, although the vicissitudes of political freedoms and repression tended to reinforce tribal links, illustrating that kinship was the only reliable criterion of trust. Another ideology, communism, has had a more difficult experience in Iraq. Communism has been curtailed, and often banned, because of its historical opposition to Baathist authority, but its principal weakness is that it is atheist rather than just secular. In seeking to dissolve family and tribal links, communism sought too much too soon. It has failed to make much progress even among the new urban working class, and almost none among the tribes.

Indeed, for Iraqis of all religious and ethnic groups, the fundamental unit of social cohesion is the family and the extended family unit, up to and including the tribe. Though the government seeks to instill loyalty to the state, people's primary loyalty is to the family, and family and tribal affiliations always take precedence over people's religious identity. Family loyalty extends into business, where relatives are considered more trustworthy, and especially into government, particularly in the regime of Saddam Hussein. From Saddam's point of view, one of the weaknesses of previous regimes was an overemphasis on political ideology and an underappreciation of family ties. When these regimes were overthrown, when ideology failed, there was no clan to fall back on in order to stabilize the regime.

The family group embraces members of different economic strata: for example, the president before Saddam Hussein, Ahmed Hassan al-Bakr, was both educated and an army officer but still felt a tie with his poorly educated and nonmilitary nephew Saddam. The dominant figure in the family group is the senior male. At one time al-Bakr took this role, but age and poor health forced him to yield to the next generation—to Saddam. Loyalty, however, does not preclude competition between different branches of a family. Often brothers stick together, while male cousins tend to be rivals. In Saddam's family, his half-brothers, the Ibrahims, have an awkward relationship with their cousins, the al-Majids. Family rivalries are curbed by self-interest, the personal authority of the senior male, and judicious marriage arrangements. (One such marriage took place a generation ago, when the Baath party was split between its military and civilian wings. The late Adnan Khairallah, Saddam's cousin and brother-in-law, married the daughter of Ahmed Hassan al-Bakr.)

As the mention of senior males, brothers, and male cousins suggests, women have a subordinate role in the traditional family. A woman's most important contribution to the family is to produce sons, for sons confer prestige on the father and are the carriers of the family tradition. Saddam's two sons, Udai and Qusai, were expected to be given a steadily increasing political role; of his three daughters, one is married to Hussein Kamel, the industry minister, another is married to Hussein Kamel's brother, a senior officer in the missile corps, and the third is still at school. Unlike most Iraqi women, Saddam's wife, Sajida, worked, as a primary school head teacher, for many years, even while she was raising five children.

Within a village or town different kin groupings might be rivals, but over the years, intermarriage, threats from outsiders, and economic and social interdependence contribute to the emergence of a shared identity. For example, people from Saddam's home area of Takrit now call themselves Takritis, even though they are not all related. Similarly, people from the town of Samarra often call themselves al-Samarrai. When Iraqis move from villages to towns or cities (over 70 percent of Iraqis now live in towns and cities) and find themselves living alongside other migrants from their home village, their tribal or kinship origins often continue to influence their personal and business relationships and antagonisms.

Since the late 1970s, the Baath party has banned the use of tribal names, although the system is still widely used in private. A notable exception, since his political rehabilitation in 1988, is Saddam's half-brother Barzan, who signs his newspaper articles "Barzan al-Takriti." The stated reason for prohibiting tribal names is that tribes have no role in the modern Baathist state, although an equally plausible explanation is that so many Takritis had entered the top ranks that use of the al-Takriti appellation might exacerbate tribal antipathy and jealousy. By one estimate, a quarter of the members of the Baath party Regional Command in the late 1970s were Takritis.

The agriculturally based rural traditions followed by Saddam's own family seem hopelessly outmoded to Iraq's second- and third-generation urban families, particularly those who have been educated. The social strain between the educated cosmopolitan elite and the rough-and-tough rural Iraqis immediately catches the attention of visitors to the country and foreigners meeting Iraqis abroad. The educated elite are often, but not always, ardently nationalist and are usually careful to hide any antagonism toward their compatriots. But some cannot stomach what they see as the crudeness of the tribal underpinnings of Saddam's regime. Those who live in Iraq do not criticize the government, but do not praise it either. Some who have the resources to do so prefer to live abroad. Their choice seems one of life-style rather than of politics per se — they are not active dissidents, nor are they necessarily disloyal.

One break with traditional mores, begun in the 1970s, has been some movement toward more equal status for Iraqi women. In 1980 women represented 19 percent of the Iraqi labor force, a figure three times that of 1976, an increase reflecting the need to fill jobs left vacant by men going into the army to battle Iran. (By contrast, in the conservative Arab states to the south, such as Saudi Arabia, social contact between the sexes outside the family is banned and women are not allowed to drive cars.) During the 1980s more Iraqi women continued to enter the labor force, although this clashed with the government's stated aim of population growth. Despite the expansion of a network of daycare centers to accommodate working mothers, a survey in 1987 showed that families were having fewer children.

That same year, Saddam, in a speech to the national women's federation in Baghdad, reminded women of their patriotic duty to have large families: "We hope that the Iraqi woman's inclination to work would not divert her from producing children. If the population of children decreases in such a way as to threaten national security, not only women's opportunities will be threatened, but also the whole country." He might have been thinking, although he did not say it, that he would prefer Sunni Muslim babies, rather than Kurdish or Shia children. For there is little to suggest that strict state education has eradicated deep family and tribal bonds or all memory of historical injustices. "One nation" still appears elusive, and Saddam is too cautious a man to believe that his education system will deliver a unified people to him.

★ ★ ★

4

Iraqi Oil:
The World's Second Largest Reserves

Oil is important to Iraq, and, until Saddam Hussein invaded Kuwait and personalized the issue, oil was why Iraq was important to the world. The oil industry accounts for three-quarters of all economic activity in Iraq; the export of oil and related products provides 90 percent of the nation's foreign-exchange earnings, and the bulk of the nation's income revenues. Before the invasion of Kuwait in August 1990, Iraq's oil reserves stood at 100 billion barrels, second only to Saudi Arabia's estimated reserves of 255 billion barrels.[1] (By comparison the United States has 34.6 billion barrels of reserves, and the Soviet Union has 58.4 billion barrels.) After half a day of sweeping military activity in Kuwait, Iraq claimed control of Kuwait's reserves of 91.9 billion barrels of reserves. The invasion thus brought Iraq's oil reserves to 191.9 billion barrels, still less than the Saudi holdings but nearly 21 percent of the known oil reserves in the world.

If this statistic is not staggering enough to signify Iraq's potential power, then only a few more figures are needed. Slightly further down the Gulf, Abu Dhabi, the chief member-state of the United Arab Emirates, has 92.2 billion barrels of reserves. Were Iraq ever to gain sufficient influence over the oil policies of Saudi Arabia and Abu Dhabi, then Saddam would effectively control oil reserves of over 454 billion barrels, or nearly half the world's known oil reserves. He would then direct more than half the production of the oil cartel and one-sixth of world production. With such power, Saddam could set almost any price — monetary or political — for oil. He could finally make the world, and especially the international oil companies, pay Iraq back for their earlier domination of its oil industry.

The earliest exploration for oil in Iraq dates back to the nineteenth century and the period of Turkish control. In the 1870s the discovery of oil in Baku, on the Caspian Sea, then a part of Czarist Russia, prompted further searches in the area to the south — both in the Ottoman lands that later became Iraq and in neighboring Iran. The territory under Ottoman control seemed a fair bet: seepages of oil on the surface in the area of Mosul and Kirkuk had long suggested underground reservoirs, but Ottoman bureaucracy proved almost impossible to penetrate for needed permissions. The first concession to explore was not awarded until 1925 (to Turkish Petroleum Company, then a British-French-Iraqi consortium), and only in October 1927 did drillers hit oil just north of Kirkuk, in northern Iraq. The oil literally gushed out, under great pressure, streaming all over the land until it was brought under control.

Having found oil in commercial quantities, the consortium had to find a way to transport it to overseas markets. Both export and full production had to be delayed until a pipeline could be completed. A pipeline to the Gulf was impractical, since the markets at that time were not in that direction. Rather, the pipeline had to head to the Mediterranean, where the oil could be loaded onto tankers bound for Europe. The two prospective pipeline routes were through French-controlled Syria and through British-controlled Transjordan and Palestine. To appease both the British and the French oil companies that were members of the oil-producing consortium, a compromise was reached. A line was built from the Kirkuk area southwest to the town of Al-Haditha on the Euphrates River. At this point the pipeline branched in two, with one branch line going through Syria to the port of Tripoli on the Lebanese coast (not to be confused with the Libyan capital of the same name), and the other line going to Haifa.

Oil was flowing through the pipeline by 1934, but expansion was inhibited by the Great Depression and the subsequent outbreak of World War II. By the end of the war, however, in 1945, exports were rising steadily. Kirkuk remained the main area of exploration, but other reserves were discovered at Mosul, also in the north, and near Basra, in the far south. The southern field required a new pipeline which terminated at the Fao peninsula, in the northern Gulf. When Israel gained independence in 1948, Iraq abandoned the pipeline to Haifa, and laid a larger pipeline to Tripoli, in Lebanon, and a new pipeline from Kirkuk to Banias, on the Syrian coast.

The development of Iraq's oil reserves is only half the story, however. The real tale concerns the rivalry between the various foreign oil companies, whose technical ability was matched by their internecine competitiveness. As the rivalry unfolded, the government of Iraq was often a mere helpless bystander, a silent partner taken advantage of by the oil companies. This situation continued until 1972, when the companies operating in Iraq were nationalized.

The first concession to explore for oil in the area was sought in 1912 by several companies grouped together to form the Turkish Petroleum Company (TPC). The British were eager to be involved in the TPC because Mesopotamia was close to Britain's military and commercial lines of communication with India; also, the British navy, then the largest in the world, had just converted from coal to oil-fired boilers and so oil supplies had to be guaranteed. The Germans initially became involved in the TPC to rival the British, and both countries sought to exclude the American oil companies. TPC was held together by Calouste Gulbenkian

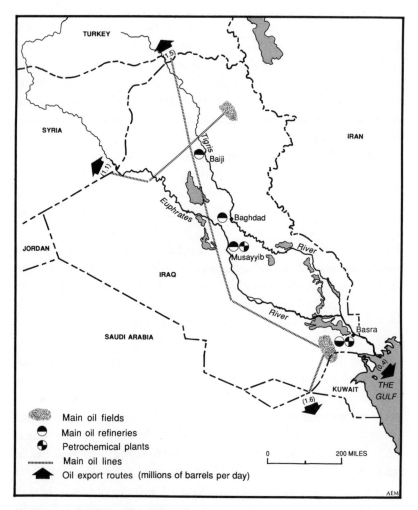

Iraq's main oil facilities and export routes

(a Turk at that time), the quintessential fixer, whose eventual nickname "Mr. Five Percent" alluded to his shareholding in TPC. Within two years the company ownership had changed so the British-controlled Anglo-Persian Oil Company held 50 percent of the shares. By the time World War I started, in 1914, TPC had a written promise of an oil concession from the Ottoman authorities.

By the end of the war the French had claimed the German shares in TPC, and the Italians and the Americans were seeking to buy shares as well. As part of the negotiations, 20 percent of the shares were promised to citizens of the new country of Iraq, although oil companies moved in quickly to buy up the shares — to the bitter resentment of Iraqi nationalists. After oil was discovered, TPC changed shareholders again, bringing in the Royal Dutch Shell Group and the Near East Development Corporation, which represented five American oil companies, principally Standard Oil of New Jersey (now Exxon) and Socony-Vacuum (now Mobil). In 1929 the anachronistic *Turkish* Petroleum Company was renamed as the Iraq Petroleum Company (IPC).

Despite its new name, the purpose of IPC was not to develop Iraq's oil reserves as such but rather to serve the interests of the foreign shareholders. The British controlled Anglo-Persian Oil Company, to take one example, was more concerned about developing its concession in Iran than about expanding production in Iraq. The comparatively slow progress in building export pipelines was interpreted by some Iraqi politicians as demonstrating IPC's indifference to Iraq. In the late 1920s, other British and Italian interests tried to break IPC's monopoly by buying concessions in northwest Iraq, but they did not have enough capital, and IPC bought them out, forming the Mosul Petroleum Company (MPC) to operate there. Recognizing that their dealings were unpopular in Iraq, IPC shareholders formed a separate company, Basra Petroleum Company (BPC), rather than take on the concessions directly, when it came to exploring for oil in southern Iraq (deemed a likely area because of newly found reserves in Kuwait and Saudi Arabia).

During the early 1950s, interest in Iraqi oil heightened when Iranian oil production fell after foreign companies protested against nationalization (the shah was pushed aside by the popular nationalist Mossadegh). Local Iraqi politicians took advantage of events to press IPC for better terms, including better training of and better positions for Iraqis in the IPC structure. But in the late 1950s the tide in Iran turned. The shah was back in power, thanks to a countercoup organized by the CIA and the British Secret Service, and Iranian oil again flowed freely, causing a slowdown in Iraqi oil production.

Ownership of oil reserves and means of production are often the grounds for revolution, but that was not the case in Iraq in 1958. The main opposition groups were preoccupied with the monarchy, and the new republican government was so unsure of itself that it was satisfied merely with continuing to receive tax and foreign currency revenues from oil production. Within several years though, matters changed. In a move that hindsight reveals as wholly wrongheaded, especially given the evolving nationalist feelings in the oil-producing countries, the international oil companies reduced the price for Middle Eastern oil, which significantly reduced local tax revenues, without bothering first to consult the various governments. This political stupidity, motivated by a world-wide over-supply of oil, was compounded by a further reduction in price in 1960. In response, Iraq's government invited representatives from all the major oil-producing nations to meet in Baghdad, a session that was the prelude to the establishment of the oil producers' cartel, OPEC (Organization of Petroleum Exporting Countries), in November 1960.

Emboldened by its success, the Iraqi government became tougher in its talks with IPC, putting more topics on the table for discussion. The talks fell apart in October 1961, and two months later the Iraqi government enacted a law expropriating all IPC concession areas not in production.

After flexing its muscle with the foreign oil companies, Iraq began to reconsider its oil-related transactions with its neighboring republican Arab state, Syria. Iraq was beholden to the goodwill of the government in Damascus for the Kirkuk-Banias pipeline and paid a fee for the use of it. When Syria unilaterally increased the transit fee in 1966, an outraged Iraq stopped pumping oil rather than pay.

In June 1967 the Six-Day War disrupted oil flows that had only just been revived by Iraq after resolving its trouble with Syria.

Blaming the United States and Britain for helping Israel achieve its great victory over Syrian, Jordanian, and Egyptian forces, Iraq joined the embargo and refused to sell oil to the US and the UK. The embargo cost Iraq dearly, in both lost revenues and dislocated supplier-customer relationships. These generally chaotic conditions formed the backdrop to the coup in 1968 by which the Baath party came to power.

Nationalization of Iraq's oil industry was inevitable considering the state-dominated economic system advocated by the Baath, which is a socialist party. In December 1972 the Iraqi government took over the northern oilfields around Kirkuk; Mosul Petroleum Company was nationalized in March 1973; and the nationalization of the Basra Petroleum Company's southern oilfields was completed in December 1975. Although the Iraqi government was victorious, the oil companies were considered to have won a good deal and had every reason to be quietly content with their compensation.

Although Iraq wanted control of its oil, it was not against securing foreign companies' help in exploration and production. Even as the policy of nationalization was being pushed, a law enacted in 1967 allowed for joint venture agreements with foreign companies. The lure for foreign companies was to win access to sources of Iraqi crude, often at concessional rates. Several oil companies prepared to enter such agreements, while their competitors were being expelled from the country. In 1968 the French company Elf signed an agreement that led to three oil discoveries. In 1973 a Japanese consortium, including Sumitomo, Mitsubishi, and Idemitsu Kosan, bought into the Elf-Iraq joint venture. In 1972 Braspetro of Brazil signed a contract for oil exploration and development. Four years later Braspetro discovered the Majnoon oilfield in the marshes alongside the Iranian border, thirty miles north of Basra. Reserves in this one field alone are estimated to be more than 7 billion barrels — an indication of Iraq's huge untapped oil wealth. (The Majnoon field is still unexploited. Damage caused to surface installations by Iranian forces who occupied the field during the Iran-Iraq War would not have affected the underground reservoirs.)

Other countries involved in the Iraqi oil business include India, whose state-owned Oil and Natural Gas Commission has had limited success in southeastern Iraq from 1973 on, and the Soviet Union. Until 1990, several thousand Soviet oil workers were employed on projects in Iraq. (A similar number of Soviet advisers and technicians were helping the Iraqi military use Soviet equipment.) Through the company Technoexport, the Soviets were involved in the development of the West Qurna oilfields, lying between the Tigris and Euphrates rivers in southern Iraq. Technoexport's other major project was to build a water-injection system for the Rumaila North oilfield, the northern part of the field from which Saddam accused Kuwait of stealing oil. (Other French and Italian companies started in the late 1960s to help Iraq develop its oil reserves. The involvement of these companies helps to explain the nuances of difference in the amount of support given to the United States during the Kuwait crisis: their involvement gave them a stake in Iraq's economic development, which they did not want to ruin by diplomatic confrontation.)

With oil comes gas, either in its own reservoirs or mixed in with the oil; the latter is known as *associated gas*. Associated gas is either flared or, more frequently, collected for treatment and use in the petrochemical industry, or used to generate electricity in specially built power plants. Compared with its oil reserves, Iraq is relatively poorly endowed with gas, possessing just 2.4 percent of the world's estimated reserves. By contrast, Abu Dhabi, Qatar, and Saudi Arabia each have roughly twice the gas reserves of Iraq, and Iran has more than five times Iraq's reserves.

Iraq has not developed any natural gas fields, so-called non-associated gas, and has had a poor reputation for flaring associated gas rather than making use of it. During the 1980s steps were taken to begin to gather the associated gas, either for reinjection into fields to improve recovery rates of oil or for industrial use. Elaborate plans were instituted to supply domestic households with bottled gas, with most other gases being used for industrial purposes and small exports of the limited remainder. (By 1986 Iraq had begun exporting associated gas via pipeline from its southern oilfields to Kuwait, where it was used for power generation.)

By the end of the 1970s Iraq was anticipating an era of great wealth. The country, and in particular, Saddam, was starting to realize that great development was possible. The government envisaged having more money than it knew what to do with, and it drew up extensive plans for industrial development and social programs to improve education and health facilities. Oil revenues were expected to more than double to $60 billion a year by 1985. The Baath party made clear its disapproval of the absurd personal riches that individuals in Saudi Arabia, Kuwait, and the other Arab Gulf states were acquiring.

But in 1979 Saddam misread the opportunity created by the surge in oil prices, which more than trebled to over $35 a barrel after the revolution broke out in Iran. Rather than seize the moment of high prices to step up oil production and propel his nation's progress, Saddam decided to wage war on Iran (see chapter 10). Constrained by enemy military activity over eight years, Iraq's oil production fell by two-thirds between 1980 and 1981. Only in 1988 did production again approach prewar levels (see table 1). By early 1990 Iraqi oil production had exceeded 3 million barrels a day again, for the first time in ten years. Production plummeted, however, after the invasion of Kuwait in August 1990—down to the 400,000 barrels a day required for Iraq's domestic needs.

Worse still for Iraq, not only did oil production falter during the war with Iran, but so did oil prices, severely diminishing the country's foreign-currency revenues (see table 1). Oil sales provide the bulk of the foreign-exchange funds with which Iraq can buy imports from abroad.

The long war with Iran repeatedly forced Iraq to reexamine its oil policy priorities. During the first few months of the war, Iranian commandos attacked Iraq's principal export infrastructure: the offshore oil terminals in the Gulf. The terminals, which had pre-

TABLE 1

Iraq's Oil Production and Revenues

Year	Million barrels a day	Billion US dollars annually
1977	2.35	9.5
1978	2.56	10.9
1979	3.48	21.3
1980	2.65	26.1
1981	0.90	10.4
1982	1.01	10.1
1983	1.11	9.7
1984	1.23	11.2
1985	1.44	10.7
1986	1.75	6.9
1987	2.09	11.4
1988	2.60	11.0
1989	2.82	14.5

Sources: **BP Statistical Review of World Energy,** 1990; **OPEC Bulletin.**

viously pumped 3 million barrels a day onto tankers, were destroyed and remained unusable until after the cease-fire in August 1988. A further setback was Syria's decision in April 1982 to stop Iraq from using the Kirkuk-Banias pipeline. Syria's formal explanation cited disagreements over the transit fees Iraq paid. The more likely reason for Syria's action is a combination of antipathy between the ruling Baath parties in both countries and personal animosity between Saddam Hussein and President Hafez Assad of Syria. Syria saw that Saddam was facing a crucial moment—his forces were about to be driven back from most of the Iranian territory they had conquered—and Syria exploited the opportunity.

After the loss of its export outlets, Iraq's main priority in its oil policy was to open new export outlets and then raise production back to the levels of the late 1970s. And, looking at its Iranian enemy, Iraq wanted its own oil output to equal and then exceed Iran's. Oil policy and military policy complemented one another, with Iraqi jets seeking to cripple Iran's oil output by hitting tankers full of Iranian oil. But Iraq's pipeline expansion policy brought it into conflict with OPEC, for the cartel wanted to ensure high, stable prices by mutual agreements to limit output. Iraq's expansion of exports would have to be at the cost of other members' quotas.

Its Gulf and Syrian outlets destroyed, Iraq was forced to depend on a relatively small pipeline through Turkey to the Mediterranean. This pipeline's maximum capacity was only 1 million barrels a day, so fleets of tanker trucks were directed through Turkey and through Jordan. But the trucks could not handle more than 300,000 barrels a day of both crude oil and refined products, and trucking was an expensive means of transport. There was also tremendous damage to the road surfaces, which were not intended to carry so much heavy traffic.

Meanwhile, as the war dragged on, Iraq tried to construct new pipelines. One was built southward to Saudi Arabia to join up with a Saudi line leading to the Red Sea port of Yanbu, and further plans were hatched to make this route carry 1.6 million barrels a day. A scheme was also considered to run a pipeline down to the Jordanian Red Sea port of Aqaba, but this idea was shelved because of the fear that Israel would threaten a pipeline running within yards of its territory. A second pipeline through Turkey was also established. All in all, at the war's end, Iraq had an elaborate system of oil export pipelines — ironically, far more lines than it would have acquired during years of peace. Enormous versatility was provided by a so-called strategic pipeline joining the northern and southern fields. Oil from any part of the country could be exported via any of the new outlets as demand changed.

In addition to the revenues flowing by virtue of these pipelines, during the war with Iran, Iraq also benefited from Kuwait and Saudi Arabia selling oil on Iraq's behalf and putting the revenues in special accounts that Baghdad could draw on. Starting in 1982, sales from the neutral zone to the south of Kuwait were earmarked for

Iraq on the understanding that Iraq would at some future unspec-
ified date give back the oil on a barrel-for-barrel basis. Production
in the neutral zone was typically between 200,000 and 300,000
barrels a day, and the revenues were handed over to Iraq until the
agreement lapsed in 1988. In addition, Saudi Arabia sold on Iraq's
behalf another 60,000 barrels a day.

By 1988 Iraq had met its goal of producing more oil than Iran, a
competitive advantage that helped give Baghdad the momentum to
force Tehran to accept a cease-fire that year. Iraq also worked to
expand the number of producing oilfields. For decades, the main
oilfields were in the north and south of the country. Now, the most
promising fields for development were those in the center of the
country: to the east of Baghdad; to the north, at Hamrin, Balad, and
Takrit; and to the west of the capital. The western fields alone held
the potential to more than replace the giant Majnoon field, which
had been captured by Iranian forces, although it was too close to the
frontline for Iran to take oil from it.

Foreign oil executives were quietly ecstatic. Not only was Iraq
going to be a major source of oil for years to come but also there
would be great opportunities for the businesses that had the special
skills needed to develop oilfields. One company undertaking
exploration work for the Iraqi ministry of oil discovered places
where one giant oilfield lay under another, and it appeared quite
possible that a third oilfield was yet deeper below. Foreign businesses were also excited by Iraq's potential development of
petroleum-related industries: refineries, petrochemical plants, fer-
tilizer plants, and factories to produce plastics, detergents, and tires.

With the expansion of its oil exports, Iraq's disagreements with
some of its fellow members of OPEC became much more apparent. Since the cartel had reintroduced production quotas in 1983, to
maintain oil prices in a falling market, Iraq's individual quota had
generally reflected its export capacity rather than its production
capacity. Successive Iraqi oil ministers have claimed that there was
an understanding with the other twelve OPEC members that Iraq's
quota would be readjusted upward in line with its improved ability

to export. After the cease-fire, Iraq reiterated this claim and demanded an allowance for the production it had forgone since the beginning of the war with Iran. This argument led to a standoff in OPEC, relieved temporarily by Iraq being placed outside the quota system.

Throughout the 1970s and 1980s Saddam Hussein did not appear to take much direct interest in oil policy, although the decline in revenues was an obvious concern. The Iraqi leader seems to have been happy enough to leave the running of the oil industry to a set of capable engineers and administrators who had evolved from the cadres trained by the foreign oil companies before nationalization.

Saddam's emphasis on administrative efficiency led him in March 1987 to appoint as oil minister Issam Chalabi, a self-confident technocrat[2] and former deputy minister, who was set the task of streamlining the operations of the oil ministry and the state-owned Iraq National Oil Company. Under the ministry's overall command, the marketing function was carried out by the State Oil Marketing Corporation (which retained its previous acronym SOMO), while the National Oil Company looked after strategic planning. Oil production was handled around Kirkuk in the north by the Northern Oil Company, and around Basra by the Southern Oil Company.

After the cease-fire with Iran, Saddam seemed to show greater interest in oil policy. Revived exports were not bringing in new riches because of the low price of oil on world markets. In an interview with the *Wall Street Journal* in June 1990, Saddam displayed the extent of his anxiety, as well as his ignorance of the oil market.[3] He declared that the inherent price of oil was $25 a barrel, at a time when supply and demand was indicating a price of around $14.

These views help explain events in a bureaucratic battle that developed between Hussein Kamil (Saddam's son-in-law and, since 1988, the head of the new superministry of industry and military industrialization) and the finance minister, Hikmat Omar Mukhailef. Hussein Kamil started pushing ahead on projects for which the financing had not been arranged and then blaming Mukhailef for incompetence. At the same time, Hussein Kamil moved to usurp some of the responsibilities of the oil ministry, winning supervisorial control over the construction of the new petrochemical complex no. 2, south of Baghdad. Rubbing salt in the wounds of the oil minister, Hussein Kamil took some of the ministry's best engineers with him.

Toward the end of 1989 Mukhailef was fired by Saddam, who later spoke at length of his incompetence. At the beginning of 1990 increased pressure started to be placed on Chalabi. His chief deputy was pushed to one side, against the minister's wishes, and a more conventional Baathist brought in.[4] Foreign oil companies were particularly dismayed when it was announced that Ramzi Salman, the head of oil marketing and the main contact with foreigners, who considered him a decent person and a known quantity, was to be reassigned to an Iraqi-controlled slot at OPEC headquarters in Vienna.

Observers of Middle Eastern affairs should have noted that Saddam himself was taking a greater interest in oil policy, but the world misread his growing irritation with weak oil prices and Kuwait's overproduction, which was partly to blame for the low prices. A logical outcome, apart from the invasion of Kuwait, was the firing of Chalabi. In October he was made the scapegoat for Saddam's mistaken policy of introducing gasoline rationing, which was resented by the general population. Saddam's candidate to replace Chalabi came as no surprise: Hussein Kamil took on the additional responsibility.

Saddam's economic ambitions for Iraq have never been clearly stated, but Iraq, with or without Saddam, will be an important country because of its huge oil reserves and production potential for years to come. The country's customers might be put off by international condemnation of Iraq, and its production and export potential might be limited by war damage, but Iraq's vast reserves remain unscathed.

★ ★ ★

CHAPTER

5

Saddam's Early Years

Saddam Hussein was born on April 28, 1937, in the village of Shawish near the small town of Takrit, which lies on the banks of the Tigris River about a hundred miles north of Baghdad. Saddam's mother, Subha Talfah, was a member of the local Talfah family. His father, whom Saddam never knew, was Hussein Abdul Majid, from the local al-Majid family. Certainly on his mother's side, and perhaps on his father's as well, Saddam was part of the local Begat clan of the Albu Nasser tribe.

The name *Saddam* comes from the Arabic root meaning "to punch" or "to strike." It is occasionally translated in officially approved biographical materials as "the fighter who stands stead-fast," but this is reading a great deal into the word. Following Arab tradition, Saddam took his father's first name as his own second name. But instead of taking on the family name al-Majid, he chose instead to call himself Saddam Hussein al-Takriti, meaning "from the town of Takrit." (Thus other people using the name al-Takriti are not necessarily relatives of Saddam.)

Some reports say that Saddam's father died before Saddam was born, while others say he died when Saddam was only a few months old. Nor is there any sure knowledge of how he died; indeed, one opposition report alleges that Hussein Abdul al-Majid simply abandoned his wife and children. In his father's absence, Saddam was brought up by a succession of uncles. A distant relative on his father's side, Ibrahim Hassan, married his mother and became his stepfather. Saddam's stepfather was reported to have beaten him regularly. Official biographies say that, despite this abuse, the young Saddam never withdrew within himself: "He faced the difficult life ahead like a man."

Life was hard in the Takrit area. There was no electricity or water supply. The intensely hot summers were unrelieved by air-conditioning even for the rich, and during the winter rains, mud spread everywhere. A photograph of the house in the village of Oujah where Saddam lived during his childhood shows a windowless single-story building made of mud, straw, and wood.

At the time of Saddam's birth the population of Takrit was probably a few thousand, although to inhabitants of the surrounding countryside and villages Takrit no doubt appeared a very important center. The townspeople specialized in making crude inflatable rafts out of animal skins, which were used by traders moving goods up and down the Tigris. But Takrit also had a long and proud history. The earliest mention of Takrit is found in inscriptions referring to the Assyrian king Tukulti Ninnurta, who ruled in the ninth century BC; the town also appears in later inscriptions concerning Nebuchadnezzar. In Roman times Takrit was called Monia Tikrides, and in the time of the Abbasid caliphs, the town's fortress dominated the Tigris. In the early twelfth century Saladin, who led the Muslim armies against the Crusaders and drove them from the Holy Land, was born in Takrit. (Ironically, Saddam today harks back to Saladin as another great Takriti, though Saladin was a Kurd and Saddam thoroughly distrusts the Kurds.)

Later there was a great monastery in Takrit, and its Christian community was famous for producing woolen fabrics. With the coming of the Mongol invaders, much of the town was destroyed; it was effectively reduced to a village.

According to the official biographies, the young Saddam always aspired to improve himself, influenced perhaps by relatives on his mother's side for, although his father and stepfather were peasants, his uncle Khairallah Talfah was in the army, and Khairallah's cousin, Ahmed Hassan al-Bakr, had been a primary school teacher before joining the army. (Al-Bakr subsequently became president of Iraq, and Saddam his chief deputy.) The nearest school was some distance away in Takrit, but, overcoming objections from paternal relatives who wanted him to work on the land, Saddam started going there every day from the age of ten, encouraged by his younger cousin, Adnan Khairallah, who had already learned to read and write.

An early influence on Saddam's thinking is said to have been the work of an Iraqi nationalist intellectual, Sami Shaukat, who in the 1930s had published *These Are Our Aims*. The volume included an article Shaukat wrote in 1932, "The Art of Death," in which he says:

Strength means to excel in the art of death.
The nation which does not excel in the art of death with iron
    and fire
Will die under the horse's hooves, and under the boots of the
    foreign soldiers.
Let us sanctify death by killing and sacrificing ourselves for
    the sake of the country.
Let us bow humbly before the art of death.

More formative than any school curriculum, however, were national and international events of the 1930s and 1940s.

Iraqi politics of the thirties was dominated by local nationalists, both civilians and military, who schemed and manipulated for power. The British mandate in Iraq had ended on October 13, 1932, when Iraq became a sovereign, independent state and was admitted as a member of the League of Nations. The monarch, King Faisal, died of a heart attack while in Geneva in 1933, bequeathing the throne to his son, Ghazi, who had just turned twenty-one. King Ghazi took a relaxed attitude to his throne, serving as a constitutional figurehead rather than a head of government. In 1939 Ghazi, driving his car while drunk, hit a power pylon at high speed and died. He was succeeded by his infant son, Faisal II, with the late king's cousin Abdul Illah appointed to act as regent. All these monarchs were greatly influenced by the wily Nuri al-Said, who was prime minister for much of the period. Nuri was charming, a shrewd politician of strong will and courage who was extremely pro-British. He stood for little but the continuation of his own influence.

Intellectually, different schools of political thought vied for supremacy in influencing Arab nationalist sentiment, mirroring in part the debate going on in Europe before World War II. Some Iraqis admired the new dictatorships of Mussolini and Hitler, while others preferred socialism on the British Labour party model. Marxists were pushing a more doctrinaire communist line, while other intellectuals sought an ideology more compatible with Islam. All these groups, however, were united in hatred of the British, who still influenced Iraq's defense and foreign policy.

Under the terms of the 1930 Anglo-Iraqi Treaty, there was to be, theoretically for twenty-five years, a "close alliance" between the two countries, and there were to be "full and frank consultations between them in all matters of foreign policy" as well as mutual assistance in case of war. Britain was entitled to move troops across Iraqi territory and to maintain air bases near Basra, in the south, and at Habbaniya, west of Baghdad. But by the late 1930s relations with Britain had deteriorated because of Iraqi resentment of British policy in Palestine, the other territory mandated to it after World War I. Under Arab nationalist pressure throughout the Middle East, Britain was restricting the number of Jews allowed to immigrate into the territory and trying to abrogate any obligation it might have had to set up an independent Jewish state. These actions were insufficient in the eyes of Arab public opinion, and independent Iraq was a hotbed of Arab nationalist sentiment, rivaling Egypt in its attempts to influence Arabs throughout the Middle East.

Although the king was recognized as overall leader, Iraqi political regimes in the 1930s were constantly changing. The ruling elite, then as now, was from the Sunni Muslim community, which predominated in the center of the country. But the British had bequeathed a system that also acknowledged the status of other communities, principally the majority Shia Muslims, who were represented by both tribal sheikhs and religious leaders. The Kurds, as well as much smaller groups — Turkomans, Christians, and Jews — also had to be taken into account by the government in Baghdad to maintain a delicate political balancing act. Each group had its own attitudes toward the king, but all considered him and his descendants to be foreigners. (Religious Sunnis, for example, held that the Sherif of Mecca, Faisal I's father, had acted improperly in rebelling against the Ottoman caliph in 1916.)

From the Iraqi government's point of view, the most troublesome minorities in the early 1930s were the Kurds and the Assyrians. The Kurds had lost an opportunity for an independent state when the spoils of victory were apportioned by the Allies following World War I. The Kurds in northern Iraq disliked Arab rule even more than Turkish rule. (Like Saddam in the 1980s, the British in the 1920s had used aircraft to bomb rebellious Kurdish villages into submission, although the British did not resort to chemical weapons.) The Christian Assyrians were particularly active in 1932 and 1933. Previously patronized by the British, who had set up Assyrian militia units separate from the Iraqi army, Christian Assyrians felt they would be discriminated against by independent Iraq's Muslim rulers. The Assyrians also feared confrontation with the Kurds because the British had used Assyrian units to police Kurdish areas. Refused political autonomy, Assyrian armed groups were hounded by the new Iraqi army, which eventually eliminated them as an armed force. A massacre of about three hundred Assyrians, including women and children, at the village of

Sumayyil in July 1933 was part of this campaign. The perpetrator of this massacre, a Kurdish general, Bakr Sidqi, was also responsible for Iraq's first coup d'état in 1936 (the first coup in modern Arab history.) Bakr Sidqi gained political control, although he allowed the king to remain on his throne. Reflecting the basic communal tensions, the Kurdish general worked with a Shia and a Turkoman politician to overthrow a Sunni politician. In the five years following, there were seven military coups in Iraq, sometimes bloodless but often involving at least one or two murders.

In the 1930s Hitler's Germany tried to capitalize on Iraqi political turmoil and hatred of the British, but with the outbreak of war between Germany and Britain in September 1939, Iraq was obliged to cut off diplomatic relations with Berlin, under the terms of the Anglo-Iraqi treaty. Iraq's prime minister Rashid Ali refused, however, to cut diplomatic ties with Italy, and the Italian embassy in Baghdad became a center for anti-British plotting. In defiance of the Anglo-Iraqi treaty, Rashid Ali also restricted the movement of British forces across Iraqi territory.

In retaliation, Britain used its influence with the regent, Abdul Illah, and the former prime minister, Nuri al-Said, to counter Rashid Ali. Rashid Ali looked to his military for support. It came faster than he expected, in a military coup against Rashid Ali himself, but he quickly made a deal with the army by which he was made regent, the titular head of state. When Abdul Illah and Nuri al-Said fled the country, Britain was left in the unstable position of having a military presence in Iraq but not recognizing the government. Meanwhile, in Europe, Britain was besieged by the forces of Nazi Germany, which had conquered most of the mainland continent.

British prime minister Winston Churchill was not disposed to put up with perceived treachery of a former mandate. In April 1941 he ordered British forces into Basra, citing Rashid Ali's infringement of the bilateral treaty as justification. Iraq's forces received some help and a few aircraft from German and Italian sources, but Hitler was just about to launch his invasion of the Soviet Union and could not be distracted by providing further assistance. Fighting began outside the Habbaniya air base on May 2 when the local British commander decided to use surprise to overcome the superior numbers of Iraqi forces surrounding the base. The battle was one of the first ever to be decided in the air. The British used their air power to decimate the Iraqi air force, mainly while it was still on the ground. Iraqi troops withdrew to the east, making a stand on the Euphrates at Falluja, but by May 19 they were overcome. An armistice signifying the end of all resistance was signed at the end of May.

As the British took control, Rashid Ali fled, along with four generals responsible for the original coup. The British sentenced all of them to death in absentia; those who later returned to Iraq were executed. The rest of the British follow-up was similarly vengeful to let the Arab world know the costs of opposing British imperial power. Many supporters of Rashid Ali were executed. Others, like Saddam's uncle, Khairallah Talfah, an army officer, were imprisoned. The more fortunate were dismissed from the army or interned without trial. British domination was such that by 1943 Iraq had declared war on Germany and Italy, as well as Japan, and its governments were fully compliant with the British.

The British remained an occupying force until 1945, using both Iraq and Iran as a bastion to support the southern Soviet Union in stemming the advance of German forces. Iraqi nationalists were further angered when other Allied units of foreigners — three Indian divisions and a division of exiled Poles — also occupied Iraq.

In an interview in 1974 Saddam said he viewed the coup that displaced Rashid Ali and the subsequent occupation as humiliating, that such events made him resentful of foreign influence "regardless of what form it may take."[1] (He seems to have maintained this antipathy toward the British, never visiting Britain and preferring to give interviews to journalists from almost any other country.) Saddam has also cited the inspiration he derived from the writings of Colonel Saladin al-Sabbagh, whose works also influenced Rashid Ali. Describing al-Sabbagh as a great nationalist with pan-

Arab aspirations, Saddam has valued his teachings for their discussion of the need for Arab unity again foreign influence.

In March 1945 Iraq became one of the founding members of the Arab League, and in December it joined the newly formed United Nations. Political stability still eluded Iraq, however, in part because the introduction of political parties into the system in 1946 increased the number and legitimacy of those wanting a share of power. Following the end of the war, the British made ready to depart, even agreeing in 1948 under the Portsmouth Treaty to give up its rights to air bases, although a joint military planning committee was to be established. The Iraqi government claimed that the agreement was between two equals, but clearly it was not: the British view was to dominate the joint committee. Furthermore, the new treaty was to last until 1973, whereas the previous treaty had been due to expire in 1957. In signing the Portsmouth Treaty, the Iraqi regime totally misread the nationalist sentiment of many Iraqis. The riots that followed became known as the *watbah*, or uprising. The regime panicked and worsened its position by allowing the army to use machine guns against unarmed demonstrators. Hundreds died. To placate nationalist sentiment, the treaty was repudiated by the enfeebled Iraqi government, but that did not bother Britain much, for the 1930 treaty still stood.

The main argument between Iraq and Britain continued to be the thorny problem of Palestine, to which Jewish refugees were fleeing in increasing numbers from Europe. As a newly independent state, Iraq vied with other Arab countries to take a leading role opposing the creation of a Jewish state. Volunteer fighters from Iraq joined forces with other Arabs against the British in Palestine. When the state of Israel was founded in May 1948, Iraq sent up to 10,000 soldiers to fight against the new Israeli army. The Iraqi forces were deployed in what is now the northern part of the West Bank, in the triangle of the area marked by Nablus, Jenin, and Tulkarm. They generally held their ground but were unsuccessful in taking new territory. All the Arab forces withdrew in April 1949, when Israel signed armistice agreements with Jordan, Egypt, and Syria.

But Iraq failed to conclude an agreement and remains, in theory, in a state of war with Israel. The Arab forces blamed their lack of military success on Western support for the Israelis, rather than on the difficulties of fighting a long way from home and the lack of coordination between various Arab armies.

As anti-Israeli sentiment rose, the situation of the Jewish community in Iraq became precarious. No doubt many remembered the rampage, known as the *Farhoud,* or looting, that had taken place in the Jewish quarter during the last few hours before the British forces entered Baghdad in 1941. About a hundred Jews were killed and many women were raped and kidnapped. In 1951 and 1952, almost all of the Jews in Iraq — 120,000 out of a total community of 130,000 — left the country. The Iraqi government acquiesced by legitimizing emigration for Jews who renounced their Iraqi citizenship in writing. But adults were allowed to take only about $20 with them, younger people proportionately less. Most emigrated to Israel, which welcomed such a community of educated Jews despite their impoverishment. Emigration was completed in eighteen months.

In 1955 Saddam moved to Baghdad to attend secondary school, a decision he has called the most important event in his life except for the Rashid Ali coup. He went to live with his uncle, Khairallah Talfah, an Arab nationalist who had been embittered by his treatment at the hands of the British and the end of his military career. Saddam studied at the Kharkh secondary school, though sophisticated Iraqis say that schooling did not rid Saddam of all traces of his peasant origins. To their ear, he still speaks with an accent that betrays the simplicity of his background, and his grammatical errors make them wince.

The political mood in Baghdad in the mid 1950s was tumultuous. Arab indignation at the establishment of the state of Israel was being whipped up to new extremes by Egyptian leader Gamal Abdul Nasser. In 1956 Nasser nationalized the Suez Canal. British and French forces responded by occupying the canal, citing threats to free passage posed by Egyptian troops, who were fighting

Israeli troops who had invaded Egypt to wipe out Palestinian terrorist bases. But, in reality, the British, French, and Israelis were cooperating in an ill-fated attempt to hold back a relentless tide of Arab nationalism. The three armies subsequently withdrew under pressure from the United States — an instance of American support for the Arab cause that is seldom remembered.

At this time Saddam became politically active. He had participated in demonstrations and riots against the government in 1956, when martial law was imposed by Nuri al-Said's government, which had failed to comprehend the strength and popularity of the Arab nationalist revival exemplified by Nasser. Clinging rigidly to old habits and postcolonial links, al-Said had signed the Baghdad Pact with Britain in 1955, a treaty designed to protect the Middle East from Soviet expansionism. (The pact also included Pakistan and Iran.) Nationalist issues fired Saddam's imagination, and he leapt into the turmoil of politics, gaining his first experience as a street fighter. In 1957, at the age of twenty, he joined the Arab Baath Socialist party.

As far as we know, however, Saddam was only a spectator to the dramatic events on July 14, 1958, when King Faisal II was swiftly overthrown in a predawn coup. The trigger for the coup was revolt in Lebanon against the Christian President Chamoun, which raised fear that young King Hussein of Jordan would be overthrown. A unit of the Iraqi Nineteenth Brigade led by Colonel Abdul Salem Aref was ordered to Jordan to support the king. En route to Jordan, Aref had to pass through Baghdad. Making a slight detour, Aref entered and seized the radio station in the capital and personally broadcast the announcement of the revolution. He sent units to the royal palace, where the regent Abdul Illah could have probably quashed the revolt but instead ordered the royal guard not to resist, out of a misguided notion that compliance would save his own life and that of the young king. When Abdul Illah and Faisal II tried to leave the palace by a back entrance in the early morning, they came under fire and were killed. Awakened by the sound of shooting, Nuri al-Said escaped by boat along the Tigris. By lunchtime

Brigadier Abdul Karim Qassem, also of the Nineteenth Brigade, had arrived in Baghdad and taken over the ministry of defense, a timing that suggested he was waiting to see whether the rebellion would be successful. Although King Hussein of Jordan considered intervention, the Iraqi army joined the conspirators, and there was no resistance.

The revolution was completed when Nuri al-Said was discovered the next day, attempting to escape from Baghdad dressed as a veiled woman. He was shot on the spot, along with the woman accompanying him; the army recovered his body and buried him at night.

Having grabbed control of the country, the plotters nearly lost it. Aref urged the liquidation of traitors, and uncontrollable mobs took over the streets. The body of Abdul Illah was taken from the palace, mutilated, dragged through the streets, and hung from the gates of the ministry of defense. Several Jordanians and a visiting American businessman were also murdered. When a mob discovered Nuri al-Said's grave, they disintered the body and dragged it through the streets.

Saddam Hussein certainly witnessed the anarchical aftermath of the coup, observing firsthand the fate that awaited a national leader who lost popularity as well as control of Iraq.

★ ★ ★

Politics after the Monarchy: Saddam as a Young Activist

The end of the monarchy in Iraq meant an end to years of corruption and to a government that had hopelessly misunderstood the tide of Arab nationalism. But the new government, headed by Abdul Karim Qassem, which promised so much, failed to deliver and soon provoked as much opposition as the monarchy had. This time, however, the political battle was different because Qassem had the army to back him, as well as communist support.

Today, official histories of Iraq tended to skate over Qassem's era, pausing only to glorify an attempted assassination of Qassem. Such an incident, botched as it was, would seem to merit only a brief mention but for one fact: Saddam Hussein was among the attempted assassins. Thus the failed assassination bid is today depicted as an act of great patriotism, with Saddam's role portrayed as particularly heroic. The reality, as best as can be pieced together, is rather more pedestrian: the assassination failed because of the incompetence of the plotters, including Saddam himself.

To understand the plot, and its failure, we must first look at the government Qassem established on coming to power. Qassem assumed the posts of prime minister, minister of defense, and commander-in-chief of the armed forces, while Abdul Salem Aref, who had led the army's first moves against the monarchy, became deputy prime minister, minister of the interior, and deputy commander-in-chief. On paper at least, the Iraqi people had reason to be optimistic about the new government for, despite the dominance of Qassem and Aref, most of the cabinet members were experienced politicians, including opposition representatives. There was also a three-man sovereignty council with representatives of each of Iraq's major communities, the Shia Muslims, the Sunni Muslims, and the Kurds.

But during the plotting to overthrow the monarchy of Faisal II, the nascent leadership had been the so-called Free Officers — some two hundred military commanders spread across the country. Their scheming and dreaming had called for the establishment of a revolutionary command council after the monarchy was deposed, but this did not materialize. Worse still, these officers now found themselves having to take orders from Aref, who had been their junior.

Within five days after the coup, Qassem and Aref began bickering about a topic that was not in itself critical policy matter, but which captivated their imaginations in the heady atmosphere of their success. At issue was the question of union with Egypt, a first step toward Arab unity, which, then as now, is a constant rhetorical theme of most Arab leaders. Aref, encouraged by Arab nationalist sentiment and the objectives of the Baath party, favored immediate unity. Qassem did not, perhaps foreseeing that unity might confer regional leadership on the Egyptian head of state, Abdul Gamal Nasser.

Aref did not let the issue lie. On a highly publicized tour of the country, he made speeches in favor of unity, frequently invoking the name of Nasser but rarely that of Qassem. On a visit to Syria for talks with Nasser to gain his support in case of a counterrevolution,

Aref allegedly called Qassem "the Naqib of the Iraqi revolution," a reference to the Egyptian general who had at first supported Nasser and then challenged him.

Qassem played a cool game in meeting Aref's challenge. Over the summer he reinforced his links with the army as well as the communists, who were against any quick union with Egypt. By September, he felt strong enough to move against Aref: he ordered that Aref be retired as deputy command-in-chief, and also removed him from his posts as deputy prime minister and interior minister. A stronger or more ruthless leader might have ordered Aref's arrest, but Qassem either knew the limits of his power or had a soft spot for his former ally. To get Aref out of Iraq, Qassem suggested an ambassadorship, but Aref declined. The two men spent an entire day in Qassem's office, locked in confrontation. At one point Aref drew his pistol. He later said he had drawn the gun to commit suicide, although Qassem claimed it was to assassinate him. Whatever happened there, the day was Qassem's, and Aref departed for West Germany as the Iraqi ambassador.

The respite in the rivalry was brief, however. Aref returned a month later, and Qassem ordered him arrested and charged with trying to overthrow the government. At this point Qassem made two political blunders: he allowed the trial to be reported to the public, thereby airing the rivalry within the leadership, and he also allowed the death sentence on Aref to be commuted to life imprisonment, thus allowing Aref to remain a potential challenger.

(A macabre feature of the Qassem era, which predated Aref's trial, was the people's court, established in August 1958 to try leaders of the previous regime for treason and corruption. The court was controlled by Fadel Abbas al-Madawi, a cousin of Qassem. After the expulsion of Aref, the court became more vigorous, picking on the opponents of the regime in a series of show trials. In tone and tenor, this people's court was not unlike the French revolutionary tribunals after 1789, the Stalinist purges of the 1930s, and Hitler's own people's court in Nazi Germany. In all these courts the hysterical bias of the judges and prosecutor, and the calmness and courage of the defendants, eventually had exactly the opposite effect of that intended: the image of the accused was enhanced and that of the regime diminished. The Iraqi show trials were discontinued in December 1959, but for the duration they acted as a focus of resentment toward the regime.)

A new challenge to Qassem came from Rashid Ali, the leader of the 1941 coup against the British. Rashid Ali had returned to Baghdad after years of exile, recently in Cairo, and his home became a center for political discussions and opposition to Qassem. At Qassem's order, Rashid Ali and others were arrested in December 1958, accused of plotting a coup. Despite disputed evidence, Rashid Ali was sentenced to death, although he was never executed and remained under house arrest. After the trial, many of the politicians in the cabinet resigned.

Qassem was becoming more isolated, even as his allies, the communists, were becoming more influential, with Qassem's blessing. But this alliance was soon strained. In March 1959 Qassem received warning of an impending army revolt in the northern city of Mosul, so he ordered his communist allies to pour supporters into Mosul. After demonstrations and skirmishes, the local army units arrested some of the communist leaders and proclaimed the revolt. At one point, air force pilots supporting the garrison attempted to bomb the radio transmitter in Baghdad. Qassem responded by ordering that the headquarters of the Mosul garrison be bombed. During the bombing, the commander, Abdul-Wahab al-Shawwaf, was wounded and taken to the hospital, where he was killed by a medical orderly while his wounds were being dressed. Leaderless, the rebellion collapsed, but for several months chaos enveloped Mosul, as the communists and their allies massacred supporters of the Arab nationalists. A special court was established, which ordered summary executions. Looting and the violent settling of past grievances were widespread.

Opponents of Qassem viewed the chances of overthrowing him by a coup to be slim because of purges in the army and firm communist support for the government. The small Baath party decided that assassination was the best alternative, and its leaders selected a group of young, enthusiastic members to train for the mission. Among them was twenty-two-year-old Saddam Hussein, who had recently been released from prison after having been accused of murdering a Qassem supporter in Takrit. To the party leadership, that must have seemed an ideal qualification.

The plan to murder Qassem involved ambushing his car in central Baghdad as he was driving either to or from his office at the defense ministry. The plotters had one advantage in that Qassem's car could take only a few routes; another advantage was that they had a man on the inside in the ministry who could tip them off about Qassem's travel plans.

Wednesday, October 7, 1959, was the day chosen. At 6:30 in the evening, while being driven to a reception at the East German embassy, Qassem fell into the trap. In the shower of hand grenades and submachine gun fire, Qassem's driver was killed, and an aide was seriously wounded. Qassem was hit in the left shoulder and was rushed to hospital in a passing taxi. One of the assailants was also killed. Qassem claimed to have shot him himself, but it is more likely that Abdul-Wahab al-Ghariri was killed by a shot from his own comrades. He was left behind in the road while the others fled.[1]

As one account describes Saddam's role, it was his job to provide cover for his four co-conspirators. Two of them were to fire into the front of the car, and two into the back. Saddam was not supposed to shoot at all, but his enthusiasm got the better of him "and he drew his machine gun from the folds of the long cloak he was wearing, and opened fire."[2] During the episode Saddam sustained a shot in the leg—it may well have been self-inflicted, for he has also been credited with shooting one of his own comrades.

Whatever its source, the wound has entered the mythology of Saddam's life. Accounts vary on how it was treated, for Saddam could not be taken to a hospital. He either dug the bullet out himself, or asked a comrade to cut into the flesh with a razor blade and pick the bullet out with a pair of scissors. A doctor later dressed the wound, describing it as little more than a scratch. Later that night he went to his uncle Khairallah's house, where he learned that the assassination had been unsuccessful.

Qassem spent several weeks in hospital but otherwise turned the assassination attempt to his advantage. He ordered his bullet-riddled car to be mounted on a pedestal at the entrance to the ministry of defense, and his bloodstained tunic to be put on display in a glass cabinet outside his office. He also decreed October 7 to be a national holiday. All in all, Qassem emerged enhanced by the experience — unlike, say, Colonel Muammar Qaddafi of Libya, who became more secretive and paranoid after his narrow escape from US bombs. (One British diplomat who has met both men says they have much in common: fondness for uniforms, a simple personal life-style, a strange rigidity of bearing, wholly unjustified belief in the power of their oratory, impulsive and irrational behavior, and a confused and incoherent political philosophy.)

Saddam meanwhile was on the run from the security forces who had arrested all his colleagues. He changed into traditional Arab dress and set off by foot, and later donkey. In addition to playing up Saddam's bravery and the pain he withstood from his wound, official Iraqi mythology also elaborates on the kindness and hospitality that he received from bedouin nomads and simple peasants.[3] At one point, Saddam swam across the river Tigris, his clothes in a bundle on his head, his knife in his teeth. Eventually, he reached the sanctuary of his home village of Oujah, near Takrit, although the security forces were looking for him and kept his home under occasional surveillance. (Saddam was sentenced to death in absentia; his arrested colleagues and other fugitives were also sentenced to death, but none of the sentences was carried out.)

From his village, Saddam soon set off again, eventually reaching the sanctuary of Syria. After six months in Damascus, he moved on to Cairo, where he enrolled at the university and immersed himself in Baath politics. Like many political exiles, he was watched by the Egyptian security forces, but they seem to have met their match in Saddam, who, according to some reports, was not adverse to giving suspected informers a savage beating. While in Cairo, he watched as Qassem threatened to invade Kuwait in 1961, and he saw Qassem's bluff called by the British, who moved reinforcements to the emirate. Though he detested Qassem, the humiliation of an Iraqi leader by a former colonial power was a lesson not lost on Saddam.

Two years later, in February 1963, Qassem's luck ran out. Early in the morning of February 8 Qassem was warned of suspicious troop movements. As he drove from his house in a southeastern suburb of Baghdad to the defense ministry, he stopped to reassure an anxious group of supporters that he had everything under control.[4]

Shortly after 9 AM the defense ministry compound was attacked by tanks, artillery, and fighter aircraft. Some tanks took up positions on the bridges over the Tigris and fired directly into the compound, while others assaulted from the eastern side. Diplomats at the British embassy, across the river from the ministry, had a grandstand view: during that day one counted 126 air strikes against forces loyal to Qassem. The thousand or so soldiers who remained loyal to Qassem held out until just before dawn the following day, when they were overrun by infantry and tanks, which crushed the twelve-foot-high railing around the ministry.

Qassem, wounded in the leg, was taken prisoner in an underground bunker. The victorious rebel forces took him to the main television station and conducted a trial of sorts. Asked whether he had signed the death warrant on the army plotters in Mosul, he replied that he had.

One of those present at this trial was Qassem's old rival, Abdul Salem Aref, whose life Qassem had spared five years earlier. Qassem told him: "You are not going to shoot me. In 1959 I had you in my power. Three times I put my gun to your head and three times I took it away. You are not going to shoot me." At that point, they shot a bullet into Qassem's head.

The rebels also executed Madawi, the head of the people's court; General Abdi, the military governor of Baghdad; and a junior staff officer. The four dead bodies were propped up on a sofa, and the television station began broadcasting. According to a diplomat who watched the transmission, Qassem looked like his usual self (he had always appeared glassy-eyed) until a soldier walked on, seized Qassem's head by the hair, and twisted it to and fro. Madawi's face was badly disfigured. He had apparently sobbed and begged for mercy; as the gun was put to his head, he had thrown himself backward to avoid the bullet.

The broadcast was probably intended to prove to Qassem's many supporters in the poorer classes that he was indeed dead, that no amount of rioting could bring him back into power.

The bloodiest day was the day following, when the revolutionaries set out to settle scores with the communists. The radio stations broadcast hysterical calls to the people to denounce communists and turn them in. But the communists were well-armed, and hundreds of street battles took place. Meanwhile, army tanks moved to demolish communist strong points. Diplomats in Baghdad at the time estimated that two thousand people died in just over two days of fighting. Under the new Baathist leadership, the purges continued for nine months. The leader of the Baath, who was also a relative of Saddam by marriage, Ahmed Hassan al-Bakr, was made prime minister. As many as ten thousand people were arrested, interrogated, and killed in secret, though there were some public executions: a diplomat recalls seeing sixteen people, mostly Kurds, being hanged in public. The viciousness of these purges is beyond words. A university professor was kept blindfolded for a week and then deliberately blinded by a powerful searchlight shone directly into his eyes. Another tale is of a doctor shot, but not killed, and thrown into a cesspit (already containing a dozen or so bodies), to die.

Saddam Hussein, who had returned to Iraq within two weeks of the coup, was not prominent at this time, although legend speaks of him taking a personal role in torture and executions, according to a diplomat serving in Baghdad at the time. Shortly after returning, Saddam married his cousin, Sajida Talfah, a primary school teacher.

The regime, made up of a fragile coalition of the military and the Baath party, was headed by Abdul Salem Aref, to give it an appearance of respectability. It was backed by a specially constituted national guard of young Baath thugs. Dressed in khaki with green armbands, and armed with submachine guns, their roadblocks were ubiquitous, and the outcome of being stopped by them was unpredictable. Many innocent people, including foreigners, were killed or wounded, accidently or deliberately, after coming across these groups.

Eventually such bloodletting brought on a reaction. On November 18, Aref, until then a figurehead president, seized total power to establish an army-backed government. In this coup, the main military target was the headquarters of the national guard. Members of the Baath, including Saddam Hussein, were forced to flee Baghdad and go into hiding.

(An interesting historical note: during the months before the Aref coup, the Baath government had relinquished the claim made by Qassem on Kuwait, signed a treaty of friendship, and established diplomatic relations. The frontier, which had been closed by Qassem two years earlier, was reopened very soon after the February 1963 revolution.)

The following year, in September 1964, Saddam was arrested for plotting against the Aref regime and was sent to prison. A biography of Saddam describes a relatively free atmosphere in the prison.[5] Indeed, although Aref's regime was not particularly liberal, it was probably the most relaxed rule of any government in Iraq during the twentieth century. A wider, though still small, spectrum of opinions was allowed to appear in the press; travel restrictions were relaxed on foreigners; contacts between foreigners and Iraqis were tolerated; and there was a genuine although unsuccessful attempt to reach a peace settlement with the Kurds. But Aref was unlucky: he died in a helicopter crash in April 1966. There was talk of sabotage, but the official version was that the helicopter had been forced down in a sandstorm. Aref's elder brother, Abdul Rahman Aref, assumed power but lacked the qualities for leadership: he was an alcoholic with no charisma and no talent for government.

Spotting an opportunity, the Baath prepared to take power yet again. This time, Saddam, who had escaped from prison, was to take a personal role, or so it is claimed.[6] At three o'clock in the morning on July 17, 1968, wearing a military uniform, he led his comrades in a tank assault on the presidential palace. Other accounts say the assault was led by Abdul Razaq Nayef, the deputy director of military intelligence, who was sympathetic to the Baath, which was still led by al-Bakr.

Determined not to have the Baath ambitions for Iraq constrained by the military, Saddam confronted Nayef in the presidential palace that night. His gun aimed at Nayef, Saddam agreed to save his life on the condition that he immediately leave the country. To make sure that the army would not move to support Nayef, it was decided that he should be sent as ambassador to Morocco. Two weeks later Saddam escorted Nayef to the airport and put him on the plane.

Back in Baghdad, President al-Bakr was appointed prime minister and commander-in-chief of the armed forces. His nephew Saddam was named vice-president of the Revolutionary Command Council. Saddam's leniency toward Nayef clearly worried him, as it left Nayef free to plot or to be selected as an alternative leader. In 1970 Nayef was sentenced to death in absentia for allegedly plotting a coup. In 1978 the execution was carried out: an Iraqi assassin murdered Nayef outside the Intercontinental Hotel in London. Saddam, in charge of security in his role as vice-president, had shown that Iraq was developing a long reach.

★ ★ ★

chapter 7

Saddam: The Popular Dictator?

Saddam Hussein has been at the center of power in Iraq for nearly twenty-two years, the first eleven as the deputy and apprentice of President al-Bakr, and another eleven years as the top man himself. How he has succeeded is a tale of patient hard work, unprincipled manipulation of allies and enemies alike, and, surprisingly, genuine support from colleagues and many ordinary people in Iraq who admire his abilities.

When the Baath party settled into power in 1968, Saddam was not immediately identifiable as the power behind the throne, although at least one report says that he was vice-president of the Revolutionary Command Council (RCC) from the earliest days of the regime.[1] But Saddam was not in the cabinet, and fifteen months passed before he started coming publicly to the fore, when his membership in the RCC was acknowledged in November 1969.

During these initial months, Saddam is believed to have played a key role in countering plots against al-Bakr, which he quashed ruthlessly, working through a mysterious organization within the Baath known as the Committee on Emergencies. His first job was to rid the Baath government of the man al-Bakr had been forced to appoint as prime minister as a reward for helping the coup, Abdul Razaq Nayef. Two weeks after the coup, Saddam forced Nayef, at gunpoint, to board a plane for Morocco. Nayef's friend, Ibrahim Daoud, another general from Aref's regime who had turned traitor and had been paid off with the post of vice-president, was also ousted.

Saddam faced tense moments in trying to make sure that this time the Baath would not be overthrown as it had been within nine months of taking over in 1963. One moment of uncertainty occurred in October 1968, when dozens of people were executed after a plot led by a General Abdul-Hadi al-Rami was discovered. Saddam is credited with personally putting down this plot.

One of Saddam's first public appearances was in August 1969, when a young Libyan army officer, Colonel Muammar Qaddafi, took over from King Idriss. Saddam led an Iraqi delegation to meet the new Arab leader. Despite the show of command, the Baath still did not feel secure at home, with good reason. Real or imagined plots were common. In January 1970, another forty-four people were hanged after a conspiracy had been uncovered.

Saddam's own position at this time was delicate because it was based on two apparently contradictory foundations. Within the Baath party he was considered to be leader of the "civil" wing. The rivalry between the civil wing and the "old guard" generals was one of the basic tensions within the party, the RCC, and the cabinet. The generals had earned a degree of respectability for their military endeavors, while the civilians had done their fighting in the streets and had often been imprisoned for it. But some of the generals were tainted by having continued to side with Aref in 1963 after the rest of the Baath had been pushed out of power. One such man was Hardan Takriti, who was serving in al-Bakr's cabinet as defense minister and deputy commander-in-chief. (Though not a relative of Saddam's, he was from the same clan.) Saddam considered the minister a traitor, yet his own position within the party was not yet strong enough to revenge such treachery, since Saddam owed much of his influence to the fact that al-Bakr was related to both his wife and his mother.

Al-Bakr was aware that Saddam was opposed to some of his closest colleagues. But the fifty-six-year-old al-Bakr seems to have taken an almost paternal interest in the career of his thirty-one-year-old relative and fellow Takriti. The younger man had so much experience and was a great debater of the issues central to Baathism — the future of the Arab world, the nature of social change. And he was willing to put his ideas into action. Both men seemed determined not to let their differences be manipulated by others; their bonds of kinship became bonds of trust. Saddam was content to pull quietly at more of the strings of power while working with al-Bakr, realizing that al-Bakr's army and middle-class upbringing would bring more support to the party than Saddam could have commanded. Al-Bakr was the acceptable, moderate face of Baathism; Saddam was the party worker who kept the regime in power with the help of activists from days in the underground.

In April 1970 Saddam's growing strength became more apparent. Two of al-Bakr's men — Hardan Takriti and Saleh Mehdi Ammash, the minister of the interior — were "promoted" to the less powerful positions of deputy presidents and replaced by two friends of Saddam: Hamid Shehab as defense minister and Saadoun Ghaidan as interior minister. The reason for the shift was the opposition of al-Bakr's two colleagues to a new agreement with the Kurds that ended hostilities and allowed for the appointment of five Kurds as ministers. Saddam, who had always been mistrustful of Kurds, is nonetheless thought to have encouraged al-Bakr to sign the pact, knowing that it would upset the old guard generals. The maneuver was completed in October 1970 when Hardan Takriti was dismissed from his post while abroad and exiled to Algeria. The following March he was assassinated in Kuwait, amid reports that he was considering a political comeback and mounting an opposition to the regime.

The plots and conspiracies of the first few years of Baath rule were nothing compared to the challenge to the government posed by the attempted coup of July 1973, when Nassem Kzar, the head of security, tried to seize power. Kzar's motivations are unclear, but he captured Saddam's allies in the cabinet, Shehab and Ghaidan, and was intending to assassinate other members of the government as they gathered at the airport that evening to greet President al-Bakr on his return from a state visit to Poland. When word leaked of Kzar's treachery, the army and Baath party were put on alert. Al-Bakr arrived and Saddam safely escorted him to the radio station, where they broadcast that the government was still in power. Kzar fled toward the Iranian border with his two hostages, but was caught after a skirmish in which Shehab was killed and Ghaidan was injured. Kzar was later executed along with twenty-two others who were thought to be part of the plot. Another prominent Baath member, Abdul Khalak Samarrai, an ambitious rival of Saddam from the city of Samarra, was placed under house arrest.

It was during these years that Saddam formed basic alliances with the men who have continued to serve him. The president of the special court set up to try the conspirators in the coup attempt of January 1970 was Taha Yassin Ramadan; in 1979 Saddam named Ramadan chief deputy in the cabinet. Although Ramadan's power later flagged, he was an important broker of support for Saddam, pulling in backing from the northern city of Mosul, his home. Tariq Aziz was chief editor of the party newspaper, *Al Thawra* (Revolution), in 1970 and was named the minister of information in 1974. Saddam made him deputy prime minister in 1979, and then minister of foreign affairs in 1983. A Christian, Aziz has made Saddam's regime more palatable to this important minority in Iraq.

Saadoun Shaker, who had spent time in prison with Saddam before the Baath took power, became a close colleague of Saddam's in party security in 1968. Saddam appointed Shaker as head of intelligence in 1972. As a Shia, Shaker helped win backing from some sections of this majority sect, who were otherwise totally opposed to the Baathists. Izzat Ibrahim, another ex-prison colleague of Saddam's, was made chairman of the special tribunal set up to try Kzar and his fellow plotters in 1973. In 1979 he was made vice-chairman of the RCC and charged with negotiating for support from those Shias and Kurds who could be partly won over to the regime. Hassan Ali, another Shia and cellmate of Saddam's during the Aref regime, also worked hard in the Baath party in the 1970s. He was a member of the tribunal that condemned eight detainees to death after Shia riots in February 1977. A minister during the 1980s, he went on to run one of the Baath regional offices.

Saddam also started looking among his relatives for aides he could trust. His own sons, born in 1964 and 1967, were too young to be considered, but his childhood friend and cousin, Adnan Khairallah, was made minister of defense in 1977 at Saddam's suggestion. During the 1970s Khairallah also occasionally acted as head of intelligence. Another relative whom Saddam groomed on matters of security was his half-brother Barzan. Theirs was an extremely close relationship and, despite a hiatus in the 1980s, has remained so.

But Saddam did not take his growing power and influence for granted. During the mid-1970s he made regular efforts to travel around the country and learn what ordinary people were thinking. These discussions also gave him an opportunity to test out opinions on people other than fawning yes-men officials. A Western diplomat posted to Baghdad in the 1970s can remember on occasion seeing Saddam, accompanied by Barzan and a few bodyguards, wandering through the streets of Baghdad, talking to people.[2]

By 1979 Saddam apparently had decided he was ready to replace al-Bakr, then sixty-seven years old. The departure of the shah in neighboring Iran, forced to flee in January 1979, and the successes of the rival Baath government in Syria suggested to Saddam that Iraq also needed a change. So, in July 1979 Saddam encouraged al-Bakr to retire on the grounds of poor health. Al-Bakr died in 1983 without revealing the exact circumstances of his retirement, but it seems likely that he knew it was wiser not to resist Saddam's proposal.

Saddam's de facto rule became official when he was installed as president on July 16, 1979. He immediately took steps to quash any rivals. Eleven days after assuming the presidency, he announced that a plot to overthrow the regime had been foiled. Alleging foreign backing (later identified as Syrian), he rallied the nation behind his new government, garnering support for the arrest of plotters in the Baath party and the army, who also happened to be Saddam's rivals. When Saddam announced to an emergency meeting of the Baath leadership that the plot had been discovered, he produced one of the alleged ringleaders, who read out a confession. As he listed his accomplices, these men, at Saddam's instruction, left the room and were arrested. Five top Baath members were detained, and a special tribunal was set. Fifty army officers and more than a hundred members of the Baath were implicated in the conspiracy. On August 7, twenty-two people, including five members of the RCC, were condemned to death. All were executed the next day, except for one, who had escaped. Among those executed was Samarrai, Saddam's old political rival, who had been under house arrest since 1973. It said that the executions were witnessed by Saddam and his cabinet colleagues. Some reports say that these men also took up positions in the firing squads.

Three of the five RCC members executed were Shias. There had been Shia riots before the plot was discovered, and Saddam was anxious to quell any thought of revolution among the Shia majority. But the plotters seem to have been primarily motivated by their personal distaste for Saddam Hussein. President Assad of Syria shared their animosity, although there was some support for a union between the two Baath-run countries (Saddam opposed such a union, probably because it would have been dominated by Assad). It was later alleged that President Assad wanted to head a union of the two countries, with Samarrai as the president of Iraq in place of Saddam.

During the 1980s, as Iraq was focused on the war with Iran, Saddam consolidated his power at home and started to gain confidence in projecting an image to the world at large. For several years,

Saddam and his colleagues had considerable difficulty in even deciding how best to present themselves to foreign audiences. An American visitor to Iraq in 1984 who met with Taha Yassin Ramadan, Saddam's top deputy, gave this impression: "The meeting took place in Ramadan's office. The walls and ceiling were painted white, the desk was of a white alabaster, and the armchairs and sofas were made of white leather. Ramadan, a short, fat man, was wearing the green uniform showing him to be a senior Baathist, with a pistol on his belt. He gave all the appearance of what he clearly was—a world-class thug."[3]

Among those who collaborated with Saddam were Iraqi intellectuals who had decided to defend the regime's worst excesses for reasons of nationalism. A stream of ambitious technocrats readily took on the responsibilities of running a government, the horrors of which they either ignored or justified as necessary. This support from a hardworking bureaucracy helped Saddam to consolidate his power and to provide greater internal stability than at any other time in the history of modern Iraq.

Saddam's position has been reinforced by a personality cult of staggering proportions. There are posters depicting Saddam everywhere. In the main cities, the posters dominate many squares; others stand alongside the highways, and it would be a foolish local council that did not make sure each town had a picture of the great leader prominently displayed. The posters show a selection of the preferred images: Saddam as soldier, Saddam as ordinary peasant, Saddam as university teacher. There is even a government department, the Very Special Projects Implementation Authority, devoted to making sure that the posters and murals are well cared for.

All over Iraq, institutions have been named in honor of the great leader: Baghdad's Saddam International Airport; the Saddam Oil Field, a new find close to his hometown of Takrit; Saddam City, the working-class Shia suburb of Baghdad. The 140-foot-long pendulum in a new clocktower in central Baghdad is surrounded by seven statues depicting the seven stages of Saddam's life, from his birth to the cease-fire with Iran in 1988.[5]

Emphasizing his links with previous golden eras of Iraqi history has been one of Saddam's habitual emphases in the past eleven years. In 1988 he surprised many by starting a process of rehabilitating the monarchy. He ordered the renovation of the mausoleum housing the remains of King Faisal I and those of his grandson, King Faisal II. When the refurbishment was completed, Saddam visited the site with King Hussein of Jordan, whose grandfather, King Abdullah, was Faisal I's brother. Why was Saddam now glorifying the monarchy? Amatzia Baram, an Israeli specialist on Iraq, has offered several possible explanations: that the early monarchs were to be respected as patriotic opponents of foreign domination; that postrevolutionary Iraq was now to embark on a new era of stability and tradition; that the legitimacy of all rulers — including, therefore, Saddam — was worthy of national tribute; that the monarchy's claims of descent from the Prophet Mohammed was to bolster Saddam's own claim to a similar pedigree.[4]

Despite signs of emerging self-confidence, there has been little easing in Saddam's regime of domestic terror. He has tortured, imprisoned, and killed too many Iraqis not to have made thousands of enemies who loathe him with a vengeance. So he continues to surround himself with security services, endlessly searching for plots against him. His intelligence service, the Mukhabarat, has many of its functions duplicated by the security service. In addition, military intelligence is thought to do more than spy on Iraq's potential enemies abroad — it also checks on threats at home. Another organization, Al Amn Al Khas, seeks industrial secrets abroad to enable Iraq to build new weapons at home. Apart from these bodies, there are the civil police and the border police.

These security services, besides terrorizing many Iraqis, also promulgate xenophobia, which raises dread in the minds of many foreigners living in Iraq. Despite wanting to be acknowledged for his political stature, Saddam has never failed to forget that his power is based on respect — and fear.

★ ★ ★

Saddam's Family Rivalries and Scandals

Writing about Saddam Hussein's family can cause more fallout than writing about Iraqi military secrets, including its various superweapons. During the seven years I have written about Iraq, I received an indirect warning of displeasure on only one occasion — after writing about the Iraqi leader's oldest son, Udai, and the death of one of Saddam's most trusted bodyguards.

According to the official version of the events of October 18, 1988, "an unexpected incident took place" on Aras Island in the Tigris, near the Jadiriya Bridge, south of the Presidential Palace, opposite a compound where senior Baath party members lived and where Udai Saddam Hussein had an apartment. Kamel Hanna Jejjo, described as a presidential messenger, was entertaining some members of his family at a dinner. Jejjo became intoxicated and started firing randomly and heavily into the air with his submachine gun. Such shots were a common way of celebrating in Iraq, but had recently been banned, after an outburst marking the cease-fire in the war with Iran caused several casualties when the spent rounds returned to earth. Udai sent one of his aides to order Jejjo to stop, but Jejjo resumed firing after a short interval. So Udai went up to Jejjo, ordered him to stop, and raised a stick to strike him across the shoulders when he did not obey. Unfortunately, the luckless Jejjo moved at the last moment, and the blow landed on his head; he died the next morning. Udai was said to have been overcome with remorse and, in the following days, tried to commit suicide three times.

Saddam ordered his justice minister to launch an investigation, and Udai was initially detained in prison. Saddam told the justice minister that he saw the incident as God's test of justice in Iraq. He also wrote in a letter to the justice minister that "Udai never killed before, as far as I know," although opposition groups claim that Udai had once killed another Iraqi in a Baghdad hotel after taking a fancy to the man's girlfriend. Udai is also known to be a keen collector of guns. In 1988 he tried to buy about $40,000 worth of expensive handguns from the United States. One official remarked that the required export license was refused "because of US policy at the time of not exporting weapons to either Iraq or Iran, still fighting the Gulf War."[1]

The unofficial version of the incident, as first heard by the author, was that Udai had been shooting in the air and had bludgeoned Jejjo when Jejjo asked him to stop. A blunt instrument was said to have been used, supposedly a tire lever (less than a foot long, but very heavy) that Udai had been carrying in his pocket. Saddam was said to have been furious about the attack: the dead man, like many presidential bodyguards, was from one of Iraq's small Christian sects, the Chaldeans, and the president was perhaps fearful that his other bodyguards would be resentful to the point of mutiny unless Udai was punished. Furthermore, Jejjo was the son of Saddam's personal cook and acted as the presidential foodtaster. (The logic of this was impeccable: Would a treacherous cook go so far as to poison his own son?)

The first report also said that Saddam had roundly condemned his son for killing the bodyguard, and perhaps had also beat his son. Saddam's wife, Sajida, intervening on her son's side, was also reported to have been beaten. Both disappeared from public view. Sajida Hussein had been attending the celebrations to welcome the wife of President Mubarak of Egypt to Baghdad, but she was curiously absent when the Egyptian first lady left the country on October 21.

The extent of embarrassment the incident caused Saddam is reflected in the chronology of reports about it. The day after the episode, on October 19, Udai's name was dropped from the masthead of the local sports newspaper of which he was nominally editor-in-chief. On November 6 Udai lost his official positions as head of the Iraqi Olympic Committee and the Iraq Football Federation. A brief announcement merely said that he had resigned for personal reasons. (Udai had been unanimously reelected to a four-year term as head of the Olympic Committee on October 15.) Presumably, he was relieved of his newly acquired post as rector of the Saddam University for Science and Technology in Baghdad. The first published report of Jejjo's death appeared in the *Mideast Markets* newsletter, then published by the *Financial Times* of London, in its November 14 issue, copies of which were available on November 11. This report probably forced Saddam to go public with the affair on November 21.

The justice minister, Akram Abdul Qadir Ali, was given an unenviable task: to make Saddam Hussein appear fair and incorruptible without incurring the Iraqi leader's wrath for exposing his son's outrageous behavior. The published text of the minister's reply rhetorically stakes out several options:

> I read [the president's letter] amid tears which I could not check and sobs I could not restrain. The feelings of fatherhood and affection did their work by tearing me apart in their struggle with the feelings of faith in God and in justice. . . .
> Mr. President, allow me to say that I am afraid you may

commit an outrage against your own son as a result of your deep sense of justice. . . . The judiciary, which you have preserved and protected, will always be what you expect it to be. . . . Thousands of cases such as your son Udai's are settled by the courts in accordance with right, law, and the essence of justice, which takes into consideration the circumstances and surrounding conditions.

The commission set up to investigate the incident was presided over by Judge Abdul Wahab Hussein al-Duri—whom opposition groups claimed was a cousin of the the vice-chairman of the Revolutionary Command Council, Izzat Ibrahim al-Duri, as well as a cousin of the justice minister. Since the official version of the incident had not suggested Udai was a criminal, he was quickly released on November 27, pending completion of the investigation. Clearly, the judges and justice minister could not challenge the facts of the incident as presented by the president. Their judicial predicament was eased slightly when the heads of some Arab states asked Saddam to show leniency; Jejjo's father also asked for the charges to be dropped.

In January 1989 Udai flew off to Geneva, Switzerland, apparently in the care of his half-uncle, Barzan Ibrahim, who was about to take up his new appointment as Iraqi ambassador to the United Nations organizations. The case against Udai had been quietly dropped. When both men applied for diplomatic residence permits, the Swiss authorities hesitated to approve Udai's. A few days later the Swiss requested that he leave the country. According to diplomats, Udai had pulled a knife on a Swiss policeman during an altercation in a restaurant. Diplomats say that Udai's departure for Iraq was so abrupt that his plane crossed paths with that of his mother, who was unaware of his expulsion and was heading for Switzerland to visit him. Saddam said in a later interview that Udai left Switzerland because "he could not endure the life and atmosphere there."

Here the story takes another turn. The details are fuzzy, partly because opposition groups tried to capitalize on Saddam's embarrassment by making up elaborate side plots. Many local diplomats believed that Saddam was becoming increasingly bored with his wife and had taken a fancy to another woman; he had been seen around Baghdad with one. For a while it was thought that Sajida was in danger, that Saddam might organize a fatal accident to be rid of her. A symbolic statement of Arab displeasure at this notion may have been the motive for a trip that Queen Noor of Jordan made to Baghdad. Protocol demanded that the queen be met by Sajida, and, according to the diplomats, Saddam understood the implicit message of the visit.

Reports of Saddam's marital infidelities had cropped up several times over the years. One report alleges that the wife of an Armenian merchant living in Baghdad was his mistress for a while; another girlfriend was supposedly the daughter of a one-time Iraqi ambassador. According to opposition claims, the Jejjo incident occurred when Saddam was having an affair with a woman who had allegedly born him a son. It was rumored that Jejjo had been involved in arranging Saddam's extramarital trysts, that Udai was furious when he found out, and that this was why he killed Jejjo. According to opposition accounts, the mistress was Samira Shahbandar, the wife of a former head of Iraqi Airways. For a time, the story went, Saddam was thinking of either divorcing Sajida or taking Samira as a second wife, a custom acceptable in Islamic law but contrary to Baath party ideology. Further episodes of this tale gave the illegitimate son's name as Ali, which meant that Saddam could be called Abu Ali, meaning "the father of Ali" but also a common Arabic idiom for "trickster." Yet a further gloss was the suggestion that Samira Shahbandar was not a member of the Shahbandar family, but a cook who had adopted the family name. This story had the dual merit of implying that Samira had stolen the name of a good Baghdad family and that the president was chasing hired help.

Rumors aside, the death of Jejjo affected the power relationships among Saddam's close relatives, all of whom owed their positions of authority to kinship. Particularly sensitive was the situation of

Adnan Khairallah, the minister of defense and Saddam's cousin and brother-in-law. The *Mideast Markets* report of the incident quoted Iraqi foreign diplomats as saying that Adnan had taken the side of his sister, Sajida, when Saddam had beaten her in his fury over Udai. Whether or not this was true, Saddam knew that Adnan would, in the Arab tradition, stand by and defend his blood relatives. Could he now trust Adnan to fulfill both aspects of his duty: to make sure the military was prepared to defend the country and to make sure the military was not a threat to the regime? There was precious little evidence that Adnan Khairallah was an annoyed brother-in-law, but there was a growing feeling among diplomats in Baghdad that Saddam might be less than happy about Adnan's professional abilities.

When Iraq Army Day, scheduled for January 6, 1989, was abruptly cancelled, rumors mounted that a coup plot had been discovered. Subsequent reports confirmed that dissident military officers had planned to attack the reviewing stand during the official march past. It was even suggested that rebellious pilots were to strafe and bomb the stand. This was precisely the kind of plot that Adnan Khairallah was expected to have discovered early on. The late cancellation of the Army Day celebrations suggested that he had been lax. (Corroboration of the plot emerged in a macabre way. One of the dissident officers was the brother of a locally hired administrative secretary to the Spanish ambassador in Baghdad. One day the officer's beaten, tortured, and bullet-ridden body was delivered to the family home for burial. The ambassador passed on details of the plot to his colleagues in the diplomatic community.)

In May 1989, four months after the canceled parade, it was announced that Adnan Khairallah had been killed in a helicopter crash, along with several others. The official story claimed that Adnan, who was piloting the helicopter, was disoriented by a sandstorm, lost control, and crashed. There was widespread disbelief of this account, although no contradictory evidence was found. Cynical Iraqis recalled that in April 1966 Abdul Salem Aref, then president, also died in a helicopter crash during a sandstorm.

The incredulity forced Saddam to set up an official court of inquiry, produce photographic evidence of the crashed helicopter, and memorialize his deceased brother-in-law by building a statue of him in Baghdad.

After Khairallah's death, two other arms of Saddam's family renewed their competition for influence: his cousins, the al-Majids, and his half-brothers, the Ibrahims. Of the various branches of Saddam's family tree, the Khairallah bough had been rather short, and clearly could no longer be relied on. The al-Majid and the Ibrahim branches were longer, and Saddam could play rival members off against each other.

The al-Majids and the Ibrahims had already become rivals in 1983, when Hussein Kamel al-Majid, then head of the presidential bodyguard, married Saddam's eldest daughter, Raghad. This was a match of which the Ibrahims disapproved. They had had their own candidate to be the president's son-in-law and deeply resented the increased clout the marriage afforded the al-Majids. At the time — it was the height of the war with Iran, and Iraq was not doing well — there was also a perception among local diplomats that the Ibrahims did not think much of Saddam's military strategy. An almighty row took place — one diplomatic report spoke of shooting being heard in the presidential palace — and the three Ibrahim brothers vanished from public eye. The most prominent, Barzan, lost his job as head of intelligence, where he had been feared for his ruthlessness; Sabawi was removed as chairman of the foreign relations committee in the national assembly; and Watban ceased being governor of Salahuddin province. It was generally accepted that the three were sent back home to Takrit and kept under house arrest.

Another reason for the brothers' fall from grace may have been Barzan's increasing greediness. Although Iraqi law strictly prohibits bribe taking by officials, Saddam has had to tolerate a large measure of corruption from those in his closest circles as a way of maintaining their loyalty. The president himself is not thought to take slices of important foreign contracts, and he has punished many officials, including the occasional foreigner, for such offences, but he puts up

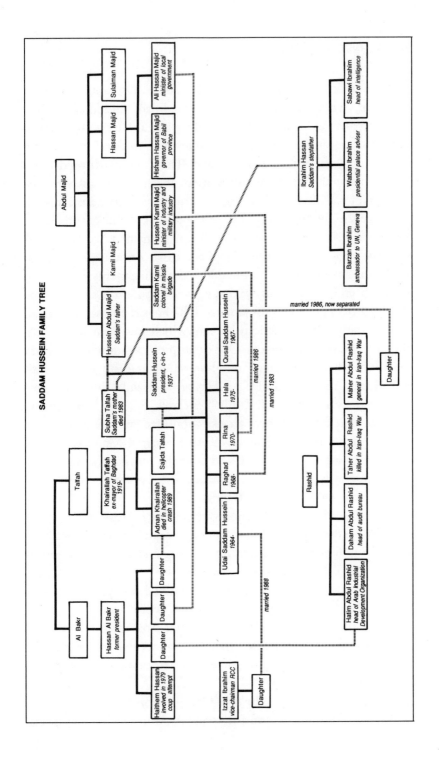

SADDAM HUSSEIN FAMILY TREE

with some lining of the pockets by his family. One retired foreign diplomat, who had been based in Baghdad, said that he had arranged business deals that included payoffs to Barzan; the money was channeled through a Greek businessman in London, working with a pro-Iraqi Syrian exile in Paris. The diplomat-turned-businessman noted with some amusement that the two go-betweens managed to facilitate deals for some time after Barzan was arrested.

Once the Ibrahims were out of the capital, the al-Majids had a clearer field. Hussein Kamel's brother, also named Saddam, married the president's second daughter, Rina. Another cousin, Ali Hassan al-Majid, scored a series of career advancements. Until 1986 he had been head of security; that year he became a member of the Baath Party Regional Command. In 1987 he was promoted to head of the Baath party's northern bureau, which gave him wide party, military, and security powers. One of his projects was to control and punish Kurdish tribes, many of whom sided, at least passively, with Iran during the war. Under Ali Hassan al-Majid's direction, poisonous gas was dropped in Kurdish enclaves, injuring both fighters and innocent civilians; these attacks continued even after the cease-fire in August 1988. In June 1989 Ali Hassan al-Majid was made minister of local government, and after the invasion of Kuwait he was temporarily given the additional post of governor of the new province created from Kuwaiti territory.

But of the al-Majids, the most outstanding is Hussein Kamel. In 1982, at age twenty-eight he was merely a captain in the Republican Guard, the unit entrusted with protecting Saddam and the presidential palace. In response to setbacks in the war—Iraq was pushed back from most of the Iranian territory it had occupied—Hussein Kamel was given the task of expanding the Republican Guard. Soon the Republican Guard was the largest corps in the army, and Saddam Hussein commented that "he was pleased to see a young man [Hussein Kamel] capable of achieving anything and everything."[2]

In 1988 the Military Industries Organization was set up to bring the General Institute for Industries and Al Amn Al Khas, the special security agency, under one umbrella, and Hussein Kamel was made its first director. He was given the rank of lieutenant general and also named acting minister for industry and minerals. The principal task of the Military Industries Organization was arms production, and Iraq's various superweapons projects — missiles, chemicals, supergun, and nuclear bomb — came under Hussein Kamel's mandate. When the agency was again reorganized, as the Ministry for Industry and Military Production, Hussein Kamel was made a full minister.

By 1988 Saddam decided that some of the al-Majids had become too prominent. He distanced himself from Ali Hassan al-Majid by removing him from the presidential entourage that met with the military command. This role was given to Hussein Kamel. (In October 1990 Hussein Kamel was also made acting minister of oil.) Saddam inaugurated the rehabilitation of the Ibrahim brothers by sending Barzan as an ambassador to the United Nations organizations in Geneva. There, Barzan used his diplomatic muscle effectively to make sure that Iraq was not condemned for human rights abuses — an irony, given Barzan's own reputation for abuses in the nation's security apparatus during the 1980s.

The next Ibrahim to emerge was Sabawi, who turned up at the Iraq National Day celebrations at the embassy in Washington, DC, in July 1988. By the end of 1989 he was head of intelligence, an appointment that must have particularly irritated the al-Majids. Watban also began to be seen around Baghdad, although his precise role was not clear. He is usually identified by diplomats as either in charge of security at the presidential palace or head of the office of Takriti protocol there, handing out presidential largesse to maintain the loyalty of the hometown power base.

Saddam also had to cope with the aspirations of his two sons, Udai and Qusai. Despite the Jejjo incident, Saddam retained an affection for his older son and wanted Udai to succeed him. Udai was partially rehabilitated in 1989, when he wrote the foreword to a local Arabic-language biography of his father, and he fully re-emerged in public in February 1990, when he was reappointed head of the Olympic Committee and the Iraq Football Federation. His photograph started to appear regularly in the Iraqi press, with never a murmur of what had happened to the bodyguard Jejjo.

Qusai's career has been less easy to monitor. Early in 1987 he married the daughter of Maher Abdul Rashid, one of the most successful generals in the Iran-Iraq War. Because of Rashid's success, Saddam began to mistrust him and ousted him. Since it would not do for the president's son to remain married to the daughter of a disgraced general, the young couple were separated in 1988. Qusai was named the second deputy of the Olympic Committee and made an official visit to Egypt to meet with President Mubarak, in October 1988. Qusai later was said to have a senior position in one of the intelligence organizations, a post from which he could keep his father informed and learn the ropes of a business that he would need to protect his own life in the future.

As Saddam's sons matured, the issue of who would be heir apparent introduced further tensions in the family. Udai seemed to have returned to his favored position. Not only is he the older son, he is also married to the daughter of the vice-chairman of the Revolutionary Command Council, Izzat Ibrahim, who is Saddam's constitutional successor. Udai, however, has many rivals and no power base. His principal rivals are all in the family—Hussein Kamel, Ali Hassan, and his own brother, Qusai—although the two sons could forge a tactical alliance against their al-Majid cousins. A potential source of support for Udai is the Baath party, but he has irritated its senior members on several occasions. For example, Udai achieved initial prominence in the Olympic Committee and Football Federation by outflanking, with his father's help, the minister of sports, Abdul Fattah Mohammed Amin al-Yassin. In 1986, fresh out of the university, Udai moved to orchestrate the dismissal of the sports minister after Iraq's poor performance in the World Cup competition held in Mexico. The sports ministry was abolished in late 1987, reportedly at the personal suggestion of the minister himself. By January 1988 Udai had assumed all the responsibilities of the defunct ministry, and the former minister had to content himself with receiving the Rafidain medal for realizing "Baath party values." Another blunder by Udai occurred at the time of the Jejjo incident. The country's vice-president, Taha Moeddin Marouf, a Kurd, was said to have been insulted by Udai when he intervened in the quarrel between Saddam's son and the bodyguard.

At present, Hussein Kamel probably thinks he is the most likely successor if Saddam were to die suddenly, before announcing a successor. Kamel has the advantage of maturity—he is ten years older than Udai—as well as good contacts and relationships with the military, because of his skill in arranging purchases of new equipment. During his service as a minister he has probably forged some alliances with other ministers, although he also has made enemies in the cabinet by demanding scarce funds at the expense of others.

A third competitor is Barzan, who has not allowed his posting to Geneva to diminish his access to the president in Baghdad; he returns frequently to the Iraqi capital. In the late 1980s Barzan seemed to have taken over handling Iraq's relationship with Iran, and he has written two lengthy feature articles on the Iranian economy, published in Baghdad's English-language newspaper, the *Baghdad Observer*. More significantly, Barzan was part of the delegation that visited Tehran in August 1990, after the invasion of Kuwait, in order to arrange a swap of prisoners of war and offer some peace-making concessions to Iran.

Self-interest would suggest that these three rivals will not plot against Saddam or each other. But the likelihood for cooperation among them also appears slight. In a crisis some other leader might emerge, though two decades of bloodletting in Iraq have left few other predictable candidates. Unless there is a complete collapse of the regime, Saddam would likely be replaced by a group of existing military and Baath leaders, perhaps including some of Saddam's relatives so as to claim, at least initially, to be carrying on his tradition, a scary possibility both for internal opponents of Saddam and for Iraq's neighbors.

★ ★ ★

9

Saddam Hussein and Israel

Saddam Hussein is obsessed about Israel and, for a while in the 1980s, some important and influential Israelis were intrigued by Saddam Hussein, whom they thought might even be the next Arab leader to sign a peace treaty with the Jewish state.[1] However, even before Saddam threatened, in a speech broadcast April 2, 1990, to destroy half of Israel with chemical weapons, Israelis had put out of their minds any notion of dealing with the Iraqi dictator.

Jewish history and Iraqi history have been interwoven since biblical times. The Old Testament patriarch Abraham came from Ur, in what is now the southern part of Iraq. Eventually his descendants established towns and villages in Canaan, and erected a great temple in Jerusalem. In 586 BC Nebuchadnezzar destroyed the temple and brought thousands of Jews to Babylon. The Babylonian exile is commemorated in Psalm 137: "By the rivers of Babylon, there we sat down; yea, we wept when we remembered Zion." After the captivity ended, when Cyrus the Great conquered

Babylon and returned Jerusalem to the Jews in 538 BC, some Jews stayed on in Babylonia. One of the basic codes of Jewish civil and religious law, the Babylonian Talmud, was written by scholars around 500 AD in academies by the river Euphrates. At various times the Jews were persecuted and antipathy was not far below the surface. In the ninth century the Jews were heavily taxed, restricted in where they could live, and forced to wear yellow patches on their clothing. In 1333 the synagogues of Baghdad were destroyed. Between 1750 and 1830 Turkish repression was so great that many Jews fled to Persia and India. But by 1920 when modern Iraq was established, the Jewish community in Baghdad was one of the largest, most prosperous, and most well-established in the Arab society. The first finance minister of Iraq, Sasun Haskail, was a Jew.

With World War II, anti-Semitism reignited in Baghdad, and a rampage of murder, rape, and plunder took place in the city's Jewish quarter just before the defeat of the pro-Nazi Rashid Ali regime British forces in 1941. When the state of Israel was founded in 1948, some 120,000 of Iraq's 130,000 Jews emigrated. Today, the Iraqi Jewish community is among the immigrant groups best absorbed into Israeli society: one Iraqi Jew, Shlomo Hillel, became police minister, and then speaker of the Israeli Knesset (parliament); another, Shimon Levy, was the chief of staff of the Israeli army in the mid-1980s.

Saddam has repeatedly played on Arab fear and hatred of Israel to outmaneuver rivals. In 1968, just after the Baath returned to power, Hassan al-Bakr put Saddam in charge of security. Saddam then had his rivals arrested, falsely, as part of an Israeli spy ring. Jews were also rounded up, and eleven were hanged, along with three Muslims, in January 1969. The executions took place in a square in the center of Baghdad and the public was invited to watch. The spectacle went on for twenty-four hours while Baath leaders, including President al-Bakr, made speeches condemning Zionism and imperialism. It is unclear whether Saddam shares the views of his uncle and former guardian, Khairallah Talfah, who in 1981 published the booklet *Three Whom God Should Not Have Created:*

Persians, Jews, and Flies. Talfah, who had been mayor of Baghdad early in Baath rule, described Persians as "animals God created in the shape of humans," Jews as a "mixture of dirt and leftovers from diverse peoples," and commented, "We do not understand God's purpose in creating [flies]."

Fewer than four hundred Jews are now living in Iraq, according to estimates by the US State Department.[2] There is no evidence of recent persecution, and one synagogue functions in Baghdad, but, as American Iraq expert Phebe Marr notes, the "position (of Jews in Iraq) today is unenviable."[3] As in every synagogue outside Israel, the rabbi offers a prayer each week for the ruler of the country. Senior members of the Iraqi Jewish community have also published letters in the press justifying Iraq's invasion of Kuwait.

There is little doubt that Iraq has remained one of the more persistently hard-line Arab states, still formally at war with Israel, having never participated in the armistice agreement in 1949. But during the war with Iran, Iraq tried to ease itself away from its isolation and win friends in the West. Yet close examination of Iraqi statements on Israel show little change in attitude. For each apparent concession there is a hard-line statement that contradicts and nullifies it. But people looking for such a change were encouraged nonetheless. The most often-quoted comment attributed to Saddam Hussein on the issue is from a meeting with a visiting member of the US House of Representatives, Stephen Solarz, who is Jewish and is also a strong supporter of Israel. The Iraqi president declared that "a secure state is necessary for both Israel and the Palestinians"—a statement that can be interpreted in many ways. Israeli officials ridiculed the notion that these words indicate Saddam's acceptance of Israel's right to exist—although that view was taken by some commentators. Iraqi diplomats have been evasive when asked about whether Baghdad was willing to recognize Israel. As Nizar Hamdoun was on the point of leaving Washington, DC, in 1987, after four years as Iraq's envoy, he answered a direct question on the subject by saying, "We cannot give away our bargaining chip before the bargaining begins." Both supporters and opponents of the

Israeli state have interpreted this remark as favorable to their own viewpoints.

During the 1980s the flirtation between Iraq and the West had prompted a renewed debate among Israeli policymakers about a basic tenet of Israeli foreign policy. The thought had long been that Israel could not achieve stable, beneficial relations with any Arab state in the foreseeable future and should therefore look further afield for support, especially to those countries that had their own disagreements with the Arab states. Hence the attention to building links with Turkey, the shah's Iran, and Ethiopia under the emperor Haile Selassie. This policy worked well until the monarchies in Ethiopia and Iran were overthrown and replaced by virulently anti-Israel regimes. So, some Israelis argued that the policy had failed and that direct contact with Arab states should be tried. Iraq was worth considering, some contended, because it had a strong leader who wanted to be seen as playing a historic role in world affairs. Saddam, they felt, would not be inhibited about making a deal in Iraq's good interests. Other Israelis said nothing had changed, either in Iraq's view of Israel or the essential soundness of Israel's long-held foreign policy. Proponents of this latter opinion had a powerful argument: the use of Israelis to facilitate contacts with senior Iranians in the Iran-Contra affair showed a continuance of some identity of interest between Tehran and Jerusalem. Further, in late 1989 Israel established relations with Colonel Mengistu's regime in Ethiopia, filling a gap left by the Soviet Union, which no longer had the will or the ability to support peripheral left-wing regimes. In the end, though, it was decided to give the policy initiative a chance, and to extend some feelers that had already been put out to Saddam's regime.

Israel's relations with Arab states other than Egypt, with whom Israel made peace in 1979, are a highly sensitive subject in Israel. The authorities deter journalists from writing about these diplomatic matters by including them in the list of topics supervised by the office of the military censor. A more effective constraint is that the number of people qualified to pass comment on the matter is small. Insiders in this group include officials at the political research center of the ministry of foreign affairs in Jerusalem, the Mossad secret intelligence agency, and military intelligence. Sometimes academic specialists and journalists are allowed on the fringe of this group, but most are tight-lipped, so as not to jeopardize their own participation in one of the more intriguing aspects of Israeli diplomacy.

Despite the harsh anti-Israel rhetoric that has streamed from Arab capitals, Israel believes that the Arab states should not be and are not totally constrained by their support for Palestinians. Jerusalem therefore tries to maintain some kind of link with most of these countries, and succeeds. Trade tries are one example: the Arab states are estimated to buy as much as $1 billion to $1.5 billion worth of Israeli goods each year. Israeli agricultural equipment, particularly irrigation equipment, has gone across the open bridges from the occupied West Bank to a middleman in the Jordanian capital, Amman, and then on to Iraq. According to Israelis familiar with the operation, the Iraqi government knows the provenance of the equipment, which is as Israel wants it, waiting to see if this seed might bear fruit.

Moreover, there are some indications that Iraq has purchased arms from Israel, though Iraq denies this and Israeli officials publicly dismiss the suggestion. Others say privately that Israel undertook the gamble to see whether political as well as commercial business could be done with Iraq. Israeli arms dealers, with the permission of their government, are believed to have delivered Israeli-made flak jackets to Baghdad in 1983 and 1984, but those shipments did not lead to any big orders.

A more indirect Israeli deal was China's transfer of Type-69 tanks to Iraq in 1983. These tanks were modified versions of the Type-59 tank, the Chinese equivalent of the Soviet T-55. Modifications included reequipment with an Israeli-made 105-mm tank gun and a laser range finder. Israel's cooperation with China on defense production is highly sensitive and kept separate from diplomatic initiatives that have succeeded in warming relations between the two countries in recent years. But officials say that Israeli permission would have been needed before the tanks were transferred, and Iraqi officials would have known that some equipment on them was Israeli.

An even more curious tale concerns an agreement that was worked on but never finalized. In 1984 Iraq was seeking international financing to build an oil export pipeline across Jordan to the Red Sea port of Aqaba. The United States was interested because Bechtel, a San Francisco–based engineering group, was a likely contractor. In addition, Chase Manhattan Bank was acting as financial adviser, the US Exim Bank was a likely source of funds, and the Washington-based Overseas Private Investment Corporation was to be tapped for loan guarantees. The contract, worth more than $900 million, would have been one of the biggest business deals of the time in the Middle East, where opportunities had dropped sharply because of the Iran-Iraq war and declining oil prices. There was competitive interest by British, French, German, and Japanese business concerns. Iraq told the foreign banks, however, that it would stop paying interest on the loans if the pipeline was rendered inoperable due to attack or sabotage. Given that condition, the banks rejected the project.

In 1988 scanty details of a potential side deal emerged. As it was courting the banks, Iraq had been trying to elicit Israeli guarantees not to attack the pipeline. Iraq offered the Israeli Labor Party, which was then in power under the leadership of Shimon Peres, a pledge of several million dollars in return for such a promise. Whether the payment was to be to the Labor Party or to the government of Israel was never clear. Peres and Israeli officials denied any payment was either offered or considered. But the pipeline idea had not been wholly discarded in September 1984, when Iraq had announced alternative plans to build the first of two pipelines across Saudi Arabia. White House backing for the Aqaba pipeline continued well into 1985, and press reports suggested that the pipeline might have been discussed by Edwin Meese, the attorney-general in the Reagan administration, when he visited Israel to meet with Peres in May 1986.[4]

The most intense period of diplomatic flirtation appears to have been in 1987. On the Iraqi side the name that keeps cropping up is Nizar Hamdoun, then completing his stint as Iraqi ambassador to Washington. During his tenure he was a favorite on the diplomatic dinner-party circuit and was not adverse to entertaining Jewish opinion formers and noted supporters of Israel at his dinner table. On at least one occasion he used the argument that since Iraq was the only obstacle preventing Iranian fanatics under Ayatollah Khomeini from marching on the Israeli capital, Iraq was worthy of American support.

On the Israeli side, the initiative was led by Avraham Tamir, a former general who was serving as one of the heads of the Israeli foreign ministry. Tamir was a protégé of Shimon Peres, who had just yielded the premiership to his Likud rival, Yitzhak Shamir, and become foreign minister in a coalition government. Tamir was a frequent visitor to Cairo, where he was trying to further normalize links with Egypt, which was supporting Iraq in the war against Iran. The details of the bid to establish contacts are obscure, but the efforts became so public that the English-language *Jerusalem Post* printed an editorial comment on the subject. By mid-1988 the efforts were less talked about, perhaps because a series of Iraqi victories on the battlefield meant that concessions toward Israel were less important to Baghdad. Some Israel officials contend that Tamir's open interest, compounded by his sociability with the foreign press corps in Egypt during his visits there, was inappropriate for a highly sensitive diplomatic initiative. "Do you call that diplomacy?" one commented scornfully.

By then, Nizar Hamdoun was back in Baghdad as a senior foreign ministry official. Asked about contacts with Israel, as described in the *Jerusalem Post* editorial, he merely said: "I read the article."[5]

In December 1987 the start of the intifada, the uprising by Palestinians living under Israeli occupation in the West Bank and

Gaza Strip, presented Saddam with a further dilemma. As Ofra Bengio, an Israeli expert on Iraq, explained: Saddam needed to present the war with Iran as the central pan-Arab issue that merited all-Arab support, but he also wanted to consider Arab unity against Israel as the central pan-Arab issue.[6] One way to make both arguments was to cast both conflicts as two sides of the same coin. Saddam put it this way: "The Zionists and the Tehran regime who are allied against our nation covet its land and seek to establish false empires."[7] The two wars were the same, he noted, except for the weapons: the Iraqis were using missiles, the Palestinians stones. There was no hint of deviation from the standard hard-line position, that Israel was a false usurper, an illegal entity, a cancerous tumor that should be excised from Palestine—but then Saddam was speaking to the Iraqi news agency, not in a conversation with visiting Americans.

At the start of 1988 twin-tracked Iraqi policy could still be discerned. Tariq Aziz, the foreign minister, declared that Iraq was against Arab pressure on Egypt to cut its ties with Israel. In September 1988 an Iraqi official suddenly backed out of an imminent meeting with the Israeli minister of energy, Moshe Shahal, an Iraqi-born Jew and member of Shimon Peres's Labor Party. But by this time Iran and Iraq had agreed to a cease fire, and attitudes in Jersalem and Baghdad were changing. Israel was becoming more worried about Iraq's arsenal of long-range missiles and chemical weapons. The Israeli military had been taken by surprise when Iraqi rockets had bombarded Tehran at the end of February: a glance at a map of the region showed that those same rockets could reach Israel if launched from western Iraq, as indeed started happening a day after US-led forces initiated military action against Iraq in January 1991.

For his part, Saddam was looking for an issue on which to push forward his claim to be the leader of the Arab world. The end of the Iran-Iraq War had also led to an increasing closeness between Saddam and Yasir Arafat, the leader of the Palestine Liberation Organization (PLO), who had been using Baghdad as a safe haven ever since Israeli aircraft bombed his headquarters in Tunisia in 1986. In Western eyes, Saddam had shown he would no longer support international terrorism when he expelled the Palestinian superterrorist Abu Nidal in 1984, as part of the price for reestablishing diplomatic links with Washington. In reality, though, Saddam continued to back the Palestine Liberation Front of Abu Abbas, whose group hijacked the Italian cruise liner *Achille Lauro* in 1986. (An invalid American Jew and his wheelchair were thrown overboard during the incident.) Afterward Abbas avoided arrest and returned to Baghdad. The West German government was convinced that members of the Baader Meinhof terrorist gang and its offshoots were taking sanctuary in Baghdad as well. And according to diplomats based in Baghdad, the Iraqi government was sponsoring a training camp for PLO guerrillas north of Hillah, a town about an hour's drive from Baghdad.

Despite all this, the need for a rapprochement between Israel and Iraq, if only to develop a strategic understanding so that a missile war did not start by mistake, gave further encouragement to Israeli policymakers of the "pro-Iraq" school during 1989. By the end of 1989, however, this effort was proving fruitless, and the Israeli initiative was being overtaken by international events. The fall of the hard-line communist regimes in Eastern Europe seemed to bode poorly for dictators in the mold of Saddam. More important, it also meant the easing of restrictions on Jewish emigration from Eastern Europe and the Soviet Union. The mass exodus of Soviet Jews seemed to upset Saddam even more: Israel was becoming stronger, at least in terms of population, a threat to the well-being and morale of Palestinians on the West Bank. In May 1990 Saddam called an Arab summit in Baghdad to discuss the issue. Many, although not all, Arab leaders attended, an encouraging endorsement of Saddam's leadership. Saddam also used the summit to publicly warn Kuwait for the first time that he was unhappy about Kuwait's overproduction of oil and its depressing effect on world oil prices.

In April 1990, when Saddam threatened to destroy half of Israel, Israeli policymakers of the pro-Iraq school were derided with choruses of "I told you so." At a meeting of Israel's top foreign policy specialists, one of the former advocates of developing links with Iraq stood up and declared that the time had come for a preemptive strike against Saddam's missiles and the chemical weapons plants. It was the end of a period of delusion. Few concessions had been made by either side, but historians may eventually term the 1980s as a time of brilliant strategic deception by Saddam. He had avoided Israeli preemptive action subsequent to the bombing of the Tuwaitha nuclear reactor in 1981. By stealth he had built up a strategic punch that put Iraq on a par with Israel. The Scud missile attacks on Israel that started in January 1991 showed — at least in Arab eyes — that Israel was defenseless. The attacks were not deterred by Israel's assumed possession of nuclear weapons; nor was Israel able to retaliate immediately, its favorite response.

Among opposition groups, mainly Islamic groups with Iranian influence, rumors continue to circulate that Saddam Hussein is Jewish. A pamphlet, *Who Is Saddam Takriti?* produced by the Islamic Union of Iraqi Students in Lawrence, Kansas, claims that the origin of the Takriti tribe is either Christian or Jewish, and that Michel Aflaq, the founder of Baathism and a Syrian Christian, had a Jewish mother. *Secrets of the Iraqi Regime,* a book published in Iran by Khalida Abdul Qahar, a former secretary to Saddam and member of the Iraqi national assembly, also claims that Takritis are of Christian-Jewish origin. There is no evidence whatsoever to support this notion, and no evidence that any of Saddam's ancestors were Jewish. The only way to interpret such stories is to view them as reflections of anti-Semitism within sectors of the opposition.

★ ★ ★

CHAPTER

10

The Iran-Iraq War

If the world was surprised when Saddam Hussein invaded Kuwait on August 2, 1990, perhaps it should not have been, for ten years earlier the Iraqi leader had attacked another neighboring state. On September 22, 1980, Saddam had ordered his troops to invade Iran.

The world was scarcely surprised then. Tensions between the two countries had been mounting since February 1979, when Ayatollah Khomeini had won control of Iran from the regime of the exiled Mohammad Reza Shah Pahlavi. Saddam Hussein, who assumed full command of Iraq in July 1979, saw the Iranian revolution and its aftermath as both a threat and an opportunity. The chief threat was the continuous calls from Tehran for revolution among Shia Muslims throughout the Middle East. Saddam's origins were Sunni, but in Iraq the Shias constituted a majority—at least 54 percent of the population.

By 1980 the danger of Shia insurrection in Iraq had become acute. After a failed assassination attempt against one of Saddam's top deputies, Tariq Aziz, then the minister of information, Saddam reacted quickly and viciously. Membership in the underground Shia Dawa party was made punishable by death. One of its leaders, Ayatollah Baqr al-Sadr, was executed, along with members of his family; most were tortured first. As many as 100,000 Iraqis of Iranian origin were summarily arrested, often in the middle of the night, driven in trucks to the Iran-Iraq border and ordered to walk across. These Iraqis were not revolutionaries; many, in fact, were middle-class businessmen whose only "crime" was their ethnic background. Possessing nothing but the clothes they were wearing, many of the expelled ended up in refugee camps close to the Iranian town of Qasr-e-Shirin, in the central border area. Although they could speak Persian as well as Arabic, Iran was otherwise almost totally alien to them: they were going to have to start from scratch.[1]

At the same time, Iran began to prepare for war. By April 1980 Iranian tanks had taken up positions east of Qasr-e-Shirin, outside Iraqi artillery range. As far back as Kermanshah, nearly one hundred miles from the border, an Iranian tank regiment was on alert, its vehicles dispersed widely across fields as an elementary precaution against air attack. Such defensive measures were also observable in the south, at Abadan, the oil center across the border from Iraq's second city of Basra. Despite the threat of armed US intervention in retaliation for the taking of American hostages in Tehran, the anti-aircraft guns defending Abadan airport were all pointed not at American forces in the Gulf, but in the direction of Iraq.[2]

This was a time of phony war and episodic artillery exchanges across different parts of the front. The prevailing view in the West as well as in Iraq was that the regime of Ayatollah Khomeini was fragile and that an Iranian resistance to it would soon be organized. Saddam welcomed to Baghdad a variety of Iranian opposition politicians and former generals of the shah, all seeking the support of Iran's traditional enemy in order to defeat the new regime at home. Saddam provided hospitality, access to radio transmitters to broadcast insurrection, and hope to opposition groups. The Iraqi leader also was caught up in the general euphoria that Ayatollah Khomeini could be overthrown.

Meanwhile Iraq claimed that Iranian troops were illegally occupying a pocket of Iraqi territory at Zain ul Qos. This land, Iraq maintained, should have been returned to Iraq under the 1975 Algiers agreement, a settlement intended to resolve the dispute over the Shatt al-Arab waterway and parts of the border. Early in September 1980 Iranian artillery stationed in Zain ul Qos shelled the Iraqi towns of Mandali and Khanaqin. When Iran made no sign of desisting, Saddam felt compelled to abrogate the 1975 agreement and to order an invasion.

Saddam's military objectives at the start of the war were ambiguous. As his forces swept into southwestern Iran, instead of calling it Khuzestan, they referred to it by its Arabic name, Arabistan. The implication was that the entire area, with an Arab population of about three million and tremendous oil wealth — most of Iran's reserves — would become part of Iraq.

A second aim was to install a new regime in Tehran, a strategy that assumed that Ayatollah Khomeini's Islamic government would collapse under popular pressure as soon as the Iranian people saw that there was an alternative. Who Saddam thought the Iranians would choose is unclear, but he probably expected the populace to endorse some element of the Iranian liberal political opposition, backed by remnants of the shah's officer corps. (To try to reestablish the regime of either Reza Pahlavi or his son was probably considered too risky.) What is known is that Saddam aided the prospect of a military coup in Iran by allowing the planning of a commando raid by Iranian exiles on the southeastern Iranian port city of Bandar Abbas.[3] The idea, according to those familiar with it, was to have Iraqi transport aircraft and helicopters carry the Iranian commandos down the southern coast of the Gulf to the state of Oman, where the commandos would await the outbreak of general hostilities. Then the commando forces would be flown over the Iranian city, some parachuting in, others landing from helicopters. Their two main priorities would be to seize the radio station and to establish contact with the officers and men at the Iranian naval base, the largest in the country. Of the three armed services, the Iranian navy was thought to be the least supportive of Ayatollah Khomeini. It was clearly a high-risk operation, perhaps even a suicide mission.

But this commando attack was never launched. The fleet of transport planes was plagued by mechanical defects as it flew from one Gulf state to another. Some of the rulers of these conservative Arab sheikhdoms clearly did not know what was being planned when they opened their airspace to the Iraqi aircraft. When American and British diplomats realized what was up, they alerted the rulers of the United Arab Emirates and Oman: if the attack failed, Iran would consider these states to be allies of Iraq, rather than neutral observers, and might attack them. Sultan Qaboos of Oman, supposedly one of the West's closest allies in the area, had "forgotten" to tell Washington and London what was being planned. He was persuaded to order the attack canceled, although, by this time, it was a moot point, in view of the number of aircraft and helicopters grounded by defects. Western diplomats, thankful at having stopped the war from spreading, leaked the story that Iraq had been intending to attack three Iranian-held islands in the southern Gulf—Abu Musa, and the Greater and Lesser Tumbs—which the shah had taken from the emirates of Sharjah and Ras al-Khaimah in 1971.[4]

On the main battlefront, more than three hundred miles long, Iraqi tanks met little resistance. Rather their main obstacle was in Baghdad: the indifferent leadership of Saddam Hussein, a commander-in-chief who had no military experience. The important targets for Saddam's armies should have been the Iranian cities of Ahwaz and Dezful, the main military bases in Khuzestan. Ahwaz had an airfield, and Dezful was the site of a huge modern air base. With these two targets neutralized, if not occupied, Iraq would have dominated the southwestern corner of Iran, and the other main cities, Khorramshahr and Abadan, would have fallen.

Iraqi forces did move close enough to Dezful, fifty miles from the border, to subject it to fierce bombardment. But otherwise, in the south, the Iraqis were content to slog away at house-to-house fighting in Khorramshahr, which by October 24 they controlled without occupying all of it. In the central sector, Iraqi forces seized the towns of Qasr-e-Shirin, Mehran, and Musiyan—important propaganda coups, but hardly significant military moves.

The Iranian response to the invasion proved stronger than expected. The country united in the face of the external Arab threat, and the Iranian air force turned out to have survived the ravages and purges of the revolution quite well. A series of damaging air attacks into Iraq, in particular against Baghdad, embarrassed Saddam, and Iranian planes also bombarded Iraqi oil installations near Kirkuk, in the north. At the same time, the Iranian army pounded the southern Iraqi city of Basra and its industrial and oil installations, causing damage equal to that inflicted on the main Iranian refinery at Abadan by Iraqi shelling.

Saddam then ordered his troops to stop advancing and dig into defensive positions. Why he did so is unclear. He could have avoided high casualties by using his superior mobile forces to gain advantageous positions, rather than having his troops simply hunt down the Iranian enemy. One problem may have been difficulties in supporting and resupplying rapidly advancing troops. Another problem—a perennial issue for Iraqi leaders—was the loyalty of the Iraqi troops. Most Iraqi soldiers were Shia Muslims, and their willingness to fight their co-religionists in Iran was open to doubt.

After a few months of a developing stalemate, the morale of the Iranians was lifted by a feeling that they had not lost and could now retaliate. In Tehran hard-line elements had started to gain control within the government, and any hope of a moderate counterrevolution against Ayatollah Khomeini had vanished. Little happened during the winter months, but by May 1981 Iranian forces were ready to launch a counteroffensive. By October they had forced Iraqi troops back across the Karun River, which flows from Ahwaz to Abadan. Saddam's forces realized that their occupation of Khorramshahr, once the Arab city of Mohammarah, had ceased to be a foothold in Arabistan and had instead become a liability.

Iraqi troops were pushed out of Khorramshahr and the surrounding territory in June 1982. Their departure was hastened by Saddam's decision to withdraw, using the fig-leaf excuse of the Israeli invasion of Lebanon as a time to call on his Arab allies to unite in confronting Israel. (Israel's invasion to repel Palestinian forces from its northern border and Lebanon had appeared almost inevitable for several months. Prime Minister Menachem Begin gave the order to invade after the Israeli ambassador in London had been shot and seriously wounded by a Palestinian acting on Iraqi orders.)

If Saddam thought that he had won a breathing space, he was wrong. A personal political crisis at home gathered momentum (see chapter 11), while Iranian forces barely had time to consolidate before launching a series of offensives to put pressure on Basra and, if possible, to cut the main road joining Basra with the rest of Iraq. Similar attacks, every few months at different points along the land border, became the norm for 1983 and 1984, putting relentless pressure on the Iraqi army. However, the need to defend Iraqi territory boosted the poor morale of Saddam's soldiers and inspired a nationalist sentiment. The Iraqi army became accomplished at building huge defensive earthworks, with surrounding mine fields and barbed-wire entanglements, from which to hold off the Iranian hordes.

Not content to seek compensation from Saddam for having started the war, Ayatollah Khomeini declared the removal of Saddam Hussein himself to be the main condition for a cease-fire. An element of personal vengeance was involved here: Ayatollah Khomeini blamed Saddam for having sanctioned the death in December 1977 of his son, Mustafa, while the ayatollah had been in living in exile in the Shia holy city of Najaf in southern Iraq. The son had died in an automobile crash at Kerbala in what were described as mysterious circumstances.[5]

By this stage in the war the Iranian air force had been so diminished in effectiveness that Iraqi troops no longer had to fear air attacks. But Iran's great strength lay in its superior manpower:

Iran's population was three times that of Iraq's. And among the Iranian soldiers were youths, often little more than boys, fired by Islamic fervor and willing to die at the call of Ayatollah Khomeini. To meet the threat of mass attack, Iraq pushed forward with the development of chemical weapons, using them for the first time against Iranian forces in late 1983.

In an attempt to find a weakness on the Iraqi side, Iran launched a series of offensives in the northern sector of the common border, in the mountains of Kurdistan. In July 1983 Iran attacked close to the Iraqi town of Haj Omran, and in October Iranian forces struck one hundred miles farther south at Penjwin. Both assaults were successful, but the casualties were high. It proved difficult for Iranian troops to hold ground in the Kurdish areas because of attacks by Iraqi helicopter gunships and aircraft. Although these actions showed the vulnerability of Iraq's northern oilfields, of greater danger to Iraq was Iranian support for Kurdish opposition groups in Iraq. But this tactic could be played by both sides: Iraq could influence Kurdish groups in Iran who were equally opposed to the Iranian central government. Fighting in the mountains of the north continued until the 1988 cease fire, but it was always clear that the war would be decided more by activities in the central and southern sectors.

While this fighting was going on, the world seemed largely indifferent to its outcome. Revolutionary Iran had its supporters in other Islamic countries, but elsewhere the harshness of Ayatollah Khomeini's rhetoric won little sympathy. Saddam's Iraq was already sufficiently notorious for its human rights abuses that the Iraqi claim of confronting Iran on behalf of the civilized world rung hollow. But Saddam realized that Iraq's ability to fight depended on its economic strength, so great efforts were put into maintaining trading relationships, and to buying goods and paying for construction contracts on credit.

The first significant advance by Iran onto Iraqi territory occurred in February 1984, when Iranian forces seized the island of Majnoon in the marshy area north of Basra. The seizure was strategic because Majnoon lies atop a huge, unexploited oilfield. Iraq again used chemical warfare to stop the Iranian advance, but it proved impossible to push the enemy back across the border. The danger of the Iranian encroachment was diminished somewhat when Iraq flooded the area around Majnoon island by diverting water from the Tigris River.

The intermittent nature of much of the fighting suggested that neither side had a comprehensive strategy. Iran's only goal seemed to be to keep pushing in on Iraq, mostly through huge offensives involving hundreds of thousands of men and several months of preparation. For his part, Saddam seemed just to want to survive, although a longer-term strategy became discernible around this time. One element of this strategy was to build oil export routes to replace those through the Gulf, which had been destroyed, and through Syria, which had been closed by Saddam's rival for Baath leadership, President Hafez Assad. A second element of the strategy was to disrupt Iranian oil exports, a tactic put into action with the first assaults on Kharg Island, the main Iranian oil-exporting termi- nal, in March 1984. Iran's response played straight into Saddam's hands: if Iraq tried to prevent Iran from exporting its oil, Tehran would cut off all the Gulf's oil exports by halting traffic through the Strait of Hormuz at the mouth of the Gulf. Iran compounded its error by attacking tankers carrying Saudi and Kuwaiti oil. Suddenly, Saddam was being portrayed as a friend of the West, even though it was hard for the US and Europe to view him and his regime sympathetically.

Also in 1984, the military balance of power shifted toward Iraq. Iran was depleting its enormous arsenal of American weapons, a legacy of Washington's backing for the shah, and no replacements or spare parts were readily available. Iraq, by contrast, was inundated by weapons from a variety of sources. After a hiatus in relations, Moscow resumed the flow of Soviet weapons, estimated to account for two-thirds of the Iraqi arsenal. France emerged as the second most important supplier, as the French government made a cynical choice of which side to back based mainly on which would provide the most business for its arms industry and secure its oil supplies. The credit terms offered by Paris were not publicly announced but appeared almost as soft as the easy terms tendered by the Soviets. Other countries also saw the war as a superb business opportunity: Egypt, boasting a large but relatively low-tech arms industry, provided a huge amount of ammunition and basic weapons as a way of currying favor with Baghdad, an attempt to win support for Cairo's return to the Arab fold after the isolation that followed Egypt's peace treaty with Israel in 1978. Brazil also became a major player, taking Iraqi oil in return for goods and a variety of weapons from its nascent arms industry. There were many opportunities for private arms dealers as well, and some dealers sold to both sides. Among the countries that did so, China quietly supplied artillery shells to both Iran and Iraq, demanding of each cash payment rather than accepting credit terms. There were limits to the scruples of some countries: the US did not allow arms exports to either side, although the Iran-Contra deal was one of several exceptions. Britain had a policy of not selling lethal military goods, but otherwise did little to stop the flow of weapons: for most of the war the headquarters of the official Iranian arms procurement agency was in central London, within a five-minute walk of both the British Foreign Office and Parliament.

During 1985 a series of Iraqi air attacks on Kharg Island seriously impaired Iran's ability to export oil and forced Tehran to open another export terminal farther down the Gulf, on the island of Sirri. But Iraq's air success against tankers was criticized by military observers as unsustained. Meanwhile, the atmosphere of stalemate was enhanced by Iraq's inability to force the Iranians out of Majnoon. Ironically, the flooded marshlands that Iraq had hoped would contain the Iranian forces enabled them to use small boats effectively. In March 1985 Saddam and his generals were rocked by the news that a comparatively small Iranian force had crossed the Tigris River and had seized a section of the main north-south highway. Fortunately for Saddam, the Iranians were only lightly armed, so they were quickly routed and forced back by Iraqi tanks. Nonetheless, the incident was a great shock.

Saddam tried to shift the emphasis of the fighting to Iran's civilian population by ordering bombing attacks on targets in and around the Iranian capital. Twenty-nine other Iranian towns and cities were also hit by rockets, aircraft, or shellfire. Iran retaliated with heavy bombardments on Iraq's southern towns and the launching of several Scud missiles, which it had obtained from Libya, on Baghdad itself. The destruction of their cities brought both sides temporarily to their senses, and a cessation of that sort of fighting was agreed upon. Saddam wanted a permanent cease-fire and immediate peace negotiations; Iran still wanted the removal of Saddam, as well as the payment of reparations, variously calculated at sums up to $350 billion. Such terms were, of course, unacceptable to Saddam. In June 1985, confident of his growing strength, he ordered the resumption of bombing attacks after Iran failed to take up the offer of peace talks. In July Iran responded by launching further attacks both in the south and in Kurdistan, and the war slipped back into its alternating pattern of quietude and skirmish. Despite Iraq's growing strength, the threat of an Iranian "final offensive" remained real.

In 1986 a series of setbacks almost finished Saddam. His failure to take the tactical initiative to crush the Iranian military threat on his borders was now looking like a serious strategic deficiency. The first hammer blow came in February 1986: Iranian forces seized the Fao peninsula, the tongue of land forming Iraq's only Gulf coastline, while, at the same time, making minor advances on the northern front. In May Iraqi forces achieved a minor victory by attacking and seizing the battered Iranian town of Mehran in the central sector opposite Baghdad. Any comfort from this victory was swiftly swept away six weeks later when Iranian forces, using a flanking movement against which Iraq had not defended, recaptured the town. Once again, an Iranian breakthrough seemed possible, either in the south, cutting the country in two, or in the center, with a march on Baghdad.

July 1986 was the gloomiest of times in Baghdad. Many in the foreign community dusted off evacuation plans. If Iranian revolutionaries began to march on the capital from the border seventy miles away, there was expected to be a mass westward flight from the city, an exodus toward Jordan. Several embassies had plans for their personnel to drive into the desert to the west of Baghdad, so as not to be caught in the chaos. They were stockpiling food and fuel, and had already hidden some caches of supplies deep in the desert. The atmosphere of near panic was not helped by the fact that July is historically the time for political change in Iraq. All sorts of rumors of coups and plots were circulating.[6]

From Saddam's point of view, the least attractive aspect of all was that it was his head that the Iranians were demanding as the price for peace. So there was the danger, short of an Iranian victory, that some Iraqis might consider deposing him as the best alternative. The plotters might also assume that a victorious Iran would not try to control the whole of Iraq, that there would remain several provinces for the plotters themselves to govern. To eviscerate internal opposition, Saddam ridded himself of two potential rivals. One was Naim Haddad, one of only two Shia members of the Revolutionary Command Council. In July Haddad was swiftly stripped of all official positions. Some reports said he was executed, but it seems that he escaped with his life.

The second prominent Iraqi dismissed by Saddam was the mayor of Baghdad, Abdul-Wahab Mohammed Latif al-Mufti. Mufti was arrested, along with several workers from his private office, and charged with having accepted bribes in the award of contracts to foreign companies working on projects in the municipality. Mufti was certainly doing this: one well-connected foreign businessman assesses that the mayor had taken $40 million in bribes over the years. The case against Mufti was solid: the Iraqi authorities used prostitutes to win the confidence of Mufti's male relatives in Britain and discover illegally held bank accounts.[7] To make the arrest appear more a criminal matter than a political one, Iraqi police also arrested a British businessman, Ian Richter, who they alleged was paying Mufti. The emphasis on corruption was deemed to be necessary because Mufti was popular with the Iraqi military, for he had organized the building of new emergency roads and fortifications in the south when the Iranians had been pressing. The military might have considered suggesting Mufti, a man with a charismatic character, as an alternative leader to Saddam: this was the theory held by some better-informed diplomats. After a trial held in secret, Mufti was executed in late 1986. Richter was sentenced to life imprisonment, and at the beginning of 1991 was still being held in an Iraqi prison.

Saddam further safeguarded his political position in summer 1986 by masterminding a special "extraordinary" conference of the Baath Party Regional Command. Although in his long speech to the conference he referred twenty-five times to a plot, it seems that he was responding to the pressure he was feeling from political and military leaders, rather than to any actual plot. There was no open manifestation of this pressure, but there were probably mutterings of discontent as the country faced yet more military setbacks. Apart from pushing out Naim Haddad, Saddam won support for the promotion of two men from his hometown, both with backgrounds in security: Ali Hassan al-Majid and Fadel Barrak.

It seems that during the summer Saddam also made a concession to his military commanders, who, until that time, were expected to seek approval for almost every military action. Military observers thought that Saddam's commanders resented this control, and that Saddam eased up when they insisted that greater freedom of action would produce better results. One difference was almost instantly apparent. Iraqi aircraft, using inflight refueling for the first time, struck the Iranian oil terminal at Sirri.

But if Iran ended the year worrying about its oil exports, revenge on Iraq was sweet. The offensive against Basra in January 1987 was the fiercest yet, although Iranian forces were stopped within sight of the city. In March the Iranians launched a new offensive in the Kurdish north. Nonetheless, the tide was steadily turning against Iran. "Operation Staunch," a US plan to use diplomatic pressure to stop arms supplies to Iran because of the threat Ayatollah Khomeini posed to the region, was succeeding. Meanwhile Iraq's arsenal was steadily growing: in 1987 Iraq was the world's principal arms importer.

At the start of 1988 many observers thought the war might continue in its desultory way for several more years. In January Iraq held off an Iranian attack on Basra, and on February 29 Iraq began launching new longer-range Scud missiles at Tehran; previously, the Iranian capital had been beyond the reach of Iraq's rockets. During the two-month onslaught, many Tehran residents fled the city. The Iranian military was particularly shocked that some missiles were made to explode in the air over Tehran, indicating that Iraq had the potential to drop poisonous gas or other chemical agents on the city. Six other Iraqi missiles, fired from two different locations, landed on the small campus of Tehran University in the center of the city, indicating terminal guidance from Iraqi agents on the ground.[8]

Iran's military forces did not collapse, however; they advanced into Iraqi Kurdistan and passed through the town of Halabja. The evidence of what happened there is disputed, but foreign military observers say that Iran used chemical weapons against the town's Kurdish citizens with the intention of blaming Iraq. But before Iran could bring in television crews and journalists to inspect the rigged atrocity, Iraq did use chemical weapons against the Kurds, even though they were Iraqi citizens themselves.[9] As many as 5,000 Kurds were reported to have died.

Saddam Hussein's regime was universally condemned for this atrocity, and its denials were not believed. But the episode proved advantageous to Iraq when, for the rest of the spring, Iranian troops, fearful of chemical attack, retreated from every Iraqi offensive. In April Iraqis recaptured the Fao peninsula, and in May they recaptured Shalamcheh, the ruins of the border post between Iraq and Iran close to the city of Basra. A further blow to Iranian morale was the bad luck of the US *Vincennes,* a navy ship that shot down an Iranian civil airplane in error. By July, with Iraqi-backed Iranian

Credit: Sygma

Saddam Hussein with his family in a photograph published in August 1988. From left to right, back row: Hussein Kamil (minister of industry and military industrialization); his brother, Saddam Kamil (officer in missile corps); Raghad (Saddam's eldest daughter, married to Hussein Kamil); Udai (Saddam's older son); Rina (Saddam's second daughter, married to Saddam Kamil); grandchild; Lama (daughter of war hero, Gen. Maher Abdul Rashid, married to Qusai); Qusai (Saddam's younger son). Front row: grandchild; Sajida (Saddam's wife); Saddam Hussein; Hala (Saddam's youngest daughter).

Saddam kissing Iraqi children during a tour of the country, a familiar pose in the Iraqi media.

Credit: Van der Stockt/Gamma (Frank Spooner)

Credit: Steve McCurry/Magnum

The Martyrs' Memorial in Baghdad consists of two glazed blue domes, parted and offset to symbolize the course to heaven along which the spirits of all Muslim martyrs are said to travel. Constructed in an open area to imitate other famous monuments from Iraq's history, such as ziggurats and the spiral minaret at Samarra, the monument is over 180 feet wide and 130 feet high. It took more than two years to build and was completed in 1983, during the war with Iran.

Credit: S. Franklin/Magnum

Giant cut-out depiction of Saddam standing above a mock-up of the Ishtar gate, one of the parts of the ancient city of Babylon that the Iraqi leader is rebuilding as a tribute to his hero, Nebuchadnezzar.

Pictures of Saddam Hussein—placed too high to be defaced—dominate the courtyard of the mosque in Najaf, one of the holiest shrines of Shia Muslims. Ayatollah Khomeini spent several years in exile in Najaf before overthrowing the shah of Iran.

Credit: © Simon Henderson

Facing Shia Muslims as they leave the mosque in Najaf is a giant mural of Saddam and Iraqi fighters, representing both the 1980–88 war with Iran and the battle of Qadisiyya in AD 637. The Arabs defeated the Shia Persians both times, a lesson that Saddam wants to emphasize to Shia Iraqis.

Credit: © Simon Henderson

Shia Muslims, who constitute an estimated 54 percent of Iraq's population, traditionally look to their mullahs (priests) for leadership on a wide range of issues rather than to the Sunni Muslim–dominated government of Saddam Hussein.

Credit: © Simon Henderson

War memorial in central Baghdad. The hands holding the swords were modeled using impressions of Saddam's own arm, enlarged forty-eight times. The metal for the memorial came from captured Iranian armor and steel helmets, shipped in slabs to Germany to be melted down and cast.

Credit: Gamma

Credit: © Simon Henderson

Giant picture of Saddam Hussein in central Baghdad, surrounded by symbols of technological progress: oil refineries, telecommunications, nuclear science, and rockets. Less-elaborate pictures are displayed prominently all over Iraq. In April 1990 a collection of Saddam's portraits were put on display in art galleries in Baghdad to mark his fifty-third birthday.

Credit: Gamma, Frank Spooner

Kurdish victims of the chemical weapons attack at Halabja in northeastern Iraq in March 1988. Iran and the Kurds blamed the attack on Iraq, but Western intelligence officials say that Iran used chemicals against the town first, followed within hours by Iraq. However, the Iranians arrived first with television cameras and exploited the opportunity to censure Iraq.

Credit: © Associated Press Photo

Iranian-born journalist Farzad Bazoft, hanged by Iraq in March 1990 for spying for Britain and Israel. On assignment for the London *Observer,* Bazoft had visited the site of a huge explosion at Qaqa State Establishment, south of Baghdad, "after being tasked for the mission by the British embassy." Western intelligence was interested in the explosion because Iraq's atomic bomb development program is conducted at Qaqa.

Credit: Crown Copyright for format

Death certificate of Abdullah Rahim Sharif Ali, who worked in London for several Iraqi-owned companies. On his deathbed Ali told British police that he had been poisoned by three visiting Iraqis, who had taken him out to dinner at a London restaurant. The inquest concluded that Ali had died from thallium poisoning. Thallium, a rat poison, is odorless, tasteless, and colorless, and is a favorite weapon of Saddam's assassins.

Credit: Kol-Al-Arab/Gamma (Frank Spooner)

Iraq's modified Scud missiles, altered to increase their range, changed the course of the war with Iran in 1988. The Iranians were shocked by the missiles' range and accuracy, which suggested that homing beacons were being operated by Iraqi agents in Tehran. Iraq also exploded twelve Scuds in mid-air over the Iranian capital, a powerful demonstration of the Scud's ability to disperse chemical agents. Iranian generals soon persuaded Ayatollah Khomeini to accept a cease-fire. Iraq's modified Scuds started landing on Israel and Saudi Arabia after US-led forces began bombing Iraqi targets in January 1991. The first rockets, armed only with high-explosive warheads, did little damage, and several fell short because modifications had made them unstable in flight.

August 23, 1990: Iraqi President Saddam Hussein is shown on Iraqi television with his arm around a British youngster identified as Stuart Lockwood. Saddam told Stuart and other Westerners that they were not hostages.

Credit: Reuters/Bettmann

exiles of the Mujaheddin-e-Khalq guerrilla group penetrating toward Kermanshah, Iran accepted a cease fire. The Iranian military persuaded Ayatollah Khomeini to take the decision, which he said was like poison, because of the risk of more casualties: the military commanders had been particularly horrified by the impact of long-range missile attacks on Tehran, and they feared the future use of chemical warheads. The cease-fire went into effect in August. The war, which had lasted nearly eight years, ended with no changes in the border or in the political leadership.

The war was both debilitating and oddly beneficial for the Iraqis. When hostilities started in 1980, Saddam was still unsure of his political position; at the war's end he emerged stronger and more in control. Although still beset by communal and ethnic dissension, Iraq came out of the war more united, much more a nation-state, according to many analysts. But with an uneasy peace came difficulties for Saddam. His troops now wanted the benefits of victory — demobilization, housing, and jobs. The continued low price of oil meant that no promises could be made. Saddam also feared the political ambitions of his victorious army commanders and quickly moved to dismiss or pension off several, including the celebrated Maher Abdul Rashid, whose daughter had married Saddam's son Qusai.[10] The emergency conditions of war were perhaps easier for Saddam to handle than his people's amorphous desires for a better and peaceful Iraq.

By the beginning of 1990 the economic strains were becoming acute, and Saddam's domestic policies were proving inadequate. In this context, an invasion of Kuwait had a double appeal: to bolster oil prices by forcing Kuwait to cut back on production and to justify Iraq's maintenance of the largest army in the Middle East.

★ ★ ★

Withdrawing from Iran: Saddam's 1982 Crisis

In the summer of 1982 Iraq's fortunes in the war with Iran were at a low ebb. The invasion of Iranian territory that had started in September 1980 had been halted, and Iraqi forces were being steadily forced back. In June 1982 Saddam's troops had to withdraw from the most significant piece of captured Iranian territory, the city of Khorramshahr. In an opportunistic move, Saddam announced that he had ordered his troops to withdraw so that the Arab nations could unite to help Arab forces in Lebanon, then under invasion by Israel. But few believed this argument, and Iran certainly saw no reason to accept Saddam's call for a cease-fire. Instead of Iraq pressuring Iran to topple the regime of Ayatollah Khomeini, as in 1980, the boot was now firmly on the other foot, and the Iranian religious leader was calling for Saddam to be overthrown and replaced by a Shia Muslim clerical regime.

The war was also having domestic repercussions. Saddam was facing almost insurmountable economic problems, and the consequent social discontent provoked a political challenge to him as well. At one point, Western diplomats thought that Saddam had been overthrown,[1] but he had already anticipated the danger. When the crucial weeks had ended, Saddam's cunning had won out, and he emerged a stronger leader than he had been before.

The main blow to Iraq's economy was Syria's decision in April 1982 to close off the Iraqi oil pipeline that ran through Syrian territory. The deep personal antipathy between President Assad of Syria and Saddam had already led Syria to openly support Iran in the war. Assad's newest decision left Saddam with just one pipeline for oil exports, a line in northern Iraq that passed through Turkey and on to the Mediterranean. But that pipeline had a working capacity of only 900,000 barrels a day, bringing in maximum revenues of around $9 billion a year, while expenditure on the war was running at an estimated $1 billion a month.

Until this time Iraq had been operating an economic policy of "guns and butter." Money "borrowed" from Saudi Arabia, Kuwait, and other Gulf states was used to finance the maintenance of the prewar standard of living within the country as a way of keeping the population happy and confident that the war would not last long. Saddam abruptly reversed this policy in April 1982. He largely postponed a new five-year plan that called for massive spending on development, and austerity became the catchword. Foreign travel was banned, imports were sharply curtailed, and large numbers of contracts with foreign companies, for construction and other projects, were canceled. In one of the Baath party's occasional shifts in favor of the private sector and away from state dominance of the economy, there was a slight slackening of restrictions on the involvement of individuals in industry, trade, and agriculture.

An additional setback was the apparent determination of the rest of the Arab world to let Iraq fight the war alone, despite Iraq's arguments about defending the Arab heartland from the threat of Persian hordes. To add insult to injury, the rest of the world was becoming cautious about supporting Iraq. Baghdad was to have hosted the seventh summit of the nonaligned nations that year, but the meeting was transferred to the Indian capital, New Delhi. Saddam had been hoping to use the meeting to win an endorsement for Iraq's fight and an implied rebuff to Iran. The change of venue also cost Saddam the leadership of the nonaligned nations for the next four years; that role passed to the new host, Indira Gandhi.

On the positive side, a measure of national cohesion had developed in Iraq during the preceding two years of war. Yet domestic support for the regime was rather shallow and likely to be further eroded by bad news from the war front. No figures were being released for casualties, but losses on the battlefield were so heavy that public funerals were banned. After a major defeat the bodies of those who had died often were not returned immediately to their families, but instead held in giant cold stores and then released over the course of weeks so that the public would not know that there had been a particular disaster on the battlefield. Particularly worrisome was the thought that soldiers from Iraq's majority Shia community would prefer to side with Ayatollah Khomeini rather than support the Sunni-dominated regime of Saddam.

The Iraqi leader attempted to strengthen his domestic position through an absolute prohibition of public criticism of either him or the regime. But he had pushed himself into a corner by identifying so closely with the course of the war, calling it Saddam's Qadisiyya, to evoke memories of the Arabs' victory over the Persians in AD 637 at the battle of Qadisiyya. This association was difficult to back away from, especially at this time of pressure.

If Saddam hesitated or doubted himself, it did not show. He decided to bluff out the domestic crisis. He rose to the challenge by identifying himself more with the war, not less, as the pace of setbacks quickened. In December 1981, as Iranian forces grabbed back as much as 70 percent of the territory previously lost to the Iraqi army, a Qadisiyyat Saddam Festival was staged. In another move to inspire public confidence in the commander-in-chief, the al-Thawra township in Baghdad was renamed Saddam City. A pliant press and officially sponsored public meetings helped reinforce this campaign, but Saddam never lost his ability to go out and meet the people to solicit their support. Although one may wonder how honest and forthright Iraqis were in his presence, Saddam remained sensitive to public opinion, at least among his basic constituency — the Sunni working class. He also used the media to project an image of a leader very much in touch with his people. By identifying with them, he encouraged people to identify with him.

Unwilling to consider any compromise with an enemy who demanded his head, Saddam, it seems, deliberately demolished the best chance for a cease-fire and negotiated peace at that time. Algeria hoped to use its good relations with both sides to try to work out a compromise. These efforts were abandoned when the airplane carrying the Algerian negotiating team, the cream of the country's foreign service, crashed in southern Turkey on May 3, 1982. It is widely assumed that an Iraqi jet shot down the plane on Saddam's orders.

Closer to home, the Iraqi leader knew that his main challenges came from the army, which was fed up with being on the losing side, and from the Baath party, which still harbored political rivals. So Saddam strengthened his personal security, even to the extent, according to newspaper reports, of hiring former British special forces soldiers to train his bodyguard. Somehow, he then managed to make peace with the army, or at least with the senior commanders. Perhaps he offered them greater independence in battlefield decision making, a concession he would have matched by reminding them that he was also willing to execute commanders who were cowardly or just performed badly on the front. (Several senior officers were shot after the retreat from Khorramshahr.) With his flank protected, perhaps only temporarily, Saddam summoned the Baath party to a secret congress for the first time since 1977.

Though Saddam had been named secretary-general of the Baath in 1979, and the party was theoretically the governing party, he had never bothered to call a meeting of the congress before. The endorsement of his decision to go to war had been made by the much smaller Revolutionary Command Council, the main decision-making body, and the Baath Party Regional Command, nominally the leadership cadre of the party. The purpose of the meeting, according to Ofra Bengio, a veteran Israeli observer of Iraq, was "pulling the party together, silencing critics, settling accounts with individual opponents and groups and, most important of all, securing for Saddam a legitimization which he had earlier scorned and now badly needed."[2] The secrecy that shrouded the meeting in Baghdad was an indication of the party's continuing clandestine nature and its unsureness, both of its agenda and how its resolutions would be received by the public. After the meeting was adjourned, though, reports of some of its proceedings were published. Ofra Bengio detected in these reports two new concerns of this congress compared with previous congresses. The first was an extensive discussion of Islam, a topic of consequence given the religious attraction Shia Iraqis felt for Ayatollah Khomeini's Islamic fundamentalism. Secondly, the congress focused on Saddam's "charismatic" leadership:

> Saddam Hussein is a symbol of freedom, independence, pride, integrity, and a hope for a better, brighter, future for Iraq and the Arab nation. This fact . . . urges us to continue to march behind the banner Saddam Hussein is raising with all possible devotion, self-denial, and courage.[3]

Rather than allowing the congress to find fault with him, Saddam found fault with the Baath, acknowledging extraordinary difficulties, deviation from the party line, and counterrevolution. Saddam spoke of "enemies of the party," by which he probably meant communists and Islamic fundamentalists, who were thought to have infiltrated party-backed trade unions and mass organizations in elections held in 1981 and 1982. Saddam also mentioned the dangers posed by "old and outdated social and religious customs and concepts" — clearly a reference to Iraqi Shias' sympathy for the ideals of Ayatollah Khomeini. The expansion of the membership of the Baath party had also led to problems, Saddam explained, for although the party had branches all over Iraq, "loyalty varies greatly from area to area, and town to town." There was an additional concern that enemies of the party were using the expansion of membership as an opportunity to infiltrate its ranks.

Saddam blamed all the Baath party's difficulties on its members and officials, alleging weakness, hesitation, laziness, incompetence, and lack of devotion to the party ideology. He called for the protection of families, friends, and relatives from the influence of counterrevolutionary trends. Everyone in the leadership had to stand together, he told them, and close cooperation with the masses was needed to counter enemy propaganda. More threateningly, he said that anti-Baath elements had to be weeded out. He then listed the criteria for choosing new members of the Baath Party Regional Command: great courage in adversity, absolute faith in the cause of the party, ability to supervise the party's lower ranks, and absolute faith in the independence of the country and the party. This latter criterion was to protect "our revolutionary experiment from the intervention and evils of Arab and foreign currents." These "evils" were probably a coded reference to Syria, which had previously tried to widen divisions in the Iraqi Baath party, as well as to Islamic fundamentalism and communism.

The congress ended on June 27 after unanimously reaffirming its confidence in Saddam Hussein, who was reelected secretary-general. A political reshuffle was immediately enacted, but without the bloody purges that had characterized Saddam's takeover of the leadership in 1979, when twenty-one high party officials were executed. Perhaps Saddam realized that such harsh measures had to be used sparingly lest they rebound against him.

The Baath Party Regional Command was maintained at fifteen members strong, but seven men were dropped, to be replaced by younger men who had risen with Saddam and remained most loyal to him. (Four of the new members were Shias, which put this sect on par with the Sunnis — seven members each. The fifteenth member was Tariq Aziz, a Christian.) A greater change took place in the Revolutionary Command Council (RCC), whose membership was reduced from sixteen to nine. All but one member of the reduced

RCC were holdovers, old political colleagues of Saddam, including two Shias. The important addition was the inclusion of a Kurd, Taha Moeddin Marouf, who had been vice-president of the republic since 1974 but with only ceremonial powers. He became the only member of the RCC who was not also in the Baath Regional Command. Although Marouf carried little weight in the Kurdish community, and was certainly anathema to opposition Kurds, his appointment was a signal of the leadership's effort to include a representative from an ethnic minority.

The third political body to be reshuffled was the cabinet, where eight members lost their jobs, and a new post, minister of light industries, was established. Most of the new ministers were technocrats rather than politicians, although one was a former army corps commander — a rare exception to Saddam's policy of complete separation between military and political command. A second, more recent exception was the appointment of Saadi Tuma Abbas al-Jabburi as defense minister in December 1990.

Other changes included the establishment of the new ministerial-level post of adviser to the president. This slot has since proved to be a temporary niche for people on the way up or on the way down in politics, usually down. But it allows Saddam to let them down lightly, with their political egos somewhat intact, so that those who have fallen are less likely to rise up in rebellion.

One member of the cabinet, however, was not let down lightly at all. Minister of Health Riyadh Ibrahim was dismissed in the cabinet shakeup for having imported tainted medicine that killed some Iraqi patients. Rumors, however, suggest an alternative motive: that he responded in the affirmative when Saddam asked his cabinet whether he should resign. Saddam then asked Ibrahim to step into a side room to discuss the matter in private, but at this point the rumors diverge. Among the versions of the tale that have been repeated by different branches of the Western media: Saddam shot Ibrahim; Saddam beat Ibrahim to death; Saddam ordered his aides to kill Ibrahim; Ibrahim's body was returned to his wife, chopped into bits.

In the wake of the Baath party congress, then, Saddam was in full command. A system of multiple and overlapping layers of government took shape (see appendix 1), which only reinforced Saddam's power. He had resolved the domestic crisis using established political channels—a feat that undermined the legitimacy of any other group of mainstream Iraqis who might have had notions of pressing for a change in leadership.

In the end, though, the strongest motive for Iraqi political unity was supplied by Ayatollah Khomeini, whose sermons regularly insisted that both Saddam and his regime be overthrown. Given that alternative, mainstream Iraqi Baathists saw no choice but to keep on fighting. The Iraqi military remained loyal, in part because several months passed without any major Iranian attack. The nation, or at least its different branches of leadership, had for the time being united to meet the Iranian threat.

Two weeks after the congress adjourned, an attempt was made on Saddam's life. On July 11, 1982, Saddam's motorcade was ambushed as it was passing through the town of al-Dujayl, a mixed Sunni-Shia community, about forty miles northeast of Baghdad. Shia forces trapped the Iraqi leader for several hours until the army came to rescue him. Many of the villagers were subsequently deported, and their houses razed to the ground. In another incident, in August 1982, a car bomb exploded outside the ministry of planning in Baghdad, killing twenty people. This was a shock to the regime, although Saddam may have been not the actual target.

For as long as the main threat to Iraq was the Islamic extremism of Iran, any mainstream Iraqi opposition to Saddam could be charged with a treasonous alliance with the enemy. So Saddam survived one of his worst crises.

★ ★ ★

CHAPTER
12

Extending Iraq's Reach:
The Development of Superweapons

Iraq's attempts at building a variety of weapons sufficient to threaten much of the Mideast predate the Iran-Iraq War. In August 1979, for example, Iraq declared its ambitions in a paper submitted in Vienna to a United Nations Conference on Science and Technology for Development. Under the section on long-term objectives to the year 2000, the last item reads: "The development of the armament industry in order to achieve self-reliance and national security for both Iraq and the Arab world." Perhaps overlooked at the time, but glaringly obvious now, this statement bespoke Iraq's desire to lead the Arab world by force of military might.

The bid got off to a faltering start. Iraq's pursuit of nuclear technology in the name of peaceful research barely disguised its scheme to equal Israel's nuclear might, which even by the end of the 1970s was widely assumed, though not openly acknowledged by Jerusalem. But whereas Israel had developed its nuclear arsenal as a deterrent against Arab aggression, Iraq's motives were to achieve

Arab leadership. Israel was not prepared to tolerate the strategic competition, and Baghdad's efforts were set back by more than eight years when, on June 7, 1981, Israeli aircraft bombed the Osirak reactor (named after Osiris, the Egyptian god of the dead) at the Tuwaitha research center, southeast of Baghdad. Two minutes of pinpoint bombing reduced the crucial reactor housing, which was within weeks of becoming operational, to twisted metal and smoldering rubble.

Saddam's nuclear weapons project was quiescent for several years after that, according to Western officials who monitor nuclear proliferation in developing countries. But in the meantime other items outside the conventional arsenal — both weapons of mass destruction and the means of delivering them — began to appeal to the imagination of Saddam and his generals, and work was started on them.

If work on nuclear weapons had been a long-term plan to match Israel's strength, the development of chemical weapons had more to do with immediate necessity. Two years into the war with Iran, Iraqi forces were being hard-pressed by more numerous enemy troops, including young volunteers who seemed fearless in their desire to fight and die a martyr's death. Mine fields and barbed wire, the threat of machine-gun fire, could not stem these onslaughts. In search of a more terrifying defensive capability, Saddam ordered the further development of chemical weapons from basic research begun in the mid-1970s.

Iraq's development of long-range missiles to transport chemical warheads had similar origins. During the Iran-Iraq War both sides were able to acquire samples of the Soviet-designed Scud missile, a straightforward development of the German V-2 missile that Hitler fired against London and other targets in the final years of World War II. But by accident of geography — Baghdad lies closer to the common border than does Tehran — the Iranian Scuds could bombard Baghdad and other Iraqi cities, while Iraqi Scuds could not reach Tehran. As a counter to the Iranian missile assaults, Iraq attacked ships carrying Iranian oil exports. But in the meantime

Saddam also ordered a program to devise modifications for the Scud that would lengthen its range so that it could hit Tehran. Much to the surprise of Iran and many other countries, Iraq's modified Scuds debuted in an attack on Tehran in February 1988. Almost immediately Iranian morale collapsed, which led Ayatollah Khomeini to accept a cease-fire in July 1988.

So far, Iraq's Scud enhancement program has produced two missiles, the Al-Hussein and the Al-Abbas, each of which significantly outdistances the original Scud. While the Soviet-supplied missile had a range of about 190 miles, the Al-Hussein can travel about 375 miles and the Al-Abbas has a range of about 560 miles. (All ranges vary, depending on the weight of the warheads.) Much has been written about how Iraq modified the Scuds using German and other foreign technicians. But most of this reporting has been guesswork. The simplest account reported in many newspapers says that the Iraqis cut up three Scuds into bits and reassembled two longer-range missiles from them.

Western intelligence agencies had their first opportunity to discover what Iraq had accomplished when two of the missiles were displayed at a military show in Baghdad in early 1989.[1] After analysis of the photographs taken there, one of which is shown in this book, Western governments decided that the Iraqis had lied when they claimed that one missile was an Al-Hussein and the other an Al-Abbas. In fact, the missiles being shown off were a basic Scud and an Al-Hussein. The measurements of the missiles, calculated from the photographs, also show that modifying the missiles was more complicated than just increasing the fuel load and diminishing the weight of the warhead. The length of a Scud is 37 feet, that of an Al-Hussein just over 40 feet, while an Al-Abbas is said to be over 41 feet long in one version and nearly 46 feet in another, according to intelligence officials. The extra length certainly accounts for the greater fuel load, but the warhead remains large. As part of the modification, according to Western intelligence officials, the fuel has been changed from the basic kerosene–liquid oxygen combination to a more powerful and compact propellant known as

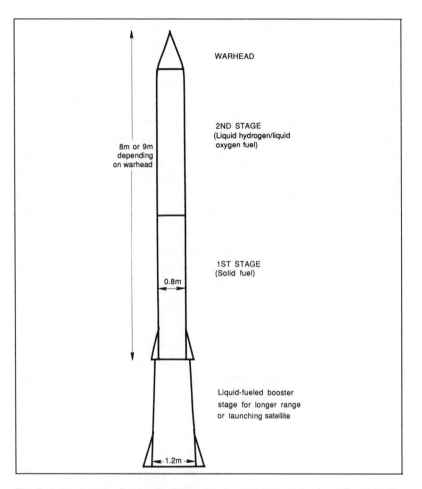

The first drawing of a Condor 2 missile, from a sketch made by the author with the guidance of an Austrian engineer who had worked on the Iraqi installations. The Condor 2 was originally conceived by European scientists working for Argentina. Egypt then joined the project, bringing in Iraq to provide funding. Baghdad has now taken over development, which is behind schedule. The missile represents a considerable technical advance over existing Iraqi rockets.

UDMH (unsymmetrical dimethylhydrazine). Experiments with other fuels are also thought to have been tried out.

While the modification of the Scud was under way, Iraq was also attracted by an Argentinian development in which Egypt, a regional ally, had taken an interest, a 650-mile-range missile, the Condor 2. Unlike the veteran Scud, the Condor 2 is intended to incorporate state-of-the-art technology. So far, though, Iraq's Condor program has been thrown off schedule by technical problems, in particular with its inertial guidance, according to Western intelligence officials. A first flight scheduled for late 1989 was postponed, but work on the project is continuing. The design calls for at least two crucial improvements over the Scud: fuel stability and accuracy. The Scud's liquid fuel is so unstable that it cannot be kept in a missile for longer than a few hours before the rocket is fired. (The crew fueling the rocket must also wear chemical warfare protection suits because the liquids are so noxious and the fueling process so crude.) In contrast, the Condor 2 can use solid fuel in both its stages, or solid fuel in one and a more modern type of liquid fuel in the other.[2]

As for accuracy, the Scud's record during the Iran-Iraq War was uneven. For every ten Scud missiles fired, only five were reckoned likely to land within half a mile of their target, although by 1988 Iraq had improved this ratio. (To explain the accuracy of some of the Scud attacks on Tehran—including two salvos of three missiles each on the Tehran University campus—some diplomats reported that homing beacons might have been used by Iraqi agents in the Iranian capital. American satellite data indicated that the two salvos had been fired from two different locations in Iraq.)[3] Military censorship in Israel and Saudi Arabia against reporting where Iraqi missiles were landing in the 1991 war made it difficult to assess their accuracy. But intelligence officials say that the lengthening of the basic Scud tended to make it unstable in flight, and a quarter of the missiles fired at Israel went out of control and fell short. The Condor 2 is supposed to be more reliable and is also designed to be fitted eventually with terminal guidance, allowing for pinpoint accuracy.

The Iraqi manufacturing sites for the Condor 2 were completed at the end of 1988. They are located in a special closed military area to the southwest of Baghdad, with its own internal road network

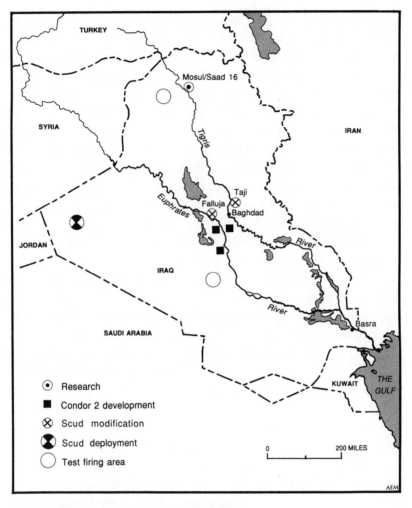

Iraq's missile research and development facilities

and even a specially built bridge across the Euphrates River. Site DO1 is the chemical plant for making the missile propellant and loading the propellant into the missile bodies. DO2 is the missile body production site. DO3 is a test area for static firing of the rocket engines and initial trials of the missile.[4]

(A by-product of Iraq's interest in the Condor is thought to be access to technology for fuel air explosive bombs, which can be dropped from aircraft as well as used in a warhead for a Condor 2 missile. The immense force of such bombs is achieved by spraying and then igniting fuel droplets. The resulting explosion has huge force, and also draws in vast quantities of oxygen from the surrounding area, threatening asphyxiation to anyone who survives the blast. The technology was tested by German engineers and handed over to Egypt, one of the participants in the Condor project. Western governments, including the United States, assume that the information was passed on to Iraq during 1987 or 1988, that is, at least two years before Egypt distanced itself from Baghdad because of Saddam's invasion of Kuwait.)

Iraq's interest in the Condor indicated a shift in priorities toward matters more important than just winning the war against Iran. Missiles with a range and accuracy to threaten any country in the region — Israel and Iran, but also nominal allies such as other Arab states and Turkey — would confirm Iraq's status as the regional Arab superpower, and Saddam Hussein as the leader of the Arabs.

(Extending the breadth of Iraq's arsenal has also been a concern. Western intelligence agencies learned that Cruise missiles were among Iraq's ambitions when two companies were approached in Britain in 1989 for equipment for a wind tunnel suitable for testing a ram-jet winged missile. The companies tipped off the British government, which warned them to steer clear of the project.)[5]

To fully assert itself as a regional superpower, Iraq resumed its efforts to make a nuclear bomb and to master the art of making biological weapons. The development of more sophisticated poisons was also logical in view of Iraq's ambitions to obtain full membership in the international club of military suppliers, which requires mastery of all means of destruction. The variety of biological and chemical weapons that Iraq has managed to develop is frightening. Since 1983 Iraq has been producing large quantities of three different chemical weapons: the blistering agent mustard gas, and two agents that attack the body's nervous system, sarin and tabun.

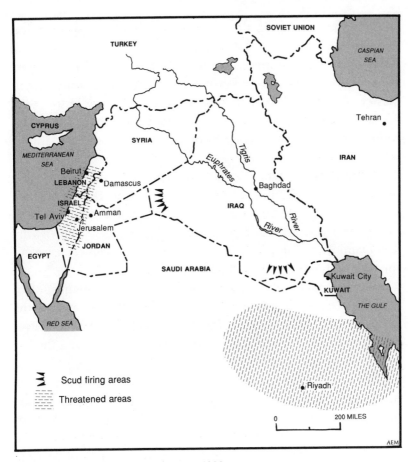

Cities within the range of Iraqi missiles, 1990

Mustard gas was first used with devastating effect in World War I. Tactically, its purpose is to maim, rather than kill, and consequently to overload the rival army's medical facilities. Making mustard gas is comparatively easy, and the process is described in open literature: mix ethylene, a by-product of oil processing and also a component of natural gas, with air to form ethylene oxide, a standard industrial chemical. Mix ethylene oxide with hydrogen sulfide, obtained from natural gas, to form thiodiglycol. Mix ethylene with hydrochloric acid to form mustard gas.

Only the last step in this process distinguishes it as chemical weapons manufacture, and it is best done in a special facility, secure from sabotage and outfitted against accidents. Newspaper reports name a wide variety of locations for Iraqi mustard gas factories, but Western officials believe that there are only two: one at Falluja, west of Baghdad, and another at the Samarra facility, about fifty miles south of the Iraqi city of that name and quite close to the Falluja complex.

Mustard gas blisters the skin, particularly in the armpits and between the legs. If inhaled, it inflames the lungs. But a suit and a mask will protect anyone caught in the open, and the gas lasts only one or two hours. Mustard gas is also soluble in water, which is why decontamination of people and equipment usually consists of spraying with water and scrubbing down.

Nerve agents, by contrast, can be fatal in small amounts, often just a drop. If absorbed through the skin or inhaled, they disrupt the body's nervous system, and death follows quickly. But the effectiveness of nerve gas may last just thirty minutes, especially in the hot desert, where it evaporates.

The Samarra plant is also believed to be where Iraq makes the nerve agent sarin and the more persistent tabun. Nerve agents are much more complicated to make than mustard gas, but the processes are still available in open literature and are well within the capability of a university laboratory. In fact, sarin and tabun were discovered almost by accident during experiments to develop pesticides. The close relationship between the nerve agents and pesticides makes production of the former easier to disguise and harder to monitor.

Iraq has been making mustard gas and nerve agents in large quantities for several years. Despite widespread use in the war with Iran, huge stockpiles remain, and inventories have been replenished and increased.

In his now infamous speech broadcast on April 2, 1990, Saddam both threatened to destroy half of Israel and proudly claimed that his forces possessed "binary chemical weapons"—chemicals that

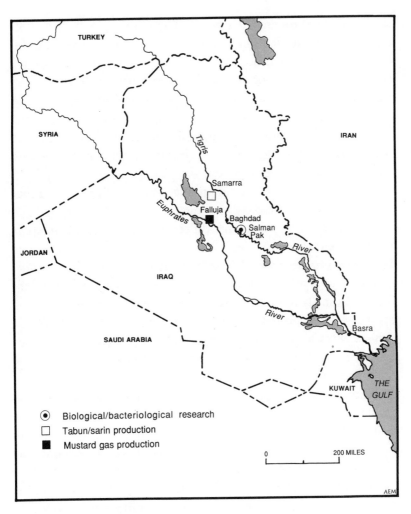

Iraq's poisonous gas facilities

are relatively harmless and stable until mixed. Foreign experts doubt this, and some are even quietly pleased that he may be working on such devices because they believe he may be wasting his time.[6] The advantage of binary chemical weapons is that materials are safe to store and handle. They become dangerous only after being fired by artillery shell or rocket when they are mixed in the course of flight toward their target. Though simple in theory, the task has proved difficult in practice. American scientists found this out the hard way. During the cold war the United States spent a considerable amount of time and money trying to develop binary weapons only to conclude that they were almost totally unreliable. US technicians could not get the chemicals to mix well in flight. But there is a danger signaled by Saddam's claim: one such binary weapon is the nerve agent VX, which is much more persistent than either sarin or tabun and could make a battlefield or city uninhabitable for weeks. If Saddam can produce longer-acting nerve agents, his arsenal becomes more dangerous.

Biological warfare is a quite different type of invisible weapon, far more lethal because it is longer-lasting. Iraq's research into biological warfare took place at Salman Pak, about fifteen miles southeast of Baghdad, in a facility located in a tight loop of the Tigris River. (It was destroyed in 1991.) There, work was done on such diseases as anthrax and botulism toxin, and perhaps even some viruses, such as West Nile fever, samples of which were exported openly to Iraq from the United States, supposedly to be used for legitimate preventative medical research.

Anthrax, in particular, is suspected of being of great interest to Iraqi military planners. It is devastating against livestock and human beings. The first symptoms are bleeding from the mouth; death follows in a matter of hours or days. Tests by British scientists on anthrax during World War II were carried out on a remote Scottish island that remained infected for forty years. (Within weeks of the Iraqi invasion of Kuwait, government veterinarians working in Britain were discreetly instructed to be alert for signs of anthrax among sheep and cows.[7] No reason was given for the caution, but one may guess that the British government feared that Iraqi agents might start spreading anthrax or other biological agents in retaliation for British support of the United States in confronting Iraq.)

The making of biological weapons, unlike chemical weapons, does not require a large industrial facility. A comparatively small laboratory is adequate, with equipment for fermentation being a standard item. After the biological agent is grown, it is dried, using cell dryers, a process similar to the making of freeze-dried coffee. Iraq had tried to buy these cell dryers and other technology in the United States, but the licenses were refused, according to a statement by US Assistant Secretary of State for the Middle East John H. Kelly before the House Foreign Affairs Committee in Washington, DC, on April 26, 1990. Kelly noted that Iraq is a signatory of a 1972 international convention banning biological weapons, although Iraq had not deposited an instrument of ratification. (International support for banning biological weapons is widespread, partly because they are so difficult to make; support for banning the development and use of chemical weapons is much weaker.)

The toxicity of biological weapons means that great care is needed in delivering them. According to Western intelligence, across the Tigris from the Salman Pak plant is a test range where Iraqi researchers are conducting experiments on how far biological agents are carried by the wind after being released. Such research is crucial to any military force contemplating the use of biological weapons: the troops unleashing the bacteria have to be vaccinated against them, but bacteria are capable of spontaneously mutating into strains against which the original vaccine is ineffective.

Despite the potency, and the dreadfulness, of chemical and biological weapons, the real test of sophistication in a modern military arsenal remains the ability to manufacture nuclear weapons. Within a few years after Israel's bombing of Tuwaitha in 1981, Iraqi efforts to make up for lost time had become apparent. For Western intelligence agencies, the work at Tuwaitha was difficult to monitor. But it was quite obvious that many young Iraqi scientists and technicians were being sent abroad to acquire skills useful to a nuclear program. Despite the deprivations caused by the ongoing war with Iran, there seemed little restraint on money and effort.

Until the Israelis bombed Tuwaitha, Iraq had been following the so-called plutonium route to a bomb. The Tuwaitha reactor would have been inspected regularly by the United Nations body, the International Atomic Energy Agency (IAEA), as part of international agreements whereby Iraq gained access to atomic know-how to be used for peaceful purposes in return for allowing the IAEA access to verify that the facilities were not also being used for military purposes. Nuclear experts believe that Iraqi researchers were hoping to cheat on IAEA inspections by using the Tuwaitha plant to "cook" uranium ore that Iraq had acquired and that was not under IAEA audit. Slipped past surveillance cameras, the cooked uranium could then be reprocessed to separate out plutonium, a potential nuclear explosive. Although the world condemned Israel for destroying the Tuwaitha reactor, France, which had originally provided much of the equipment, was not prepared to replace it, and so, in the view of Western experts, Iraq then decided to try other means to produce a nuclear bomb.

Apart from plutonium, there is essentially one other nuclear explosive, highly enriched uranium. But one must devise a method to convert uranium, which contains only 0.7 percent of the fissile isotope U-235, to a metal containing 90 percent. There are two techniques for this conversion, both of which involve converting the uranium ore into uranium hexafluoride gas, and then sorting out the smaller U-235 atoms from the larger U-238 atoms, which are not required. This is the process the United States used to manufacture the atomic bomb dropped on Hiroshima in 1945. At a huge plant in Oak Ridge, Tennessee, highly enriched uranium was obtained by passing hexafluoride gas through diffusion barriers, but the cost was enormous — at one time the plant consumed 10 percent of all the electricity in the United States.

A much more efficient way to collect the U-235 atoms is to process the hexafluoride gas in ultra-high-speed centrifuges, a system adopted by a consortium of Britain, the Netherlands, and Germany, which has used the method for years to make low-enriched fuel for power stations. The same process yields highly enriched uranium if the gas is left in the system for longer periods.

Despite the dangers of misuse of this technology, the European consortium has a sad record for security. Secrets have leaked steadily over the years from the consortium's plant and from its subcontractors. Pakistan's controversial uranium-enrichment plant at Kahuta, outside the capital, Islamabad, uses centrifuges based on early European designs. Iraq is now believed to be following a similar route to developing a nuclear explosive; it investigated the diffusion-barrier method in the late 1980s, but gave it up after failing to acquire the special nickel powder of a particular size most suitable for the diffusion barriers.

An equally complicated but separate task is the design of an effective atomic bomb. A crude bomb can be made by slamming one piece of highly enriched uranium into another; just such a bomb was dropped on Hiroshima. But a much more sophisticated bomb allowing for more technical features relies on a technique known as implosion (used in the bomb dropped on Nagasaki), and mastering implosion is the real indication of nuclear proficiency. In an implosion device pieces of highly enriched uranium or plutonium are squeezed together into what is called a critical mass, that is, a sufficient amount of fissionable material to sustain a nuclear chain reaction. The difficulty is to squeeze the uranium tightly enough and long enough for the reaction to start and sustain itself. The tendency is for the uranium to blow itself apart without starting a chain reaction, a disappointing failure that scientists call a "fizzle."

In an operative implosion device, segments of explosive are shaped to form a casing that resembles a hollow soccer ball, in the center of which are placed subcritical masses of highly enriched uranium. When the device is detonated, the explosive forces are directed inward, and the uranium achieves critical mass. Western officials are convinced that Iraq is working on such a bomb design, and were able to monitor at least part of these efforts by a sting operation that resulted in the seizure at London Heathrow airport in March 1990 of a consignment of nuclear components and the arrest of several people (see chapter 18). The components were

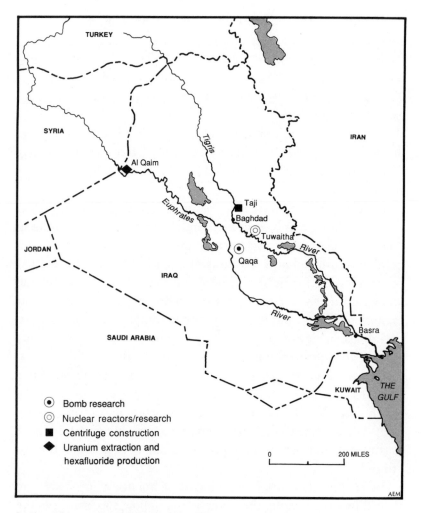

Iraq's nuclear research and related facilities

capacitors of a special type suitable for providing sufficient electricity to fire the detonators that set off the conventional explosive in the outer shell of an implosion bomb. (There was some confusion in news reports, which named the components as *krytrons,* the high-speed switches that release the capacitor's charge. Shipments of krytrons to Israel and Pakistan are believed to have helped in these countries' nuclear bomb programs. Iraq may have ordered krytrons as well, but these were not intercepted at this time.)

Although the sites of Iraq's chemical and biological weapons research are well known, its nuclear project is shrouded in secrecy. Much military work was thought to be done at Tuwaitha, ten miles southeast of Baghdad, though it was nominally a civil facility. IAEA inspectors could examine only mutually agreed places in the plant's compound, which was surrounded by high sand embankments on which anti-aircraft guns were mounted. One Western official with access to intelligence material said that a large, new building in the compound aroused much interest, mainly because it was the only building on the site to be camouflaged.[8] Another possible site for a uranium-enrichment plant was an area alongside the Badush Dam, being built on the Tigris, north of Mosul.[9]

Bomb design is thought to be carried out at the destination for the capacitors seized in London, the Qaqa State Establishment, at Iskandariya, about half an hour's drive south of Baghdad. This is where a mysterious explosion took place in August 1989 and hundreds of people, including Egyptian workers, were thought to have been killed. When the Iranian-born journalist Farzad Bazoft, who was reporting for a British newspaper, visited the site he was arrested and prevented from leaving the country. He was subsequently charged with spying and, in March 1990, was hanged, despite a chorus of international protests. (For a detailed discussion of Bazoft's plight, see chapter 18.)

Iraqi projects to develop explosives for an implosion bomb include research into two forms of conventional explosive, HMX (high melting point explosive) and RDX (rapid detonation explosive). Intelligence officials know that Iraq has been trying to build a production facility for both forms of explosive, possibly at Al Qaqa. Bomb designers say that RDX could be used, but HMX is better.[10] Work on producing uranium hexafluoride gas was being done in early 1991 at Al-Qaim in western Iraq, while the metal centrifuges to separate out the fissile isotope were being made at Taji, a few miles north of Baghdad.

Unless Iraq severs its international agreements and misuses highly enriched uranium fuel under IAEA safeguard at the Tuwaitha reactor, it seems unlikely that it can make an atomic bomb quickly. Fear of such misuse was bruited by various senior US officials after the invasion of Kuwait, although an inspection by the IAEA in November 1990 indicated that no uranium had been misappropriated. Until it is known that Iraq has a functioning uranium-enrichment plant, it is more reasonable to assume that the country is at least two years away from producing a nuclear bomb, two years being the time needed to obtain sufficient quantities of enriched uranium.

One further possibility must be considered: that another country will give Iraq sufficient highly enriched uranium to make a bomb. This is not a wholly implausible scenario — intelligence officials firmly believe that China gave Pakistan enough weapons-grade uranium for two bombs in the latter part of 1984,[11] and Pakistan, at least before the invasion of Kuwait, had become noticeably closer to Iraq. Iraq, for example, has supported Pakistan in its confrontation with India over the disputed territory of Kashmir,[12] a long-smoldering argument that flared in early 1990. Additionally, intelligence officials say that Pakistani nuclear scientists have visited Iraq, and Iraqis have been to the unsafeguarded enrichment plant at Kahuta.

Iraqi–Pakistani cooperation may have been part of the reason that President Bush refused in November 1990 to sign a memorandum saying that he did not believe Pakistan had a nuclear device; under US policy, his refusal caused an immediate suspension of US aid to Pakistan.

An additional, unreported, pressure on Pakistan was applied by the British government in the same month. Ahmed Jamil, a member of the Pakistan embassy staff in London, had been the London fixer for Dr. Abdul Qader Khan, Pakistan's leading nuclear scientist, for more than ten years. The British declared Jamil persona non grata and gave him less than a month to leave.[13]

Slightly separate from Iraq's weapons research is the work under way to develop a rocket capable of launching a satellite. On December 5, 1989, Iraq claimed to have successfully tested a satellite launcher, the Al-Abid. Western intelligence was surprised by the claim, made two days after the launch, mainly because of a foul-up within the US military bureaucracy. The firing had been detected by satellites that had transmitted the warning to the US early warning center, dug deep into a mountain outside Colorado Springs, but the message had not been passed on to Washington.[14] Analysis of the US satellite data revealed that the Iraqi rocket had soared thirteen miles into the air before falling back to earth; its second stage had not separated and no satellite had been launched. The Al-Abid appears to be a genuine satellite launch vehicle, rather than a strategic weapon, and a potentially powerful one. Its first-stage booster was, according to Western intelligence officials, a cluster of five Al-Abbas rockets strapped together. The launch failed, but it caused the world to sit up, perhaps still doubting Iraq's capability but not Saddam's ambition.

chapter 13

Project Babylon: The Supergun

Few tales to come out of Iraq in the last few years better illustrate the grandiose ambitions of President Saddam Hussein than his bid to acquire for his country a massive gun capable of firing a projectile weighing 1.5 tons at a target more than six hundred miles away. Filled with explosives, chemical weapons, or an atomic bomb, such a gun could strike any city in the Middle East, and even parts of southern Europe. In theory, such a gun-launched warhead would dwarf any missile-launched warhead in Iraq's arsenal, and, Western intelligence experts say, would be much harder to intercept than a missile warhead. A supergun system could also, in the long run, be cheaper than a missile arsenal: a gun barrel can be used many times, while missiles can be used only once, and their launchers just a few times.

Iraqi officials have denied that the country has a supergun project, saying that pipes intercepted by British Customs in 1990 were for a petrochemical plant. But some of the foreign technicians who helped Iraq say that the country is conducting a top-secret supergun project named after the city of Babylon, in tribute to the period when Mesopotamia was ruled by Saddam's role model, Nebuchadnezzar.

In late 1989 the United States, several European countries, and Israel—each with its own concerns about how an Iraqi supergun would further increase instability in the Middle East—gave high priority to stopping Project Babylon. The main obstacle was that although reports suggested that parts for the gun were being manufactured all over Europe, intelligence officials did not know where, or even what the parts looked like.

The first interception illustrated the uncertainty.[1] On April 10, 1990, a group of officers from the British Customs service huddled together on the dockside at the northeast British port of Teesport wondering what to do next. They were there in response to a tip-off: parts of an alleged Iraqi superweapon were about to be loaded or had been loaded onto a Bermuda-registered freighter, chartered by the Iraqi government, tied alongside the dock. The powers of the British Customs are extensive, but so are its potential liabilities. Customs agents can order that a ship be searched, and even unloaded, but if no contraband is discovered, the Customs service may be liable for the costs and even compensation for any delay in the ship's sailing.

Quandaries about searching vessels are more suited to senior bureaucrats in their warm offices, than to their dockside subordinates caught in the cold wind and rain. So there was a fair amount of muttering among the waiting men at Teesport about what should be done. Matters were not made any easier by the supposed target of their inquiry—parts for a supergun about 150 meters (480 feet) long, with some pieces of piping having a diameter big enough for a person to kneel inside, and with walls a foot thick. The British Customs officers were used to searching for drugs or similar contraband, but the mere mention of a supergun seemed surrealistic. The only immediate guidance to solving their predicament came from a bearded, youthful official from "one of the security services" in London, who had joined them minutes before they set out for the dock. Though he had donned a Customs jacket and cap, he appeared gauche in comparison to the self-confident, conservative types who join the Customs service. Nor did the uniform hide his enthusiasm for what was otherwise a routine interception. He was fully obsessed with superguns, whatever they were.

The waiting and muttering came to an end within half an hour. Through the dock gates appeared two large truck-and-trailer units, each loaded with four huge pieces of piping. The trucks were flagged down and ordered to unload their cargo in a nearby warehouse. The consignment was labeled as petrochemical pipes for a new petrochemical plant in Iraq known as PC2. The Customs officers ordered that wooden planks protecting the pipes be removed so that the man from London could inspect them. Within minutes the expert declared that the pipes were probably intended for a supergun; within a few hours he announced that he was sure. The Customs officers impounded the pipes and set about investigating who should be prosecuted for attempting to export a gun without a license.

The on-the-spot analysis by the man rushed in from London was based on a thorough reading of one of the more obscure books in the English language, *Paris Kanonen — the Paris Guns (Wilhelmgeschütze) and Project HARP,* written by two scientists, Gerald Bull and Charles Murphy, and published in Bonn in 1988. The ends of the pipes at Teesport had rims — flanges that enabled sections to be bolted together. These, and the smoothly finished inner walls of the pipes, were almost identical to pictures in Bull and Murphy's book.

To understand the significance of the seizure at Teesport, we can do no better than to begin with the two stories — that of the Paris guns and that of Project HARP — presented in that book. The Paris guns were German-designed weapons used in 1918, in the closing months of World War I, to bombard Paris from German-held territory seventy-five miles away, a range far beyond the capabilities of conventional artillery in that day as well as this. More than forty years later, in the 1960s, Bull, a brilliant Canadian scientist, led an attempt to develop this technology for the US and Canadian governments. Known as Project HARP (High Altitude Research Program), Bull's work was intended to produce a supergun that could be used to launch small satellites.

Bull and Murphy's book is replete with technical explanations and full of photographs of working test beds, one in Arizona, another straddling the Quebec-Vermont border, and a third on the Caribbean island of Barbados. The principle of making a gun powerful enough that projectiles such as satellites could be launched into space depended on slowing the speed by which the propellant charge was detonated. For a 1,000-mm bore gun, about nine tons of charge was needed, but the propellent would have to be detonated steadily as the projectile flew along the barrel, rather than exploding all at the same moment, as in conventional artillery. The projectile would be still accelerating as it left the barrel, enabling it to reach the high speed necessary to achieve at least a partial orbit of the earth.

But in 1967 Washington decided to stop backing the project. Rockets seemed a cheaper way of launching satellites, and safer for the often delicate payloads, which could not bear the rapid acceleration of being fired along a gun barrel.

For several years Bull instead concentrated on conventional artillery, and he made a significant contribution to the development of base-bleed shells, shells that extend the range of conventional artillery from around twenty miles to well over thirty miles. The constraint on range was the turbulence caused by a shell in flight; the turbulence upset the shell's aerodynamics, reducing its speed. Under another contract to the United States and Canada, Bull worked out an elegant solution: having a small rocket in the base of the shell "bleed" a exhaust jet during flight, thereby reducing the turbulence and extending the range. But in the mid-1970s the contract ended, and Bull had to look for other clients. One client was Israel, another was South Africa, to which he sold artillery gun technology in contravention of United Nations sanctions. Caught and prosecuted by the US, Bull was fined and jailed for four months, and his Quebec-based company, Space Research Corporation, folded. Bull claimed that he had been working on behalf of the CIA and remained embittered about the affair for the rest of his life. Whatever happened, South Africa's famous artillery guns, the towed 155-mm G-5 and the self-propelled 155-mm G-6, are a legacy of Bull's efforts.

After his release from prison in 1980, Bull was determined to continue his research with the help of any country that would fund him. Western officials believed he was dismissive of any suggestion that moral considerations should limit his choice of business partners.

Little more was heard of Bull, other than the occasional visible evidence of his having given advice to manufacturers of 155-mm howitzer guns. During the Iran-Iraq War, Iraqi arms dealers scoured the world for the best artillery. Samples of the G-5 and G-6 were bought from South Africa, a country with which Iraq did not have diplomatic relations, through the Chilean arms company Cardoen, which held a license to manufacture the guns. But more direct evidence of Bull's work was displayed at the first Baghdad International Exhibition for Military Production in late April 1989. Among the exhibits was the Al-Fao, a locally produced self-propelled 210-mm howitzer that bore an astonishing resemblance to the South African G-6. The Iraqi Military Production Authority also showed off what it claimed was a successful conversion of a Soviet-produced 130-mm artillery gun to 155-mm specifications. The cognoscenti, including the world's intelligence agencies, realized that Gerald Bull was almost certainly dealing extensively with Iraq.

That might have been the end of the story, and Project Babylon might still be a top-secret, but for information that began to emerge during 1988 and 1989. Just when is unclear. (In late 1990 the British Parliament opened an inquiry to find out what the British government knew, and when.) One British official says a request from London to learn more about Iraq's interest in extra-long-range guns was made of diplomats in Baghdad as early as summer 1988.[2] Another official was more circumspect, and declined to state when the British government first knew that Iraq was working on a huge long-range gun, saying that the information was sometimes so vague and the notion so unlikely that it took weeks for London to understand what was taking place.[3] (Apart from Germany's Paris gun of 1918, the only other example in history of an extra-long-range device was the German project in 1944 to build a V-3 gun to bombard London from occupied France. This was a technical failure, although one such gun did lob a few shells at advancing American troops in the Ardennes during the Battle of the Bulge in late 1944.)

Working backward, British officials deduced that the Iraqi supergun project was started in late 1987 or early 1988.[4] One crucial piece of evidence was information gained from a British-based explosives and propellant company, Astra, that in September 1989 had taken over a Belgian company in the same field, Poudrière Réunie Belge (PRB). Examining the PRB books, Astra executives discovered orders for propellant charge suitable to fit inside a gun 1 meter (just under 40 inches) in diameter, and another order, partially filled, for similar propellant for a gun with a bore of 350 millimeters (about 16 inches). The second order had been from Jordan, but the delivery had taken place at the Amman airport, and it seemed likely that the intended recipient was Iraq.

Other parts of the jigsaw puzzle soon began to fit together. By March 1990 it was fairly obvious that Iraq had a supergun project organized by a team of foreign engineers under the leadership of Gerald Bull, who was working out of his reconstituted Space Research Corporation in the Belgian capital, Brussels. Any doubt in the minds of the Western intelligence services was dispelled by the news on the evening of Thursday, March 22, 1990, that Bull had been fatally gunned down outside his apartment in Brussels. No witnesses came forward. Two bullets had been fired at close range to the back of Bull's neck and, while he was on the ground, three more bullets had been fired into his body. The murder weapon, a

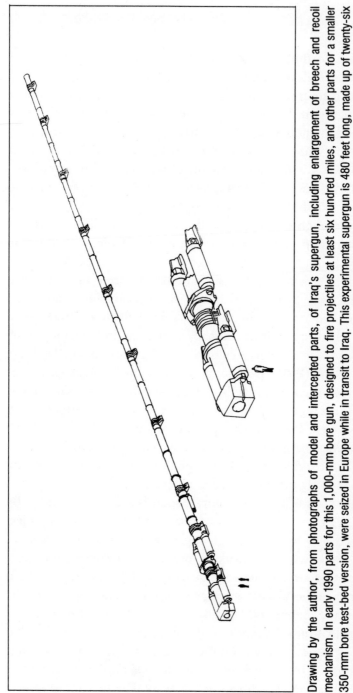

Drawing by the author, from photographs of model and intercepted parts, of Iraq's supergun, including enlargement of breech and recoil mechanism. In early 1990 parts for this 1,000-mm bore gun, designed to fire projectiles at least six hundred miles, and other parts for a smaller 350-mm bore test-bed version, were seized in Europe while in transit to Iraq. This experimental supergun is 480 feet long, made up of twenty-six sections of pipe. At its firing angle of 52 degrees, fixed on the slope of a hill, it would have stood higher than a twenty-five-story building. Western intelligence officials believe that Iraq is eventually hoping to put into service a 600-mm version, which could threaten every city in the Middle East with high-explosive, chemical, or nuclear warheads.

silencer-equipped 7.65-mm pistol, was left lying beside the body. Theft was immediately ruled out as a motive when Bull's wallet, containing a variety of foreign currency worth in total $20,000, was found in his pocket.

No individual or group claimed credit for the murder, but it bore all the hallmarks of a classic assassination by the Israeli intelligence agency, the Mossad, although press speculation also suggested that the Iranians or the Iraqis might have done it, the latter because Bull's business relationship might have soured. Within intelligence circles, though, the Mossad was believed to be responsible. Neither the Iranians nor the Iraqis were considered by intelligence officials to have the professionalism, and a hired killer would have probably stolen the wallet as well. Asked whether Mossad was responsible, a senior Israeli official said, "No."[5] For intelligence insiders, though, the telltale sign was the two bullets to the neck. Bull's legs would have started to crumple as soon as the first bullet shattered his spinal cord. The police report suggested the second bullet was fired while Bull was still standing, indicating a very proficient gunman: "Mossad was showing off," according to one British intelligence official.[6] The three bullets to the body were just to make sure—certainty being another Mossad hallmark.

There is little indication that the Israelis were ahead of other intelligence agencies in discovering Iraq's supergun. But the Israelis were certainly quicker off the mark than other countries in deciding to do something about the gun. Clearly, the prospect of an Iraqi supergun with a range of six hundred miles gave Israel more cause for concern than most countries—Jerusalem and Tel Aviv are less than three hundred miles from Iraq. Some Western officials also credit the Mossad with causing a mysterious explosion at the PRB factory in January—two months before Bull died—which delayed the shipment of some supergun propellant. And the Mossad had outpaced the British government in discovering that some of the supergun's components were being manufactured in Britain. The information that put British Customs onto the Teesport shipment had come from the Israelis. ("Who tipped you off?" a British official was asked afterward. "The same people who killed Bull," he replied.)[7] The Israelis had named the manufacturer of the pipes, the port of shipment, and the ship. As a finesse, perhaps, to indicate the depth of their knowledge, the Israelis gave the previous name of the ship and its port of registration, both of which had recently been changed. This forced British Customs to rush about in near panic before deciding which ship to stake out, rather than lose face by going back to the Israelis to ask for the current name of the ship.

After the Teesport seizure, a string of interceptions took place across Europe. The general public was amazed, and the manufacturers and others involved in the shipment of the parts professed similar astonishment, with varying degrees of genuineness, at what the Iraqis had ordered. Part of the shock was the sheer dimension of the gun: at 480 feet long, it was intended to be tilted to an elevation of 52 degrees. Thus the top of the gun's barrel would stand higher than 355 feet, about as tall as a twenty-five-story building.

Another source of confusion was that there were two types of guns: one whose barrel was 1,000 millimeters in diameter, and the other with a barrel 350 millimeters in diameter. The former seemed to be the preferred production model, with a potential range of 600 miles boosted to 2,000 miles if the projectile also carried a rocket motor. The smaller was thought by Western intelligence officials to have been the experimental test bed; its barrel was in three sections with a total length of 30 meters (32 yards), although the potential range of this type was still a creditable two hundred miles.

The sections of the barrel for the bigger gun were made by Sheffield Forgemasters, a British company. Sections for the smaller gun had been made by another British company, Walter Somers, which had also helped machine finish the larger tubing. The breech block for the large gun had been manufactured by Società delle Fucine, of Terni, Italy. The recoil mechanism for both types was manufactured by Von Roll of Switzerland, which also made the breech block mechanism for the smaller gun. The propellant charge came from PRB of Belgium. The slide bearings that would have supported the larger barrel and allowed it to move backward in recoil were being constructed by Trebelan of Spain, according to British officials, although the company denied any knowledge of this.[8] Western officials say that Trebelan was also making the foundation beams on which the slide bearers rest. After press publicity, officials were satisfied that the orders had been stopped.

One of the reasons the Western countries had failed to realize that Iraq was working on a supergun was that the supergun project was being conducted separately from Iraq's other superweapons projects, such as its nuclear, chemical, and biological weapons development. The normal paraphernalia of telephone intercepts and information from agents planted in the Iraqi networks thus had not elicited any information about a supergun. Western officials think that the Iraqi government gave Gerald Bull the task of providing Iraq with the superguns, and, to satisfy his own concerns about security, let him get on with it by himself. (By most accounts Bull was a tough and eccentric negotiator who would sit cross-legged on the floor and harangue everyone in the room with a two-hour monologue.) The work was carried out at the reconstituted Space Research Corporation and at a sister company known as ATI. The identity of ATI caused considerable confusion. Some European governments took ATI to mean the Advanced Technology Institute, based in Athens, while other sources thought ATI referred to the Amalgamated Trading Industries of Belgium. The splitting up of the orders for components across much of Europe added to the confusion and made the operation very difficult to penetrate.

What never emerged in the international investigation of the Iraqi superguns was any sign of the projectiles that either gun would fire. The absence of projectiles enabled at least one man charged with illegally conspiring to export gun parts from Britain to say that he thought that the parts were for launching satellites and had no military purpose. The difficulty of proving the parts' military purpose without disclosing intelligence sources—whose information, at any event, might not be good enough to serve as evidence in court—led the British authorities to drop pending prosecutions associated with the Teesport seizure. (Iraq then made a bid for the seized parts to be sent on to Baghdad, but the invasion of Kuwait, and the resulting trade embargo, halted all action on that score.)

Though the projectile component was never discovered, investigators knew what they were looking for because Bull had devoted much of his book to the subject. The superguns were not intended to fire shells, as such, but winged darts, which Bull called *martlets*. Smaller than the gun barrel, the martlet would be held stable as it was shot along the 480 feet of tubing by sleevelike pieces of shaped padding known as *sabots*. At the end of the barrel, the sabots would fall away from the martlet, leaving the projectile as an almost perfect shape to bear the aerodynamic stresses of high-speed flight. (Some tank shells use the same principle, their darts designed to force their way through enemy armor by their sheer momentum.) A dart fired from the 1,000-mm gun was judged by Western officials as capable of carrying 1.5 tons of high explosives or, more effectively, given the lack of pinpoint accuracy for such a weapon, a large quantity of chemical weapons that would spread widely on impact. More troubling was the possibility that a supergun dart could carry a crude atomic bomb, about two feet in diameter. (A major task in developing a nuclear weapon is to master the fusion or fission technology and then miniaturize the product so that it can be placed atop a missile or under the wing of a strike aircraft. The supergun, however, would have obviated the need for miniaturization.)

Western officials believed that the darts were being manufactured in Europe, because their exterior surfaces had to be carefully machined to specifications beyond the capabilities of Iraq's own industry. But it would have been hard to disguise the essential military purpose of the darts, and engineering companies could not have pleaded ignorance as they so often did after being caught making supergun parts. Whatever company was involved could not have claimed that this was a device for a petrochemical plant.

Despite the successes of European intelligence agencies and customs services in intercepting so many supergun parts early in the summer of 1990, Western officials do not believe that Project Babylon is dead.[9] The small group of Western engineers who had worked with Gerald Bull dispersed across the world after his death. Some have been tracked as far as South America, where presumably they were hoping they would be outside the reach of Israeli assassination squads. There is evidence, according to Western officials, that some members of the group want to work together again to finish the project they started. In the murky world of international arms manufacture, they have been looking for a patron, perhaps an arms company. Their aim remains to produce a viable supergun that will not be as immobile as the 1,000-mm version, which can be aimed only at one target. Western officials believe that a gun with a bore of between 600 and 660 millimeters was being designed even as Saddam's occupation of Kuwait was being played out.[10]

To date, it remains unclear what happened to those parts of the superguns that did reach Iraq. Sheffield Forgemasters had a contract to produce fifty-two sections of piping, twenty-six of which made up a single gun. In the six months before the Teesport seizure forty-four sections had already been delivered, twenty-six for one barrel and eighteen for another. (Only the shipment of the final eight sections was seized.) One of the smaller guns had also reached Iraq, along with the propellant, but it was damaged during testing at a range outside Mosul.

Despite an intensive search by US spy satellites, the intended sites for the superguns have not been located, according to officials with access to the distribution of such information. The 350-mm guns would have been relatively easy to hide, but the 1,000-mm gun was intended to be embedded in concrete on a hillside, pointing permanently at its target. The positioning of the gun was shown in a scale model made in England as part of the contract, and exported to Baghdad so that Saddam could review it. Photographs of the model show small figures of men working on the barrel and loading mechanism, a launch control center, and a helicopter landing pad, with a model helicopter sitting on it.[11] Such a ground installation would be easily detected by US spy satellites, which can be programmed to identify any construction 480 feet long and straight. The installation is also likely to be on the side of a hill, pointing either at Iran or Israel. And not just any hill, but one that has a slope of about 52 degrees — the slope of the gun barrel in the scale model.

It would also be likely, Western officials say, that the barrel would be sunk in a trench of reinforced concrete, which would protect it against all forms of air attack, bar the use of a ground-penetrating nuclear weapon. This form of defense is easier to construct than a tunnel into the side of a hill, and it provides the same measure of protection. Well-protected by anti-aircraft missiles, on the surface or underground, the supergun would be virtually impregnable. The tunnels for the V-3 gun, which the Germans had dug in northern France during World War II, were destroyed in 1944 only when the British air force dropped ten-ton bombs from 20,000 feet. Those huge bombs, larger than any conventional bombs in existence today, knifed deep into the ground before exploding, creating a minor earthquake.

The assassination of Gerald Bull in Brussels was a blow keenly felt by Saddam Hussein. Just over a week later Saddam gave a long speech contrasting the world's condemnation of Iraq for having executed the Iranian-born journalist-spy Farzad Bazoft and the world's silence about the murder of Bull. The speech is better remembered, though, for Saddam's assertion that Iraq possessed binary chemical weapons. "By God," he threatened, "we will make fire eat up half of Israel if it tries anything against Iraq."[12] It was a significant step up in the level of tension in the Middle East, although few observers at the time believed that it was Kuwait that was in the most immediate danger.

★ ★ ★

chapter 14

Smuggling Superweapons Technology

What sort of a person helped Saddam Hussein build up his superweapons arsenal? Otto Schmidt (not his real name) is a fun-loving Austrian engineer who in 1988 and 1989 helped construct Iraq's facilities for the Condor 2 missile. (The facilities for manufacturing, fueling, and testing this missile are complete, although development of the missile itself has been delayed by technical difficulties.) Explaining what he had done, in immense detail, while sitting back home in Austria in his modest apartment, Schmidt expressed no guilt.[1] He was speaking, in May 1989, because he had fallen out with his former employer, who he alleged owed him money. Speaking on condition that his real name was not revealed, and that his face was obscured on television, Schmidt spoke soberly and truthfully, as far as it could be discerned, about what he had done. He was vaguely puzzled that no Western intelligence agency had ever contacted him to ask about the Condor project.

Schmidt knew that the Condor 2 project was intended to make Iraq the dominant military power of the Middle East, a competitor whose strength would match or exceed Israel's. He certainly was not ashamed of his work for Iraq. Indeed, he took pride in describing how well he had built the installations, and provided photographs as proof. Although carrying a camera in a militarily sensitive area is to risk arrest, Schmidt had taken several rolls of film of the missile fueling depot that he had built. Asked why he had taken the risk, he replied: "I have taken pictures of every project that I have worked on as an engineer, and so I was determined to have pictures of this project as well." Schmidt also contributed to the drawing of the Condor 2, shown on page 127. He revealed that a booster stage was also planned to convert the missile into a satellite launcher, or boost its range beyond 650 miles so that Iraq could threaten not just Israel, Iran, and Saudi Arabia but also the southern Soviet Union or American bases in Turkey and British bases on the island of Cyprus in the Mediterranean.

Schmidt was not the sort of man to scare easily; still, he knew that in talking to journalists he was taking a risk, the more so because he had a wife and young family. He thought, however, that he would be safe from Iraqi retribution because he was about to go abroad again, on a contract to build a ski resort in the US. He was particularly pleased that he avoided incurring the wrath of the Israelis. He recalled that the previous summer the car belonging to the general manager of Consen, a European company supplying technical advice on Condor 2 to the Iraqis, was blown up in the south of France. No one was hurt in the incident. The engineers working for Consen in Iraq believed that the Israeli Mossad was probably responsible, though a previously unknown group, the Guardians of Islam, claimed the credit. With Iraqi permission, and at Baghdad's expense, the European engineers in Iraq had their wives and families flown out to stay with them, instead of going home that summer on leave to Germany and Austria.

A hint of Schmidt's motivation came from his remarks about Iraqis whom he had met. Although he had taken on the contract for money — about $4,000 a month, plus accommodation — he had obviously enjoyed working in Iraq. He clearly respected the ability of Iraqi engineers and technocrats, and their insistence on maintaining high standards of finish on the various facilities. He compared this perfectionism with the laxness of Egyptian officials, for whom he had also built Condor facilities. The wiring and anti-spark paint in the missile fueling plant outside Cairo, he said, were wrongly specified to save money, no matter that this shortcut entailed a high risk of explosion once the plant was in operation.

(The Egyptian link in assisting the build-up of Iraq's military strength was substantial and extremely close throughout the 1980s. Indeed, Egypt brought Iraq into the Condor 2 project, initially to help finance it, under an agreement called Badr 2000, meaning "Victory 2000." Iraq pushed on with the Condor development after diplomatic pressure, mainly from the United States, forced Egypt and Argentina to stop all but clandestine cooperation. Egypt's earlier assistance is now especially ironic since President Mubarak has condemned Iraq's invasion of Kuwait and provided troops to the international force in Saudi Arabia. An additional irony is that the United States has forgiven nearly $7 billion worth of Egyptian debt in recognition of Egypt's support for Washington's position.)

Another European engineer involved with Consen, and still believed to be connected with the organization, Adolf Hammer (his real name) is a German rocket specialist. Hammer's record of helping Arab states acquire military high technology dates back to the 1960s — before Israel had a nuclear and technical edge over its potential adversaries. At that time Hammer worked for Messerschmitt, a German company that in 1959 placed a team, which included former Nazi scientists, in Egypt. Their job, with others, was to help Egypt build jet aircraft and long-range rockets to threaten Israel. The project eventually collapsed, partly because of technical difficulty and also because the Israeli Mossad began a campaign of sending letter bombs to some of the scientists. Hammer returned to Germany and rose in his company, which became the conglomerate Messerschmitt-Bolkow-Blohm (MBB). When

Chart showing role of Consen group in developing the Condor 2 missile for Iraq, Egypt, and Argentina, by making use of links with European aerospace companies. The chart was drawn by German television journalist Egmont R. Koch, using internal Consen documents and intelligence sources. The Consen group fell apart after saboteurs, thought to be Israeli agents, blew up the car of its general manager in the south of France in 1988. Only Iraq is believed to be still working on the missile.

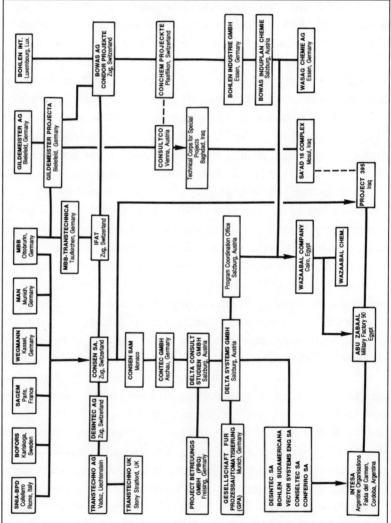

Consen won the contract to develop the Condor 2 missile for Argentina, Hammer was the MBB executive in charge of his company's contribution. After the United States put pressure on the German government to stop MBB's involvement, Hammer left the company and joined part of the Consen group, Delta, in the Austrian city of Salzburg.

Another link in the European-Eygptian-Iraqi armaments chain is Keith Smith, a British computer expert and a former executive with the British arms company Hunting. Hunting makes a variety of weapons such as mortars, artillery shells, and bombs; the company is also a subcontractor to the British nuclear weapons program. At Hunting, Smith was the computer systems manager and a specialist in battlefield analysis. His expertise lay in calculating the likely effect on buildings and people of a weapon's warhead, and suggesting design changes to achieve particular effectiveness against a target. Smith left Hunting in the early 1980s. He says that he set up as an independent consultant, although the company records of Ifat, based in Zug, Switzerland, show that he joined Ifat as a director; Ifat is a subsidiary of Consen, with which it shares a building.[2] Smith denies working for Ifat other than on a consultancy contract to buy a computer and software for the Egyptian army. (The contract was almost certainly connected with Egypt's work on the Condor 2, and, according to the US manufacturer of the computer, Prime Computer, paid for out of US aid funds to Egypt.) However, Smith's signature appears on a letter of intent to buy rocket nozzles from a California company, Space Vector Corporation, in 1984, for the Argentinian version of Condor 2. Smith was signing on behalf of another Consen company, Desintec. But in 1989 Smith insisted that the signature was a forgery and he denied that he had been a director of Ifat—the Swiss company's records were wrong. He acknowledged having known Ekkehard Schrotz, the Consen manager whose car had been blown up in the south of France: they had worked together when Schrotz had been assigned to an MBB team working with Hunting in Britain in the 1970s.

On November 30, 1990, NBC News identified Keith Smith as the man who had tried to acquire fuel air explosive secrets from the American defense contractor Honeywell. The information had been passed on to Egypt by Consen's Ifat subsidiary and is now thought by Western intelligence officials to be in the hands of Iraq. Smith was also named in court documents as having accompanied an Egyptian military officer to meet Abdul Qader Helmy, a naturalized American of Egyptian origin who was sentenced to prison by a US court in 1989 for smuggling Condor rocket technology to Egypt.

What is Consen? The company refuses to answer questions about its involvement in the Condor project, but American officials describe Consen as a group of rocket specialists and scientists who quit their jobs with some of Europe's biggest aerospace companies to set up an organization ready to sell its knowledge to the highest bidder. Western officials dub such people "technomercenaries." Consen's original client was the Argentine air force, which wanted to progress from the Condor 1 (a sounding rocket used to monitor atmospheric conditions) to a ballistic missile. Egypt joined in on the venture in 1984 and brought with it Iraqi financing.

The origins of the Consen group can be traced to Bohlen Industrie, a German industrial company, although its management maintains it was deceived by an unnamed person who used it as a "good will shield." For several years Consen employees maintained frequent links to their previous companies, and indeed brought them in on crucial phases of missile development in 1988 and 1989, until US pressure on various European governments put an end to such collaboration. Snia-BPD of Italy did work on the propellant for Condor. Wegmann of Germany worked on the launch cradle. MAN, a German industrial giant, and MBB were both specialists in a wide range of rocket technology and contributed their expertise. An MBB subsidiary, MBB-Transtechnica, equipped the rocket research establishment, known as Saad 16, built under contract by a Chinese state-owned construction company outside the northern Iraqi city of Mosul. Some of the electronic testing equipment for this facility was purchased in the United States before Washington realized what Iraq was up to.

The Helmy affair and Iraq's attempt to buy US-manufactured nuclear weapon capacitors (see chapter 18) are prominent among the relatively few instances when either Egypt or Iraq tried to buy military high technology illegally in the United States. Although some equipment did reach its destination, the United States has been quite effective in controlling strategic exports. The capacitors were stopped, as were specialized pumps suitable for use in a uranium-enrichment plant, which Iraq tried to buy from a New Jersey company in 1989. Generally speaking, Iraq has not tried to involve US companies in its clandestine activities to build an arsenal of superweapons. Otto Schmidt, the Austrian engineer on the Condor missile facilities, said that the Iraqis wanted neither American nor British citizens on the project: they were considered too likely to talk to their governments about it. (The Egyptians, however, were willing to work with Keith Smith.) Gerald Bull took a similarly cautious view of US suppliers in ordering parts for Iraq's superguns.

But Iraq slipped up when it decided to use US banks for some of the transactions. By allowing payment transactions to pass through the United States, Iraq gave American intelligence a window on its dealings in the United States and in Europe.

The circumstances are still under investigation. At least one American grand jury heard evidence and brought indictments in February 1991. Official inquiries focus on the Atlanta, Georgia, branch of Italy's second largest commercial bank, Banca Nazionale del Lavoro (BNL).[3] Contacts between the BNL and Iraq were so good that Baghdad seems to have dropped its guard and concentrated its banking business for its otherwise top-secret superweapons projects in Atlanta, instead of the ultra-confidential banks in Switzerland or the Caribbean.

The heart of the grand jury investigation is a series of letters of credit confirmed by the Atlanta BNL. Letters of credit are a staple of an assurance to the exporter that the importer has the means to pay for the goods. Typically, when the goods are delivered the bank that confirmed the letter of credit issues payment to the exporting company and the central bank in the importer's country then transfers funds to the creditor bank. For providing this service, banks charge a commission, which the exporter pays, as a form of insurance, as it were, to cover the risk of the importer's defaulting on the payment.

During the 1980s, Iraq's financial position was so strained that Baghdad often arranged to make payments for goods two years after they were delivered. Iraq's credit rating was so poor that many banks either severely limited the amount of Iraqi business on their books, or refused to confirm letters of credit for Iraq. Those banks that continued to confirm letters of credit for Iraq charged a high premium for doing so: bankers say a typical figure was between 15 and 20 percent of the value of the goods above the normal rate of interest.

The Atlanta branch of BNL, however, was confirming letters of credit for Iraq for as little as 1.5 percent over the normal rate of interest. It is this anomaly that the grand jury is investigating. The question is whether anyone in the bank acted improperly in these arrangements. Particular attention is being paid to the former manager of the BNL branch, Christopher Drogoul, who was fired, along with several other executives of the bank, when suspicious transactions were discovered in 1989.

Not surprisingly, many companies, both in the United States and abroad, that were exporting goods to Iraq came to Atlanta to arrange their letters of credit. If any of these companies thought it strange that the commission was so small, none has so far admitted it, though it must have been a subject of discussion in boardrooms. Nonetheless, as long as the paperwork for the letter of credit was in order, the exporters were assured of payment, and all the financial risk was BNL's. In 1990 that risk stood at nearly $2 billion — the sum of all the outstanding credit that BNL Atlanta had extended to finance general business with Iraq.

It remains unclear how much officials at BNL's main US office in New York or its head office in Rome knew about the goings-on in Atlanta. The suspicion among other bankers trying to do business with Iraq at this time, but on a much smaller scale, is that the credits were part of a larger political understanding between the Italian Socialist Party, a coalition party in the Italian government, and the regime of Saddam Hussein.[4] (BNL is the trade union bank in Italy and backs the Italian Socialist Party.) The motives for such a relationship can only be guessed at: perhaps some Italian politicians were amassing a slush fund, or perhaps they hoped to ensure a favorable trading relationship for Italy in the longer term.

One certain loser in the BNL affair is the US Commodity Credit Corporation (CCC), an arm of the US Department of Agriculture. BNL Atlanta's first business with Iraq was to arrange financing for the export of US agricultural surpluses. Highly dependent on food imports, Iraq preferred to buy on credit even though the price of some American farm commodities was higher than the international price. In 1985, after bidding for the business, BNL Atlanta provided some $300 million in CCC-related financing for Iraq; in 1987 it financed the entire CCC-backed program of $680 million, yet charged such a small commission that competing banks were amazed. By 1989 Iraqi purchases of US farm products reached $1 billion. When the Iraqis stopped making payments for goods already received, in 1990, the CCC had to assume the burden of paying American farmers.

In addition to procuring foreign goods, Iraq had the longer-term ambition of setting up a bank in London that would finance its foreign trade. According to one banker familiar with Iraq's thinking, the idea was to recycle some of the money made available through BNL Atlanta.[5] In 1989 Iraqi bankers went as far as approaching the Bank of England (the British central bank) on the matter, knowing that they would need official permission to set up a bank office. But the Iraqi bankers received no sympathy at all from British officials.

One of those attending the meeting was Sadiq Taha, a senior official from the Central Bank of Iraq, who spent many months in

London in 1989 and 1990. Part of this visit was spent convalescing from heart surgery; the rest was spent sitting in the offices of Iraq's front organization in Britain, known as the Technology and Development Group (TDG). One fax sent by Taha to BNL Atlanta shows that he was in regular contact with the branch manager. Addressed "Dear Chris [Drogoul]" and signed "best regards, Sadiq," the fax asks BNL Atlanta to provide "best methods currency and instruments for implementing purchase by TDG and sell to Iraqi organization so as to include in the contract being signed." The second sheet of the fax message lists twenty-four European companies and the value of goods being bought from them, for what appears to be a munitions factory worth around $40 million.

Taha died in London on June 6, 1990. The cause of his death is unclear; it was probably related to his weak heart. But one London banker, who knew him well, remains suspicious, fearing that Iraqi agents murdered Taha on Saddam's orders rather than risk the chance that a US court might indict Taha and that he would divulge Iraq's funding operations. "He knew everything about Iraq's bad financial position and the tricks being used to circumvent it," the banker said, speaking on the condition that his name not be disclosed. As for Taha's motives, the banker said that the Iraqi official was a fervent admirer of Saddam Hussein and of what Saddam had done for Iraq.

A second Iraqi who played a crucial role in the financing schemes appears to be Fadel Khaddoum, who was identified in the British parliament as an Iraqi intelligence agent. Khaddoum regularly worked out of the TDG offices in London, but he would appear all over the world whenever there was a financial question to handle, and not always on military projects. In South Korea, he was involved in talks with contractors for the plans to expand Iraq's Gulf naval base at Umm Qasr, on the border with Kuwait. In Italy, Khaddoum was considered a key player in arranging deals on a new steel works in Iraq and a petrochemical complex that, besides serving civil purposes, was to greatly expand Iraq's ability to produce mustard gas. Elsewhere, Khaddoum was involved in trying to

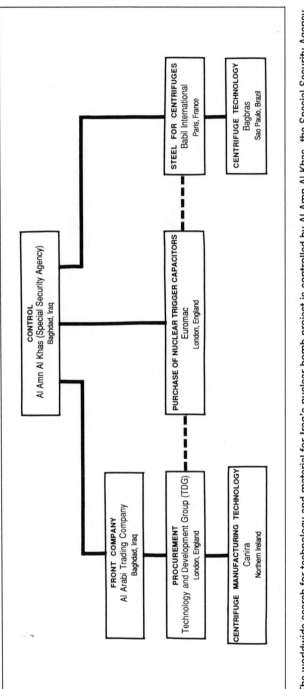

The worldwide search for technology and material for Iraq's nuclear bomb project is controlled by Al Amn Al Khas, the Special Security Agency, headed by Hussein Kamil Majid, the minister for industry and military industrialization. In 1989 the main procuring company was TDG in London, owned by Al Arabi Trading Company, which operated out of the headquarters of the Technical Corps for Special Projects in Baghdad. TDG's attempt to buy a plastics composites factory in Northern Ireland was terminated by the British government because such a factory could be used for making ultra-high-speed centrifuges and missile parts. TDG, Euromac, and Babil International were run by members of the Iraqi al-Khafaji clan, according to Western intelligence sources.

arrange financing for new aircraft for Iraqi Airways, the state-owned airline. A lawyer by profession, Khaddoum was totally at ease in the international business community.[6] Some reports say that he attended the university in France with Chris Drogoul, the BNL manager in Atlanta.

One of the other important Iraqi executives operating out of London was Safa Habobi, who was also an official of the Nasser State Enterprise at Taji, to the north of Baghdad, where Iraq was building an industrial facility and some munitions plants. Habobi had been a crucial negotiator in the 1987 purchase of Matrix Churchill, a British machine tools company, by the Iraqi government using front companies.

When British officials started investigating Habobi, they found he had family as well as commercial links with other Iraqi concerns. More interestingly, while most of his activities in London had to do with machine tools for industrial purposes and sometimes for munitions factories, his activities outside London were often connected with Iraq's bid to make a nuclear bomb. Habobi had married into the al-Khafaji clan, and a senior executive of the Paris office of Babil International, a steel company, was a member of the same clan. It was in Paris that funds belonging to Habobi's London company, Technology and Development Group, were held at a branch of the Arab consortium bank Ubaf. Babil International controlled Bagbraz in São Paulo, Brazil, which did much perfectly legitimate work but also had contacts with the Brazilian uranium centrifuge program and links with the University of São Paulo, where research on centrifuges was conducted. A further al-Khafaji connection was Euromac, a small trading company in northern Italy run by two Iraqis from the clan. It was Euromac of England, a separate but related concern, that ordered on behalf of Iraq the nuclear weapon capacitors stopped at Heathrow airport in March 1990 (see chapter 18).

As the extent of Iraqi arms purchasing has become known, more Western companies have been implicated. The activities of firms operating in what was West Germany stand out, partly because the

German media have undertaken energetic investigations. The resulting furor led the government to produce a special report for the German parliament in August 1990. In a confidential briefing it was revealed that 170 German companies had been investigated and that criminal proceedings had started against 25 of them. A German intelligence summary produced in May 1990 lists 117 current investigations of possible contraventions of German export regulations, of which 18 refer to Iraq.[7]

Apart from missile development projects like the Condor 2, German engineers are thought to have worked on Iraq's modification program of the Soviet-supplied Scud missile. German companies were also more involved than other foreign firms in helping the Iraqis set up chemical weapons factories. In one so-called pesticide production plant, which was built to produce the nerve gases tabun and sarin, German engineers installed an air-tight chamber for toxicity tests. Such a chamber might have a use in a bona fide pesticide factory to test a product's effect on rabbits or mice, which farmers might not want to kill while they were ridding their fields of other pests. But in one Iraqi research facility, German engineers installed a chamber large enough for humans. The purpose of the chamber, as revealed by the German media, was to test gas masks and protection equipment. It was reported that Iranian prisoners of war were used in these tests, and many of them died during the experiments.[8]

No German company has been prosecuted for selling such chemical weapons to Iraq (although a company that sold a chemical weapons factory to Libya was prosecuted). The German company Karl Kolb, which installed a chemical weapons plant south of Samarra, was compensated by the German government when it broke its contract with Iraq at the request of the Bonn authorities. Another legal lacuna was discovered in the case of two engineers from the German corporation MAN.[9] Walter Busse, age seventy-eight, had been a department head at MAN, and after leaving the company he visited Iraq in 1988 and 1989 to offer advice on centrifuge technology, which Iraq was using to produce enriched uranium for a nuclear bomb. Sometimes Busse was accompanied by Bruno Stemmler, age fifty-seven, an expert at MAN in the manufacture of centrifuge rotors. German investigators found that neither Busse nor Stemmler had signed a confidentiality agreement with MAN, and therefore could not be prosecuted for revealing proprietary information. (Civilian companies in Germany were supposed to have imposed tougher security measures after a major scandal in the Netherlands in 1978, when it was discovered that a Pakistani scientist had gained access to centrifuge technology at the Urenco enrichment plant, operated jointly by the Netherlands, Britain, and Germany to produce reactor fuel for nuclear power plants. The Pakistani at the center of the inquiry was Abdul Qader Khan, who is now his country's top nuclear scientist and credited with producing the nuclear explosive for Pakistan's nascent bomb project.)

Western officials who had been involved in disrupting Pakistan's clandestine purchasing of nuclear equipment after the earlier blunder were dismayed that there had been another security lapse, for they considered Iraq a far richer, more ruthless, and more ambitious country than Pakistan. Using their earlier experience, they judged that Iraq would have a nuclear bomb in much less than the ten years it had taken Pakistan.

★ ★ ★

CHAPTER

15

Who Armed Saddam?

American soldiers on duty in the Saudi desert in late 1990 did not have to speculate about who was responsible for making Iraq one of the best-armed countries in the world. Soon after arrival, each soldier was provided a copy of *How They Fight; Desert Shield; Order of Battle Handbook,* published in September 1990 by the United States Army Intelligence Agency. This pocket-sized 146-page guide to the Iraqi military, its tactics and equipment, included 83 pages of line drawings and brief specs of Iraqi tanks, artillery, missiles, and aircraft. The overwhelming preponderance of equipment was of Soviet origin, with France as a second-place supplier, and a smaller range of items from European and Chinese sources.

Contrary to press speculation that the United States had been one of Iraq's major arms suppliers, the only American items in the handbook listed were M-60 armored personnel carriers (APCs); M-109, M-110, and M-107 howitzers; and the Bell 214 helicopter. Most of the APCs and probably the howitzers were Iranian equipment captured by Iraq during the Iran-Iraq War. The Bell helicopters were supplied ostensibly for civilian use, as were some Hughes helicopters not listed in the handbook. Both types were widely used as transport helicopters by the Iraqi military, and some of the Hughes vehicles might have been used as gunships, although American officials say that this is a risky proposition since these helicopters are not armored — or, at least, not delivered with such protection — against ground fire.

The handbook did not indicate how many pieces of each type of equipment the Iraqis had. This more basic intelligence was given to front-line units as the need arose. But the handbook indicated that much of the equipment was comparatively old or not state of the art in design. By comparison, the equipment in the hands of the coalition forces confronting Saddam was generally more modern. But any advantage here might have been offset by the fact that most of this equipment was not designed specifically for desert warfare. Of course, the bulk of Iraq's equipment was also not initially designed for the desert, but Iraqi forces fought with this equipment against Iran during the 1980s, and they knew its strengths and weaknesses in a desert environment.

The organizational charts of the Iraqi army shown in the handbook might have particularly worried the arriving American troops. From corps level down, through division to brigade level, every Iraqi fighting unit had a chemical weapons company or platoon. The handbook explained that any Iraqi offensive that might entail chemical weapons had to receive prior approval from high command headquarters in Baghdad. The field officers then judged whether fire support and force size were sufficient to gain the particular objective, or if chemical rounds, delivered by artillery, were to be used. The three types of chemical weapons mentioned in the handbook were a lethal mustard agent, an incapacitating agent, and tear gas. The Iraqi army's defensive use of chemical weapons to stop an enemy attack was not covered in the handbook, but the chemical defenses provided for Iraqi soldiers were. Each Iraqi soldier was given a gas mask and a Soviet decontam-

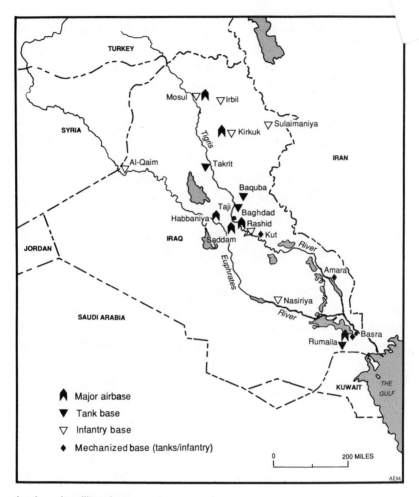

Iraq's main military bases

ination kit, which included an atropine injection to counter nerve gas, and a blister decontamination agent.

As well as describing basic offensive and defensive moves, which must have seemed familiar to American troops brought in from Europe, the handbook listed some essential strengths and weaknesses of the Iraqi forces. It rated the Iraqi army as the world's eighth largest, and one of the best equipped and most experienced in combat. It said the Iraqi army was distinguished by its flexibility, unity of command, and high level of mobility. It could operate in coordinated maneuvers over a front seventy miles wide, coping with the complicated logistics requirements and the coordination of air and artillery. Individual commanders were not given high marks for initiative, especially in exploiting success, though the Iraqi army was said to be highly qualified in planning, command, control, and communications, as well as logistics and maintenance. Further weaknesses, detected in the Iran-Iraq War, were Iraqi concern over the political impact of excessive losses, fear of punishment for failure, and lack of cooperation between the services. Poor Iraqi morale during night fighting was noted, as well as the difficulties of conducting night operations in the desert.

Special mention was made of the Republican Guard Corps, the elite strategic reserve that had performed well in the war with Iran. Armored units of this corps, with mechanized units and special forces components, were responsible for the blitzkrieg invasion of Kuwait in 1990. The Soviet influence on Iraqi military thinking was not emphasized in the handbook. Initially modeled on the British army, and still retaining many traditions of this heritage, the Iraqi military had adopted tactical thinking that was almost pure Red Army.

Another US government publication was also a good source of material on Iraq's military strength. *World Military Expenditures and Arms Transfers, 1989,* published in October 1990, was the latest assessment by the US Arms Control and Disarmament Agency (ACDA) on the flow of arms in the world. A table of leading military powers, based on 1988 data, ranked Iraq twelfth in the world in terms of military expenditures, and sixth in the size of its armed forces, which were the largest in the Middle East. (The difference in ranking compared with the *Order of Battle Handbook* exemplified the dificulty, common to intelligence work, of forming definitive judgments.)

The ACDA report also revealed that in 1988 Iraq was the largest importer of arms in the Middle East, accounting for 31 percent of the region's weapons imports. And from 1984 to 1988, Iraq was again the largest importer in the region, purchasing nearly $30 billion of armaments — almost three times the amount bought by Iran, whom Iraq was fighting during that period, and about five times the value of arms bought by Israel. These amounts, it should be noted, did not include clandestine sales.

Iraq's chief arms supplier in the mid 1980s was the Soviet Union, which provided almost 30 percent of Iraq's arms imports. And Iraq was the Soviet Union's principal customer, taking in $15 billion worth of weapons, almost twice the amount that Moscow was transferring to the rest of its clients put together. The ACDA report noted that the Soviet Union's dominant position in the regional "dense goods" market dated back as far as 1978.

The second and third largest arms suppliers to the region were the United States and France. The United States supplied no arms to Iraq, while France supplied $3.1 billion in arms to Iraq between 1984 and 1988, or one-fifth of what Moscow provided. The last significant volume supplier was China, which sent about a third of its $8 billion in sales to Iraq — and a comparable amount to Iran in the same period. The United Kingdom, West Germany, Czecho-slovakia, Poland, Italy, and Bulgaria round out the list of arms suppliers to the Middle East during this period.

An essay on diversification of arms supply, in the same ACDA volume, elaborated on the sources of Iraq's arsenal. Iraq instituted a policy of diversification after suffering an arms embargo by the Soviet Union in 1980 and 1981. Moscow's tendency to supply obsolescent weapons may have also irked the Iraqis. By 1988, according to the ACDA, Iraq was semidiversified, but still more than 50 percent dependent on one source, the Soviet Union. An advantage of diversification, besides reducing the threat of embargo, was that it created competition among exporters, enabling the importer to obtain more modern equipment, better-quality equipment, and better financial terms. The ACDA essay predicted that Iraq would seek to fully diversify its arms sources as it concentrated on modernizing its forces and expanding its arms industry.

TABLE 2

Value of Arms Transfers to Iraq, 1984–1988

Supplying country	Millions of current dollars
Soviet Union	15,400
France	3,100
China	2,800
Poland	750
West Germany	675
Czechoslovakia	675
Bulgaria	650
Italy	370
United Kingdom	30
United States	0
Others	5,200
TOTAL	29,650

Source: **World Military Expenditures and Arms Transfers, 1989** (Washington, DC: US Arms Control and Disarmament Agency, 1990).

ACDA analysts expected the Iraqis to look mainly to the West for advanced arms, such as French fighter aircraft—but that commentary predated the invasion of Kuwait.

The ACDA volume also looked at the economic constraints on the growth of Iraq's forces. By 1988 Iraq was bearing the cost of having a million soldiers under arms, yet its gross national product (GNP), in constant terms, was the lowest it had been in ten years, except for 1986. Given that Iraq's population had increased by nearly 50 percent in ten years, a falling GNP meant a substantial drop in living standards. By 1988, though, the main burden of military expenditures had passed. In 1988 the value of arms imported by Iraq was $4.6 billion, half as much as it had been in 1984, and Iraq had even begun to export arms itself, although their economic value, about $80 million, was relatively insignificant.

Another source for answers to the question Who armed Saddam? was *The Middle East Military Balance,* the standard text on

Middle East arsenals and arms transfers produced annually by the Jaffee Center for Strategic Studies at Tel Aviv University. The volume published at the end of 1989, covering the period up to June 1989, had extensive lists of equipment believed to have come from different countries, though the value, quantity, and date of acquisition were not specified. Regarding material supplied to Iraq: Austria was said to have sent artillery pieces via Jordan; Belgium provided ammunition; Brazil sent armored personnel carriers, armored recovery vehicles, trucks, multiple rocket launchers, and trainer aircraft. Britain sent electronic equipment and light vehicles; Chile supplied bombs; China sent tanks, artillery pieces, combat aircraft, and anti-ship missiles. Egypt sent ammunition, Soviet-made combat aircraft, anti-tank guided missiles, small arms, tanks, armored personnel carriers, surface-to-air missiles, multiple rocket launchers, mortars, trainer aircraft, and helicopters; and Ethiopia sent secondhand arms. France sold combat aircraft, artillery pieces, anti-tank missiles, surface-to-air missiles, air-to-ground missiles; West Germany sold tank transporters; Greece sent artillery ammunition. Italy sold missile frigates and corvettes, aircraft electronics, artillery pieces, radars, helicopters, small arms, land mines, and spare parts, and an unconfirmed report alleged that chemicals for the production of poison gas came from private Italian firms. Morocco sent secondhand arms, as did the Philippines; Portugal sent ammunition; Saudi Arabia transferred US-made artillery pieces and ammunition; South Africa provided artillery pieces and ammunition. Spain sold mortar ammunition as well helicopters, partly made in West Germany; the United States sold civilian helicopters, and the USSR and Soviet bloc provided combat aircraft, tanks, surface-to-surface missiles, helicopters, artillery pieces, ammunition, and surface-to-air missiles. The list concluded by noting that Yugoslavia sent small arms.

The Jaffee Center also reported that there were foreign advisers or instructors in Iraq from Britain, Brazil, Egypt, France, Jordan, Morocco, and the Soviet Union and Soviet bloc, while Iraqi trainees were abroad in Egypt, France, Italy, Jordan, Turkey, and the

TABLE 3

Suppliers to Iraq's Armed Forces

Item	Estimated Iraqi strength	Source
Tanks		
T-72	1,000	Soviet Union
T-62	1,200	Soviet Union
Type 59/69	1,500	China
Other	1,300	
TOTAL	5,000	
Artillery	5,000	2/3 supplied by Soviet Union
Surface-to-surface missile launchers		
Frog	25	Soviet Union
Scud	25	Soviet Union
al-Hussein	50	European modified
TOTAL	100	
Anti-aircraft missiles		4/5 supplied by Soviet Union
Combat aircraft		
MiG 25	30	Soviet Union
MiG 29	26	Soviet Union
MiG 21	170	Soviet Union
MiG 23	90	Soviet Union
Mirage F1	72	France
Su-24	15	Soviet Union
Other	302	
TOTAL	705	
Attack helicopters		
Hind	45	Soviet Union
Gazelle	60	France
Bo-105	30	Germany
Other	25	
TOTAL	160	
Naval gunboats, Ossa	8	Soviet Union

Sources: Estimates derived from **The Middle East Military Balance, 1988–1989** (Tel Aviv: Jaffee Center), and **The Military Balance, 1989–1990** (London: International Institute for Strategic Studies).

Soviet Union and Soviet bloc. Foreign forces in Iraq supporting the regime included other Arab nationals in both the army and the popular army (a militia), and volunteers from the Yemen Arab Republic (now Yemen).

The reasons for each country's support for Iraq are as diverse as the countries themselves but include such factors as political affinity and desire for hard currency. The cases of the Soviet Union and France are worthy of closer examination.

Moscow's links with Baghdad go back many years: relations were established as soon as the Iraqi monarchy was overthrown in 1958. In 1972 the two countries signed a friendship and cooperation treaty. It was obvious that Soviet arms would be an important ingredient in this relationship because, for many years, military aid was the basic mechanism of Soviet foreign policy in the third world. But having started the relationship, Moscow was not able to control it as well as it might have liked. Saddam's purging of the Iraqi communist party in 1979 was a bitter blow for Moscow, and many of its ideological friends were imprisoned or executed; the lucky ones fled the country. To express its displeasure, Moscow instituted a partial arms embargo in 1980 and 1981. But weapons supplies soon revived because Moscow wanted to maintain leverage and influence in Iraq, especially after Saddam began to probe for links in the West. Thus in 1982 Iraq received some of the very best in Soviet equipment, including MiG-25 aircraft, T-72 tanks, and Sam-8 anti-aircraft missiles. As the Iran-Iraq War continued, Soviet equipment still poured in, including MiG-29 interceptors in 1987, and advanced ground attack aircraft. The credit terms associated with these weapons deliveries are thought to have been generous until 1989, when the changes in foreign policy effected by President Gorbachev, and his desire to improve relations with the United States, are believed to have included tougher payment terms for Iraq.[1]

France's policy toward Iraq has been to take advantage of any hiatus in relations between Moscow and Baghdad. This policy was in effect even before the start of the Iran-Iraq War: in 1968 France tried to sell Mirage jets to Iraq, although it was not prepared to sell the same aircraft to Israel. In 1979, when the anti-Western regime of the Ayatollah Khomeini came to power in Iran, France became eager to improve contacts with Iraq in order to secure a substitute supply of oil. The main architect of the closer relationship is thought to have been the French prime minister Jacques Chirac, who not only was genuinely warm to Iraq but also wanted to bolster the French arms industry. By the end of the Iran-Iraq War, this policy had backfired. About $10 billion worth of French arms had been delivered, but Iraq had fallen behind in payments and owed France $5.5 billion, mainly for the arms. Worse still, France had become too dependent on Iraqi business, which accounted for 40 percent of French arms manufacture; the decline in Iraqi orders after the 1988 cease-fire dealt a severe blow to French exports.

There is as yet no authoritative assessment of how to apportion blame in the clandestine supply of equipment to Iraq for its superweapons projects: chemical and nerve agents, nuclear bomb technology, and long-range missile programs. Evidently, a major role was played by German and Austrian companies, with support from French and Italian companies. The involvement of American and British companies was minimal — owing more to Iraqi suspicions than to any unwillingness by at least some individuals to become involved. Exports from American companies did end up in Iraqi weapons development plants, but it is difficult to judge the contribution this material made.

The Poison Gas Connection, a special report commissioned by the Simon Wiesenthal Center in Los Angeles, listed all companies that were mentioned in the press as being involved in Iraq's unconventional weapons programs, without attempting to judge the companies' awareness of how their exports were used or to differentiate between goods of direct and indirect use. The report, written in 1990 by Kenneth R. Timmerman, who edits the *Middle East Defense News* newsletter in Paris, listed 207 companies from twenty-one countries: 86 German firms, 17 Austrian, 16 French, 12 Italian, and 11 Swiss. The list also included 18 British companies and 18

American companies but, given Iraq's distrust of UK and US nationals, these entities were probably unaware of the end use of their products.

With the end of the Iran-Iraq War, Western countries could no longer justify their arms supply relations with Iraq by citing the need to contain Iranian fanaticism, and the Iraqis canceled many orders or asked for slower delivery. The political changes in the Soviet Union and Eastern Europe in 1989 and 1990 reduced those lines of supply as well. But arms salesmen still saw Saddam's regime as a legitimate customer. Ironically, one of the consequences of Iraq's invasion of Kuwait was to stop the flow of arms merchants who were eager to sell Iraq new generations of high-tech equipment for delivery in the late 1990s. Iraqi forces were put at even more of a disadvantage by the United Nations embargo that prohibited the delivery of arms supplies, including spare parts.

Questions remain about the puzzling role of Soviet technicians who stayed on in Iraq after the invasion of Kuwait, but it is likely that Iraq's arsenal was already subject to a steady degradation in maintenance and battle readiness because of a slowdown in the supply of spare parts and little new equipment to replace Iraq's oldest stock.

★ ★ ★

CHAPTER 16

Washington and Baghdad: Fools and Good Intentions

A discreet daylong conference was held on May 19, 1988, at the Vista International Hotel in Washington, DC. It was not just another think-tank gathering of the sort held every day in the nation's capital. This conference was organized by the Central Intelligence Agency (CIA), and on the two-page attendance list[1] the affiliation of nineteen of the fifty-nine participants was given as "Agency." In addition three people were listed as coming from the Defense Intelligence Agency, the intelligence analysis arm of the Defense Department; two from the super-secret National Security Agency, which listens to and decodes the secret communications of other nations, as well eleven from the State Department; and two from the Department of Commerce.

The title of the conference was "Charting Iraq into the 1990s," and those attending listened to a series of papers presented by a variety of scholars, journalists, and consultants. According to one person who was present that day, there was a constructive air of trying to figure out how the United States could develop a working diplomatic relationship with Iraq, and very few illusions about how difficult that task was. Another person commented that the CIA officials tended to ask few questions and gave away very little about what their real concerns were.

There were no Iraqis at the gathering, but several foreigners had been invited. It is extremely unlikely that the Iraqi embassy in Washington did not know that the conference was taking place, and within a few days a fairly detailed report of the presentations and discussions was probably on its way back to Baghdad.

Although the CIA periodically organizes similar conferences on various countries and topics of interest, Baghdad would not have viewed the conference as routine. Instead, Saddam Hussein and his advisers would have seen the conference as confirming their worst suspicions about the nature of official US attitudes toward Iraq. The Iraqi leadership would also have thought that the United States was plotting to diminish Iraq's importance in the Middle East, if not to overthrow Saddam's regime itself. Any Iraqi official sufficiently savvy about American ways to realize the relatively innocuous nature of the conference would have kept his thoughts to himself, rather than risk an accusation of being at least an American sympathizer or a CIA agent.

By this time, Saddam was well aware of comments about him that emerged during Congressional inquiries into the Iran-Contra affair, the scheme by which weapons were sent to Contra fighters in Nicaragua using profits from US arms sales to Iran. In trying to persuade Iran to facilitate the release of American hostages in Lebanon, Lt. Col. Oliver North, an assistant to the president's National Security Adviser, had also listened to Iranian demands that Saddam Hussein be overthrown. "Saddam Hussein is a (expletive)," North told an Iranian official at a secret meeting in Frankfurt, Germany, in October 1986.[2] The expletive North used was not given in the report of the Congressional committees, but it must have been strong, for Albert Hakim, an Iranian expatriate who was acting as interpreter, "demurred at the harshness. . . . but North urged a faithful translation saying, 'Go ahead. That's his (the President's) word, not mine.'" Although North was operating largely independently of the State Department, his view of Saddam Hussein was shared by many U.S. officials.[3]

As the negotiations continued, North declared, "We also recognize that Saddam Hussein must go." The Congressional report says that North described how this could be accomplished, but this detail is omitted. In further discussions later that month in Mainz, Germany, the Iranian team continued to press for the removal of Saddam Hussein. This time Richard Secord, a retired air force general and former deputy assistant secretary of defense, said that "we" would talk to another country in the region, adding, "it's going to take a lot of talk, a lot of talk." Both meetings were attended by George Cave, a CIA consultant and former employee of the agency.

Saddam had already heard other threats to his leadership and other predictions of his demise. In 1986, when North was testifying to Congress, Iraqi troops were suffering defeats on the battlefield, and Mideast experts speculated that Saddam might be overthrown by the Iraqi army, which would replace him with a new leader more congenial to Iran. The speculation was that the Gulf Arab states would prefer this outcome to a complete Iraqi collapse, which would be an additional threat to their security, and so they might be prepared to help organize it.[4]

Contrary to some comment after the invasion of Kuwait that recent US-Iraqi relations had been warm, most officials and experts on Iraq regard the relationship as always having been at best extremely difficult. Diplomatic ties had been broken off by the Iraqis in 1967, when Baghdad accused American and British aircraft of having helped Israel achieve its surprise victory in the Six-Day War. An American interest section was maintained under the protection of the Belgian embassy, but it was not until 1977 that a diplomat of ambassadorial rank in all but name was assigned to this office, and full relations were not established until 1984.

When the Iran-Iraq War began in 1980, the attitude of many American officials was that the combatants could not have been better chosen. Most American foreign service officers despised the regime of Ayatollah Khomeini in Tehran for having held diplomats of the US embassy hostage for 444 days. American officials also detested Iraq's abysmal human rights record. Once it became clear that the Iran-Iraq War would not spread to other Gulf states, many officials in Washington were content to sit back and watch Khomeini and Saddam slug it out.

But observers noticed that the United States did not condemn Iraq's invasion of Iranian territory and only responded verbally to Iraq's first use of chemical weapons against Iranian forces in November 1983.[5] Indeed the first US condemnation of Iraq was not made until March 1984. The desultory nature of US reaction to the first sustained use of chemical weapons since the Geneva protocol of 1925, which banned the use of chemical weapons, undermined the message of condemnation. Instead of a cooling in US-Iraq ties, efforts were being made to improve them: the removal of Iraq from the State Department's list of countries supporting international terrorism, the provision of guarantees on US credits, and the reestablishment, in 1984, of full diplomatic relations.

In hindsight the United States can be criticized for not having taken a tougher position, particularly on Iraq's gross violations of human rights, which placed it among the very worst regimes in the world. But US officials were trying to take advantage of a reduction in Iraqi support for international terrorism between 1978 and 1980, and also to exploit the freeze in Baghdad's previously close relations with Moscow subsequent to the purge of Iraqi communists in 1979. After all, one approach to foreign relations is that diplomatic recognition does not imply approval of a country's regime. A corollary of this argument is that good diplomatic relations would enable one country to influence another for the better.

In the 1980s US-Iraq relations developed momentum because of the Iran-Iraq War. As the years of fighting lengthened, the specter arose of an Islamic fundamentalist regime in Tehran that would dominate the region. None of the conservative Gulf sheikhdoms — Saudi Arabia, Kuwait, Bahrain, Qatar, the United Arab Emirates, and Oman — wanted this. They were all allies of the United States and the West for reasons of oil and business, and it was impossible for them to reduce financial and moral support for Iraq, which was bearing the burden of confronting Ayatollah Khomeini. Revolutionary tentacles were appearing all over the Middle East: Hezbollah Shia extremists were active in Lebanon, the French and American embassies in Kuwait had been bombed and an assassination attempt was made on the emir, and a coup had been attempted in Bahrain.

Trade with Iraq was encouraged, although Iraq was short of money and US corporations were reluctant to accept credit terms. But the potential market in Iraq was so huge that many oil and contracting companies felt that they could not ignore it. In 1984, with the encouragement of the new Iraqi ambassador to Washington, Nizar Hamdoun, a US-Iraq Business Forum was set up to act as intermediary between Iraq and US corporations.[6] Over the next several years the forum, which achieved a corporate membership of over fifty, attained considerable success in bringing together Iraqis of ministerial level, such as the oil minister, Issam Chalabi, and chief executive officers of major US corporations.

Improved diplomatic and business contacts encouraged US officials, who ignored or misinterpreted information that might, on reflection, have caused a radical review of US policy toward Iraq. The most serious test of US accommodation occurred in May 1987, when a French-built Iraqi Mirage fighter fired two French-made Exocet missiles at the USS *Stark,* a frigate steaming in international waters in the center of the Gulf. In the resulting explosion thirty-seven sailors were killed and many were injured. The frigate began to list and was so severely damaged that it was nearly a write-off. In the aftermath, Iraq was tardy in its apologies and even slower in paying compensation for the dead and injured. The United States moved quickly to commit naval forces to the region to escort oil tankers, but it blamed Iran—not Iraq—for the dangerous environment that allowed the accident to occur in the first place.

The incident served as a way for the US to make up to Iraq for Washington's actions in the Iran-Contra affair, selling anti-aircraft missiles and anti-tank missiles to the Iranians. Saddam had been furious when these adventures had come to light in November 1986. He did not ignore the change of attitude, although he always remained suspicious. American intelligence information, including satellite photographs of Iranian troop dispositions, was welcome, but was used cautiously. The revelations of the Iran-Contra affair had shown that Oliver North was ready to hand over intelligence to the Iranians, but that some of it was erroneous. (When Iran launched one of its last offensives near Basra at the end of 1987, Iraq complained that the United States had not given advance warning.) Saddam probably also suspected that the US military liaison with Iraq was a way for the United States to become better acquainted with the Iraqi officer corps, perhaps to select a suitable officer to back a coup attempt against the regime.

The US Congress was generally skeptical of an Iraqi alliance, though members of Congress did not want an Iranian victory in the Gulf. A staff report to the Senate Foreign Relations Committee in November 1987 said that an Iraqi defeat "would be catastrophic for Western interests."[7] But Congress was also upset by Saddam's use of chemical weapons, especially against civilians, and particularly after the cease-fire in August 1988. At that time legislation was proposed for trade and financial sanctions, but the Reagan administration successfully amended the bill so that the question of sanctions was left to the president's discretion.

Officials at Exim Bank, the federal agency that provides credits and credit guarantees to American exporters, also viewed Iraq with suspicion. In October 1989 analysts at the bank were given the opportunity to put Iraq in its place when the Iraqi delegations attending the annual Washington meetings of the World Bank and the International Monetary Fund, asked for a meeting.[8] The Iraqi's, led by their finance minister, Hikmat Omar Mukhailef, were hoping to make a high-level presentation of their country's needs: Iraq was intending to spend much more on domestic projects in the postwar period and wanted Exim Bank to help US exporters win contracts by issuing new credits and guarantees.

Exim officials, whose priorities may lead them to take different policy lines than the State Department, were blunt in their response. They told the Iraqis that Baghdad must first reschedule its debt with its major trading partners on a multilateral basis, rather than trying to make separate deals with each creditor. Exim officials also told the Iraqis that they were spending too much on the military, given the weakness of oil prices and Iraq's oil production quota. The toughness of the bank's response, and the detail of its analysis, is said to have shocked the Iraqi delegation. Mukhailef lost his ministerial position shortly afterward; Saddam subsequently accused him of incompetence and of having presented incorrect figures at Iraqi cabinet meetings.

Some of Saddam's actions at this time suggest genuine puzzlement about the poor state of Iraq's relations with the United States, and an effort on his part to repair them. In June 1989 a visiting delegation of thirty corporate leaders from the US-Iraq Business Forum held discussions with all three of Iraq's deputy prime ministers, in addition to the oil minister and the information minister. They were then treated to a surprise reception by Saddam himself, who posed for a group photograph, as well as individual photographs with each member of the delegation.[9]

A further gesture was Saddam's willingness to meet with a five-member delegation of senators, led by Robert Dole, the Republican minority leader. The April 1990 meeting was controversial; the senators appeared too conciliatory in the minds of some critics. To the embarrassment of the Americans, the Iraqis published a transcript of much of the conversation. Saddam deflected the critical questions, and, according to the transcript, the senators failed to press him on crucial items like chemical weapons and human rights.[10]

By the time the senators paid their visit, US-Iraq relations were heading toward terminal decline, but the administration failed to recognize it, preferring instead to try to counter the attacks by members of Congress demanding trade sanctions and cancellation of credit arrangements for agricultural products. Some officials privately dismissed the attacks as partisan against Iraq and in favor of Israel, and not helpful to diplomacy. Despite the recent arrests at London's Heathrow airport in connection with an attempt to smuggle nuclear weapons components into Iraq, and despite Saddam's threat to destroy half of Israel, the assistant secretary for the Near East, John Kelly, spoke proudly of the achievements in US-Iraq relations in a speech to the House Foreign Affairs Committee Subcommittee on Europe and the Near East on April 26, 1990. He noted that Iraq had stopped supplying arms to the Christian leader in Lebanon, General Michel Aoun; that Iraq was discussing a new constitution that "potentially would provide greater recognition of human rights"; that Iraq had participated in two disarmament conferences on chemical weapons; and that in the "Middle East peace process" trying to solve the Israeli-Palestinian dispute, Iraq was deferring to the parties more directly involved, including Egypt and the Palestine Liberation Organization. After mentioning the many disquieting developments of the previous months, including human rights abuses, work on nuclear weapons, and threats to Israel, Kelly argued against trade sanctions: "We believe Iraq has clearly received the important message of unanimous US Government concern over its recent actions, and we are hopeful that the Government of Iraq will move quickly to bring US-Iraq relations back to a positive level."

Much of the blame for the Bush administration's failure to understand Saddam has been apportioned to the US embassy in Baghdad and the US ambassador, April Glaspie. After all, these diplomats were placed there, in part, precisely to anticipate what Saddam was thinking.

By several accounts, the US embassy in Baghdad was a most unusual embassy.[11] While the British embassy, for reasons of historical legacy, stands proudly on the banks of the Tigris, the American embassy is well away from the center of the capital, in a villa converted into a small fortress in the same suburb as the Palestine embassy. The embassy's main contact at the Iraqi ministry of foreign affairs was Nizar Hamdoun, the former Iraqi ambassador in Washington; Hamdoun, however, preferred to communicate directly with American officials he had met in Washington, rather than through Ambassador Glaspie.

Outside the US embassy, Iraqi intelligence agents checked visitors and occasionally harassed them by such tricks as taking possession of their cameras and exposing the film while the visitor was inside the embassy. Iraqi intelligence officers regularly tracked the movements of diplomats and broke into their homes while they were empty. Sometimes these officially sanctioned burglars would steal a few items or reposition books or furniture; other times they would trash the premises. Complaints to the police would be recorded but not otherwise investigated.

It is easy to see that Baghdad was not a popular posting for American foreign service officers. For talented officers eager to push their careers, there were many more attractive postings where their work could be recognized by their seniors at the embassy and back in Washington. Some of the US diplomats sent to Baghdad in the late 1980s were considered "oddballs" by other diplomats and American visitors to Iraq. One used to take long walks around the streets of Baghdad, unintentionally giving the impression to Iraqi intelligence that he was servicing dead letter boxes, where messages can be left for or collected from spies without personal contact. Another spent spare hours at home learning Hebrew, which might have been good preparation for a future posting but would have confirmed the worst suspicions of Iraqi intelligence when they burgled his house. In the mid-1980s one US political officer, whose job was to monitor domestic change in Iraq, reported that 80,000 Iraqi deserters were avoiding the war with Iran by taking refuge in the marshes of southern Iraq. The report was passed back from

Washington to other embassies via the capitals of friendly countries, where it was ridiculed as an absurd exaggeration.

The US embassy's poor reputation for straightforward diplomacy was matched by its bungled attempts at spying. In 1987 the military attaché, Mark Po, was expelled by the Iraqis after being caught red-handed monitoring the arrival by ship of a consignment of Soviet MiG-29s in Kuwait. Po's mission was to watch crates of aircraft parts being unloaded from Soviet freighters in a Kuwait port and driven up to Iraq. The convoys of trucks carrying the crates were leaving the port under cover of darkness, so Po found himself a convenient spot from which to observe traffic, at a turn on one of the highways skirting Kuwait City where the trucks had to slow down to almost a halt. It was Po's job to write down the numbers and markings on the crates so that "crate-ologists" back in Washington could assess how many aircraft and which models were being delivered. People familiar with intelligence gathering say that the standard procedure is to sit quietly in a vehicle with locked doors, so that if one is questioned by police, one can offer excuses about reading a map or the engine having overheated. But Po was standing outside his vehicle, writing in his notebook by the beam of his headlights. After he was arrested by the Kuwaitis, he was held incommunicado for thirty-six hours before being handed over to the Iraqis. When he was released in Baghdad, he expressed puzzlement that the Kuwaitis should have done this. His diplomatic colleagues knew that the Iraqis had decided to expel him when he received a special greeting from an Iraqi officer at a diplomatic cocktail party. The Iraqi officer, in charge of liaison with foreign military attachés, offered Po the warmest salutations, going so far as to kiss him on both cheeks. Po was declared persona non grata the following day, and quickly left Iraq.

Other US intelligence slipups included the granting of visas to important Iraqis without realizing who they were. The first that American officials knew of the visit to the United States of Saddam's half-brother, Sabawi Ibrahim, was when he attended the Iraq National Day celebrations at the Iraqi embassy in Washington in

July 1989. Soon afterward, Sabawi was made head of Iraq's intelligence service. Another member of Saddam's Takriti elite, Fadel Barrak, had been in New York for several days before the FBI was tipped off. From 1984 until 1988 Barrak had been head of Iraqi intelligence, and he has remained one of Saddam's closest advisers. Western intelligence officials say that in late 1990 he was put in charge of Iraq's links with international terrorists.

Into the American embassy in Baghdad in 1988 came April Glaspie. Admired by her colleagues for her professionalism, Glaspie was one of the few US diplomats who really saw the posting to Baghdad as a good career move. She had won the job against tough competition and some opposition. What the Iraqis made of her, the first American woman ambassador in the Arab world, is hard to judge, although Iraq's own good record in giving women an opportunity to pursue professional careers, especially in comparison to the rest of the Arab world, made the posting seem sensible.

Glaspie speaks Arabic fluently and has split her career between assignments in the Middle East and rotations in Washington and the American embassy in London. She was in Amman, Jordan, in 1967, when Israel defeated three Arab armies in the Six-Day War and King Hussein of Jordan lost the West Bank. In Damascus, Syria, she won the reputation of being an excellent political reporting officer. She had also served in Egypt, Tunisia, and Kuwait. Immediately before being sent to Baghdad she had been working in Washington at the State Department handling Lebanese, Jordanian, and Syrian affairs, a job that brought her into contact and occasional confrontation with Israeli diplomats. One Israeli intelligence officer who sat in meetings with her to discuss Lebanon said, outraged, "She used to try to lecture us." At this time the State Department's legal counselor, Abraham Sofaer, was urging the closure of a PLO-sponsored Palestine Information Office in the capital. Pro-Israel and Jewish lobby groups backed Sofaer, but some US officials wanted the office to remain, hoping it would encourage the PLO toward diplomacy and away from terrorism. Sofaer won, and the office was closed. Glaspie is said to have been keenly disappointed; a State Department colleague said that Glaspie "found it almost impossible to speak to Israelis" after this episode. The Baghdad posting solved the problem, but her nomination met some opposition in Congress. One report says that American supporters of Israel made it clear that Glaspie would not be acceptable as a US ambassador in any country bordering Israel.[12]

April Glaspie came to Baghdad and worked very hard at diplomacy, but other aspects of her performance raised eyebrows. Some American business executives invited for lunch were surprised when the meal consisted of canned tuna on a lettuce leaf, followed by a fruit bowl. Complaints and tales of unhappiness among embassy personnel had predated Glaspie's arrival, and they reached such a pitch that a State Department inspector was sent out twice within twelve months to investigate. The solution chosen by the State Department was to leave Glaspie to diplomacy and bring in an administration officer to handle day-to-day operations. Joseph Wilson, who had a reputation for making difficult embassies function, was chosen for this position and was posted to Baghdad as deputy chief of mission in September 1988. Wilson found himself running the embassy single-handedly after the invasion of Kuwait because Glaspie was caught abroad on vacation, having misjudged Saddam in her first one-on-one interview with the Iraqi leader shortly before August 2, 1990. She misread Saddam's comments, thinking that he wanted to negotiate with Kuwait and that his toughness was merely rhetoric.[13]

In testimony before the Senate Foreign Relations Committee on March 20, 1991, Glaspie said that the transcript of her comments had been edited by the Iraqis, removing her insistence that Iraq's dispute with Kuwait should be settled "in a non-violent manner, not by threats, not by intimidation, and certainly not by aggression." But she offered no explanation of why the State Department had not corrected the false impression earlier. Justifying her alleged remark in the transcript that an American television interview with Saddam had been "cheap and unjust," she said that she meant the edited interview shown on television in Baghdad.

★ ★ ★

Opposition and Human Rights

Each year the US State Department submits to Congress its *Country Reports on Human Rights Practices,* a country-by-country survey of human rights conditions. Though numbingly bureaucratic in style, the analyses are fuller and more dispassionate than reports published by such private organizations as the London-based Amnesty International and the New York–based Middle East Watch. The most recent edition of *Country Reports,* published in February 1990, states baldly: "Iraq's human rights record remained abysmal in 1989." According to the report, internal opposition to Saddam's regime is stifled, all publications are subject to censorship, there is no freedom of speech, there is extensive surveillance of the civilian population, and various intelligence services use extralegal means, including torture and summary execution, to suppress antigovernment activity. There was a time when every typewriter in Iraq had to be registered, but this is no longer the case for Iraqis, although foreigners must register them. The Iraqi security services monitor all people who possess word processors and computers, so as to control the possible dissemination of political leaflets.

One question that the State Department report does not address, however, is the degree of personal responsibility that Saddam Hussein has for this state of affairs. Is the president fully aware of what his security services are doing in his name? Doubtless, the answer is yes, given Saddam's earlier political career and his habit of appointing close relatives to top positions in the security services. As a young man, Saddam ran the security arm of the Baath party, both before and after it took power in 1968. He himself is said to have been a torturer, and he was certainly the organizer of strong-arm tactics to silence dissent within the party and to paralyze opposition to it. Both of Saddam's sons, Udai and Qusai, are believed to hold senior positions in different security organizations, and Saddam's half-brother, Sabawi Ibrahim, is head of intelligence, while his son-in-law, Hussein Kamil Hassan, is head of Al Amn Al Khas, the Special Security Agency in charge of clandestine arms purchases abroad.

It is not known whether any of these men personally have blood on their hands, but allegations of personal involvement in torture have been made against Saddam's half-brother Barzan Ibrahim, who was head of intelligence until 1983 and is now ambassador to the United Nations organizations in Geneva. Dr. Sahib al-Hakim, an Iraqi exile living in London, where he runs the Organization of Human Rights in Iraq, says that Barzan set fire to the beard of a leading Shia mullah, Professor Mohammed al-Sadr, in order to coerce him into professing allegiance to the Baath party. When the clergyman's sister, Ameena, was also tortured in front of him. When the clergyman refused to make the required statement, Barzan shot him.

Sahib al-Hakim's family is one of the most prominent Shia Muslim families in Iraq. After Ayatollah Khomeini came to power in Iran in 1979, the al-Hakims were identified by Saddam as potential leaders of a Shia revolt against his largely Sunni-dominated government. Ninety members of the family living in Iraq have been arrested, and twenty-two executed. In 1988 a relative, Sayed Mehdi al-Hakim, was assassinated in Khartoum, Sudan, by men who fled in an Iraqi diplomatic car.[1]

Killing or kidnapping opponents outside Iraq, as well as within the country, has been a hallmark of Saddam's regime. In the Gulf state of Dubai in 1981, Sahal Mohammed Salman was shot in the head. Police captured the assassin as he was running away and identified him as an Iraqi security agent who had arrived in the country earlier that day on a diplomatic passport. In 1985 the body of an Iraqi living in exile in Sweden was discovered in a plastic bag. He was a former army officer who had given interviews to the Swedish media about the atrocities carried out by Saddam's regime. In London in 1978 a former Iraqi prime minister, Abdul Razak Nayef, was shot down outside a hotel by a man who had had his target identified by an Iraqi security agent. The assassin, Abdul Ahmed Hassan, is serving a long prison term in Britain, but Iraqi diplomats frequently ask for his release, making it clear that English prisoners in Iraqi prisons would be freed in return.

The murder of Nayef showed that the Baath were targeting not only active members of the opposition but also others who have had differences with the Baghdad regime. Nor are members of Saddam's own clan safe. In 1970, two years after the Baath had taken power in Baghdad, the first Baath defense minister, Hardan al-Takriti, was shot dead in Kuwait, where he had taken asylum after a falling-out with Saddam and other Baathists. In 1988 Abdullah Rahim Sharif Ali, an Iraqi who worked in England, was murdered in London after being taken out to dinner by three Iraqis who were visiting from Baghdad. One of them slipped thallium — an odorless, tasteless, and colorless poison usually used to kill rats — into Ali's vodka while he was in the cloakroom. The three visitors returned to Baghdad, and their victim fell ill and died eleven days later. (A photograph of Ali's death certificate appears in this book.) Before Ali died, however, he told the British police about his visitors. A British police request for the help of Iraqi police went unanswered. Members of the Iraqi opposition say that Ali did not belong to any of their groups but had an argument with the officials of the regime.

On several occasions Iraqis have been kidnapped abroad and brought back to Iraq to be tortured. A Shia clergyman, Sayed Abdul Moneim al-Shawki, was kidnapped in Kuwait in 1979 and reportedly held for several days in the Iraqi embassy in Kuwait City before being forcibly taken across the border to Iraq. Sometimes the torture takes place outside Iraq. Two Iraqi students studying in Karachi, Pakistan, were abducted in 1987. Their decapitated bodies were found two days later near the local Iraqi consulate. Their fingertips had been cut off, to hinder identification, and there were signs of burn marks on the bodies.

The types of torture used in Iraqi prisons are well chronicled: beatings, starvation, sleep deprivation, electric shocks, and a variety of devices designed to maim and kill. The motive for torture is not simply to discover information, but also to inculcate lifelong fear among survivors and the family and friends of those who do not survive. Torture breeds a climate of terror that makes it easier for the regime to control the country.

In the testimony of freed prisoners, various forms of physical torture are mentioned time and again. The booklet *Human Rights in Iraq, 1968–1988*, written by Walid al-Hilli, an Iraqi who was himself a victim of torture by Saddam's security forces, uses line drawings to illustrate some of the more common methods:

1. Burning by oil heater. The seated victim is tied firmly to an oil heater, and the heater is turned on.
2. Burning by an electric ring. The victim's hand is tied to an electric ring of the type used for cooking, which is then turned on.
3. Suspension from ceiling. The victim is suspended by his feet, perhaps from a ceiling-mounted fan, and is beaten with truncheons and whips. Sometimes the fan is turned on, so the victim revolves while being beaten.
4. Amputation. A foot or hand is clamped and cut off, without anesthetic, using either a manual or electric saw.

5. Falaka. The victim's feet are bound, and the soles are beaten continuously until they bleed.
6. Electric drills. Drills are used to bore holes in the hands, feet, or head of the victim.
7. Confinement in a metal cylinder. The victim is stood inside a metal tube that is too narrow for him to sit down, and is left there for hours or days.
8. Hanging by hair. The victim, usually a woman, is suspended from the ceiling by her hair.
9. Head clamp. A metal clamp is tightened on the victim's head until the skull fractures.
10. Needles. Needles are pushed under the victim's fingernails or through the victim's tongue.
11. Burning. The victim is tied to a metal bed and a fire is lit beneath it.
12. Pinning of ears. The victim is pinned to a wall by nails driven through his ears, which tear when he falls down exhausted.
13. Being pulled apart. The victim's legs are tied to different cars, which then drive off in opposite directions.
14. Suspension by wrists. The victim's hands are tied behind his back and he is suspended from a roof.

According to too many accounts, women and children are tortured in order to bring pressure on male relatives. The women are sexually assaulted, sometimes in front of their husbands, and children are tortured or threatened with torture as a means of gaining information from their parents. In one reported case, a torturer heated an iron rod until it was red hot and then touched a baby's tummy with it.

Though some victims would welcome the respite of death, the executions are painful and drawn out. The most common form of execution is hanging, but sometimes this becomes instead a slow strangulation. Other reports say that victims are cut to pieces using machetes or axes, or are savaged by specially trained dogs. At least one man is thought to have been executed by being immersed in a bath of strong acid. Thallium poison is used either to kill outright or to bring about debilitating illness and a lingering death. Firing squads are also used; it is reported that Saddam has executed dissident members of his cabinet in this way.

For those confined to Iraqi prisons, daily existence can be a constant battle for survival. Conditions are unsanitary, and food is often not provided; it is the job of relatives to bring it in, though visits are restricted. (A British businessman in an Iraqi prison was supported by weekly visits from diplomats bringing essential food-stuffs.) Prisoners are regularly assaulted and harassed by officials. During the heaviest fighting of the Iran-Iraq War, criminals were allegedly taken from Iraqi prisons so that their blood could be pumped out and transfused to wounded soldiers. The prisoners died in the process.[2]

After twenty-two years of state-waged domestic terror, it is scarcely surprising that opposition to Saddam within Iraq is muted. But opposition groups still exist. The Shia majority and the Kurd-ish population have many reasons to distrust Saddam and his coterie of supporters, who are predominantly Sunni and Arab. (Of the forty-two political figures listed in this book's Brief Biographies section, only seven are Shia and two Kurdish. The Sunni Arabs account for an overwhelming 74 percent of the national leadership, but less than 20 percent of Iraq's population.) Nominally, Iraq tries to play down sectarian and ethnic differences, and the Iraqi consti-tution prohibits "any act aimed at undermining the national unity of the people, provoking racial, sectarian, and regional bigotry." But, almost inevitably, the main opposition groups are non-Sunni or non-Arab.

Among the Kurdish underground political groups of long standing are factions that support the government, and two groups that do not, the Kurdish Democratic party (KDP), headed by Massoud Barzani, and the Patriotic Union of Kurdistan (PUK), led by Jalal Talabani. The latter two groups fought against the Iraqi army during the Iran-Iraq War. The attitude of pro-government Kurds to the Kurdish opposition is, as far as can be surmised, that

Kurdish separatism is an anachronism, an unattainable dream that is better ignored.

As a dispensation to the Kurds who do not attempt to oppose the regime, Saddam allows three provinces—Dahuk, Irbil, and Sulaimaniya—to be nominally autonomous. Indeed, provincial elections were held as recently as September 1989. Two Kurdish political parties are sanctioned by the regime: the Kurdistan Democratic party and the Kurdistan Revolutionary party. In theory these two parties join with the Baath party in Iraq's ruling coalition, the Patriotic and Progressive National Front, but this coalition is totally dominated by the Baath. The vice-president of the republic, Taha Moeddin Marouf, is a Kurd, but his powers are minimal. Saddam's personal bodyguard until June 1990 was Sabah Mirza, a Kurd, and the new Iraqi chief of staff, appointed in October 1990, is Hussain Rashid, another Kurd.

Barzani's KDP is the heir to the heritage of Mullah Mustafa Barzani, who confronted several successive Iraqi governments in the 1960s and 1970s with the help of the shah's Iran and Israel. (Jerusalem provided clandestine military advice and medical support as a way of forcing Baghdad to remain preoccupied with domestic troubles.) During the Iran-Iraq War, the KDP fighters allied themselves to the Ayatollah Khomeini's Iran. Their political ambition is independence, but most of the time they settle for an existence high up in the valleys and mountains of Kurdistan, where they are generally not bothered by the central government.

The PUK also allied itself with Tehran during the war, but at a crucial time Talabani flirted with switching sides. That Saddam was even prepared to contemplate dealing with the PUK was an indication not only of his desperation but also of his feeling that Talabani was a man with whom negotiations could take place. In late January 1985 the putative deal collapsed, apparently because Saddam no longer felt the need to make concessions, especially after he signed an anti-Kurd agreement with Turkey in October 1984. A condition of this pact was that Baghdad should not bolster any Kurdish separatist trend in Iraq that might arouse the substantial number of Kurds who live in Turkey.

(A curious tale, not reflecting well on the PUK, is associated with this period. The Kurds say that, as part of his inducement to the PUK, Saddam ordered the payment of $12 million to the London account of a British offshore company, Algom Universal, which was a front company for the Kurds. The money was transferred in early January 1985. Within days Iraq claimed that the money had been embezzled and transferred fraudulently. A British court froze the disputed money. The case came to court in June 1990, but in a pretrial settlement the Kurds agreed to repay the money. Neither side was prepared to comment on the affair, and both were relieved that the story went unreported. The Iraqi government would have been embarrassed by the embezzlement, and also by the revelation of negotiations with the Kurds, which had never been admitted officially. For its part, the PUK was anxious to avoid criticism from rival Kurdish groups over its willingness to deal with Saddam, and the out-of-court settlement precluded any risk that the PUK would be labeled a group of embezzlers.)

During 1987 and 1988 Saddam's regime reintroduced a policy of forced resettlement of many Kurdish villagers in closely supervised encampments near the main towns of the Kurdish areas. About half a million Kurds were relocated, along with some members of the small Turkoman community nearby. As many as three thousand Kurdish villages were destroyed, blown up by explosives and bulldozed into ruins to prevent villagers from returning. The Iraqi authorities explained that they were clearing a zone several miles deep along the border with Iran, so as to give a free range of fire to Iraqi soldiers defending the area. But many of the villages destroyed were well back from the border.[3] Apparently, the government wanted no Kurdish settlements near strategic roads in the area, fearing that Kurdish fighters would attack Iraqi military traffic. Large numbers of Kurdish men were also reported to have been transported to detention camps in southern Iraq, along the borders with Saudi Arabia and Kuwait. No information has come from such camps, leading to speculation that they hide a darker purpose.[4]

The most notorious incident in Saddam's campaign to repress the Kurds was the use of chemical weapons against Kurdish civilians living in the town of Halabja in March 1988. According to Western officials, however, the Iranian troops used chemical weapons first, with a plan to blame Iraq and then claim a propaganda coup. The Iraqi forces did use chemical weapons in Halabja as well, but only after the Iranians had done so.

However, after the cease-fire with Iran chemical weapons were dropped on Kurdistan by Iraqi aircraft, the first known use of such weapons in peacetime against a country's own population. The Kurds claim that the Iraqi army made no attempt to differentiate between Kurdish fighters, and women and children, deliberately bombing villages rather than the mountainsides where the fighters were taking refuge. Tens of thousands of Kurds fled north across the border to Turkey. Ali Hassan al-Majid, Saddam's cousin, who was in charge of security in the northern region, is accused of organizing the campaign of repression and terror. He later became minister of local government and was temporarily the governor of Kuwait after the invasion, at a time when some of the worst incidents of repression and pillage were recorded.

The Shia opposition to Saddam has not been as militant and combative as the Kurds', but the Shias' religious fervor and better financial backing give them another kind of power. There is absolutely no discernible broad Shia support for Saddam Hussein, although individual Iraqis of Shia origin have risen to high office in his regime. For example, Saadi Tuma Abbas al-Jabburi, the defense minister appointed in December 1990, is believed to be a Shia. The American-educated Saadoun Hammadi, a deputy prime minister, is also a Shia by origin, though his fluent defense of Iraq's case for invading Kuwait shows his total loyalty to Saddam.

During the Iran-Iraq War, the readiness of Iraqi soldiers, most of whom were of Shia origin, to fight against their Iranian co-religionists was one of the great puzzles often debated by analysts. The explanations ranged widely: possible distaste for revolutionary Islam, a feeling of being Arab rather than Persian, fear of the consequences of refusing to fight. Shia soldiers were seldom trusted as a group though; none are believed to be in the Republican Guard units that form Saddam's elite combat troops and personal guard.

In the Shia cities of Najaf and Kerbala, both of which contain important religious shrines, Iraqi security forces keep a close watch for any sign of insurrection. Saddam occasionally makes payments to the local religious authorities, claiming the money comes out of his own pocket, so that the shrines can be maintained and repaired. Pictures of Saddam are common in these Shia cities, although they probably reflect a desire to avoid trouble with the police rather than loyalty to the president. In the street the body language between local Shias and government officials indicates a desire to avoid any contact.

During the years of the Iran-Iraq War, the Shia opposition to Saddam was based in Tehran, working under an umbrella organization known as SAIRI, the Supreme Assembly of the Islamic Revolution in Iraq, which was headed by a Shia cleric, Mohammed Baqr Hakim. Extravagant claims were made for the fighting strength of this organization, which was also assumed to be the power behind the Dawa party operating underground in Iraq. SAIRI was also thought to have operated under Iranian orders, pursuing the war aims of Tehran. It is credited with attacks in Kuwait, where its members tried to blow up the US and French embassies, and a later attempt to assassinate the emir of Kuwait. Relatives of Shias arrested by the Kuwaitis later seized Western hostages in Beirut, hoping to effect a swap. But the taking of hostages only reinforced US antipathy toward Iran and helped to justify Washington's move toward Baghdad.

Apart from the Shias and Kurds, the rest of the organized Iraqi opposition is an assembly of small parties. An opposition meeting held in Damascus, Syria, in October 1990, two months after the invasion of Kuwait, was attended by the Islamic Front, an alliance of six Shia parties, the biggest of which was the Dawa; the Kurdistan Front, also an alliance of six parties, including both the KDP and the PUK; representatives of the Iraqi Communist party, which was part of the regime in Baghdad until 1979, when its members were purged; and dissidents from the Baath party, who were treated with the greatest suspicion.

The Iraqi Communist party has received little support over the years from Moscow. Although the Soviet Union cooled its ties with Iraq after Saddam's purge of communists in 1979, ties were revived by 1984, particularly as far as the all-important arms supply relationship, without any apparent Iraqi concessions. The Baath opposition dates back to internal arguments over who was to blame for the party's loss of power to the army in 1963. The credentials of this splinter group are now weak: opposition Baathists were purged heavily in the years immediately after the 1968 takeover, and, after two decades of Baath rule, there is little political leverage in the claim that the ideology itself is appropriate, that only the present leadership is faulty. Moreover, the argument about present leadership is moot, since Iraqi citizens have no peaceful means to change the leadership.

Most of the bits of the Iraqi opposition have offshoots operating in Western capitals, of which London is a favorite. One such Iraqi opposition group is the New Umma party, led by Saad Jabr, a wealthy London-based exile who made his money as a businessman in Saudi Arabia after fleeing Iraq in 1968. Jabr says his party seeks support from a broad constituency and brings together Kurds, anti-Saddam Baathists, and Islamic fundamentalists. His party gained a new, higher profile in May 1990 when it started to fax a regular series of one-page newsletters to news organizations across the world. The newsletters contained inside information, which often could not be corroborated, indicating good sources in Baghdad. (The newsletter reported the dismissal of General Abdul-Karim al-Khazraji before it was officially announced.) The newsletters are also a good source of biographical detail, some of which is as good as that collected by foreign government agencies. In 1987 Jabr claimed that some of his speeches were broadcast on illegal radio stations operated by Kurdish groups. He made a similar claim in January 1991, when it became known that a new anti-Saddam radio station was broadcasting into Iraq using transmitters and frequencies made available by Egypt and Syria. In February 1991, the New Umma party announced that it had suspended its activities and was joining forces with a new body, the Free Iraq Council. The move appeared to be little more than a change of name, as the president of the council was Saad Jabr.

Some of the opposition factions have operated underground for so long that they may be ill-prepared to take over the government should Saddam's regime collapse. Often the credibility of their individual leaders is untested as well. And while opposition groups occasionally cooperate with one another, their differences are sometimes greater than their common ground. Saddam has turned this divisiveness to his advantage by implying to Iraqis that his leadership and that of the Baath party are the nation's only safeguards against chaos and civil strife. The high proportion of Iraqis employed in the government bureaucracy and in state-run factories may be understandably reluctant to swap Saddam for an unknown. Outsiders might be forgiven for recommending that the best alternative for Iraq is a broadly similar government structure headed by someone other than Saddam. But the removal of Saddam would not necessarily dismantle the apparatus of terror that is the distinguishing characteristic of contemporary Iraq.

★ ★ ★

CHAPTER 18

Death of a Journalist:
The Spy Bazoft

On August 17, 1989, a huge explosion rocked the Qaqa State Establishment, a plant operated by the Iraqi military between Latifiya and Iskanderiya, on the road south from Baghdad. The shock of the blast was felt by many people in the center of the Iraqi capital, about twenty-five miles away, and several embassies reported the blast. Big explosions had been relatively frequent during the years of the Iran-Iraq War, when Baghdad came under Iranian attack or there was an accidental explosion at one of the many ammunition dumps around the capital—but the country was no longer at war.

There was no mention of the incident in any of the local newspapers. Nor was it in the realm of possibility for Western diplomats to visit Qaqa to find out what happened. But the CIA and other Western intelligence agencies were especially interested in Qaqa, which seemed a central facility in Iraq's clandestine nuclear weapons program. Qaqa was already the focus of at least one intelligence operation, for it was thought that crucial design work on Iraq's first nuclear bomb was being conducted there. But there were many other military projects under way at the facility as well. The explosion might have been related to another project in one of the many buildings spread over a large area.

The US intelligence operation already in progress involved a clandestine Iraqi purchasing bid, through a British front company, for US-manufactured electrical capacitors suitable for detonating a nuclear bomb. (These particular capacitors store an electric charge that, at a flick of a switch, provides the surge of current needed to detonate the conventional explosive that initiates a nuclear explosion.) People unfamiliar with intelligence operations might suppose that as soon as US agents realized that the capacitors were destined for Iraq, their export would have been banned. But to have done that would have been to forfeit a rare opportunity to learn about the Iraqi project. Sophisticated electronics are seldom bought "off-the-shelf," and between the initial inquiry and the actual delivery there are often months of negotiations on price, as well as greater details of the specifications required. The US government knew it could stop the shipment at the last moment, while in the meantime learning much about Iraq's nuclear weapons project. In particular, American intelligence wanted to obtain information about Iraq's clandestine procurement network abroad, the crucial personnel in Iraq, the site of different facilities, and the actual bomb design. So the US Customs Service, with the agreement of the manufacturer, CSI Technologies, of San Marcos, California, placed an undercover agent, Daniel Supnick, as an employee at CSI Technologies, where he was known as Daniel Saunders.

The Iraqi attempt to buy the high-grade capacitors had started a year before, in September 1988, when representatives of a British-registered company, Euromac, contacted CSI Technologies to inquire about the price and delivery of coaxial, high-voltage, low-inductance capacitors for ultimate export to Iraq. The company or organization wanting them was not initially clear. Contact and inquiries about details of the order went on intermittently; there had been another twenty-three telephone or telex contacts, according to the court record of a grand jury convened in southern California in November 1988, within weeks of the first Iraqi inquiry, before the information emerged that the capacitors were destined for an establishment called Qaqa. That telex was sent September 8, 1989; one hundred capacitors were needed, a comparatively small purchase of $10,500.[1] Additional, albeit slender, information in the hands of the CIA also pointed to Qaqa as being possibly important to nuclear weapons research: three Iraqi scientists from Qaqa attended a conference on "The Physics of Detonation" in Portland, Oregon, in 1989. The conference was sponsored by three US nuclear weapons laboratories.[2]

Now that there had been an explosion at Qaqa, the question was how to find out what had happened. Several European businessmen were working on projects in the vicinity. One British company, the 600 Group, had even installed equipment at Qaqa. Nearby, Europeans were helping to run a tractor factory, where farm tractors were assembled from kits imported from Brazil. It is quite possible that one of them confirmed that the explosion had occurred at the Qaqa facility, and perhaps he even estimated the rough location of the blast.

What was fascinating about Qaqa for US intelligence was the belief that Iraqi experiments on different explosives for the conventional, nonnuclear part of an atomic bomb were being conducted at the facility. American intelligence was particularly interested in whether Iraq was using RDX (rapid detonation explosive) or HMX (high melting point explosive). The choice of explosive would indicate how quickly the imploding shock wave was expected to move when it compressed the nuclear core to a critical mass, and therefore indicate the sophistication and power of Iraq's atomic bomb. A sample of explosive debris from close to where the explosion had occurred might reveal what kind of explosive was being made.

The problem was therefore simple — but nevertheless a problem: to acquire a soil sample from near the site of the explosion. Into this problem walked an opportunity: Farzad Bazoft, a naive, Iranian-born journalist, working regularly (but not on staff) for a British Sunday newspaper, *The Observer*. The thirty-one-year-old journalist was to arrive in Baghdad in early September on a tour arranged by the Iraqi government for journalists to observe elections in the Kurdish provinces. Bazoft was already on the books of British intelligence, which cooperates closely with the CIA. He had been sent to school in England before the Iranian revolution in 1979 and stayed on afterward. Short of cash, and generally a mixed-up kid, he had attempted to rob a building society (a quasi-bank that makes mortgage loans) in 1981. Bazoft was caught, tried, and sent to prison for eighteen months. When Britain moved to expel him and send him back to Iran, he pleaded that his life would be at risk because of his links to Iranian opponents of Ayatollah Khomeini; no doubt, he also mentioned that his father was an official with the state-owned National Iranian Oil Company. His patrimony would have made him of interest to British intelligence, which along with the CIA was almost obsessed at the time with learning more about Iranian oil production, in order to calculate the country's export earnings and construct hypotheses on how long Iran could stand up to Iraq in the Gulf war.

Bazoft was a dreamer, and unreliable. But he was keen and pliable, which made him of potential use as an agent. He was also plausible, able to talk his way into opportunities, and probably out of difficulties. By 1989, he had already shown his ability by managing to acquire semipermanent status at *The Observer*, where he wrote regular by-lined stories. (There is no indication that *The Observer* knew that it was employing an intelligence agent. The newspaper would have most certainly fired Bazoft had that been known. In the 1960s *The Observer* had had a bad experience when it employed the former British intelligence officer Kim Philby, later identified as a Soviet agent.)

To give Bazoft a legitimate journalistic purpose for digging around at Qaqa, the story of the explosion had to break in the international press. This happened, intentionally or otherwise, when the London newspaper *The Independent* carried a front-page story on September 6, the day that Bazoft flew to Baghdad. The newspaper reported that an explosion had occurred near Hillah, about fifty miles south of Baghdad and twenty-five miles beyond Qaqa; that hundreds of Egyptians working at the plant had been killed or injured. The plant affected was said to be related to the Condor 2 missile project. The source of the story was given as the Kurdish opposition. Although many of the details were wrong, the story served its purpose: every newly arrived foreign journalist in Baghdad wanted to rush to Hillah and Qaqa to get the full story.

Several went and were turned back. Bazoft made no secret of his intention of going, but journalistic inquiry was part of his cover. Foiled in his attempt to receive approval from the Iraqi authorities, he was briefed by a contact at the British embassy in Baghdad to go independently.[3] Although Bazoft was unreliable as far as written reports went, the task was otherwise ideal for him. The crucial issue was to obtain soil samples, and Bazoft was given special containers to collect them in. (Plastic containers, like those that protect 35-mm film, cannot be used because the plastic contaminates the sample.)

Bazoft went down to Qaqa, along with a British nurse, Daphne Parish, who was working in Baghdad and whom he had met on a previous visit. (There is no indication that she knew he was spying.) He made one visit on one day, another the day after. It seems that on the second day he reached the crater where the explosion had occurred, destroying a building. The hole was eighty feet across. He took soil samples from around the crater and photographs of the area. They returned to Baghdad; Bazoft handed over his samples and photographs to his British embassy contact, who sent them back to London via diplomatic pouch; and he prepared to leave Iraq.

Then things started to go wrong. Bazoft was detained at the Baghdad airport after Iraqi security agents had monitored the handing over of the material, and a few days later Daphne Parish was arrested as well. They were charged with spying. Within weeks,

Iraqi newspapers were saying he was spying for Britian. In November, Bazoft appeared on Iraqi television, confessing this time to having spied for Israel.

A trial followed, and in March 1990, Bazoft was sentenced to death. Parish was sentenced to fifteen years, and an Iraqi to whom Bazoft had spoken was also imprisoned. British public opinion was horrified, as were human rights groups across the world. People assumed that Bazoft was a simple journalist, a little foolish perhaps, and that any confession to spying was false, a result of torture or the threat of it. Although the British government pressed for his release, it seemed strangely reticent, seeking clemency for Bazoft but never claiming that he was an innocent journalist. Bazoft was executed on March 15, 1990. After his death, the information that he had robbed a building society was released, and the British foreign secretary, Douglas Hurd, told the House of Commons that Bazoft had contacted the police in London four times between 1987 and 1988 offering information about Iranian opposition groups in Britain.[4] Hurd claimed that these approaches — never taken up — were the extent of Bazoft's contacts with officials.

The British media did not put much credence in the confession that Bazoft wrote, and which was released in part by the Iraqis. The reluctance of journalists to credit the rambling text to Bazoft is understandable. It had almost certainly been dictated to Bazoft by his Iraqi interrogators, who would have been more concerned about what it did not say than what it said. It did not reveal Bazoft's British contact, other than to mention his first name, Michael. It did not say where Bazoft met his Brtish contact. Bazoft did admit that he had been spying on his five previous visits to Iraq, and the Iraqis also showed maps that Bazoft had drawn, and a photograph that he had taken of a road sign near Qaqa. Since his original maps and photographs would have been sent to the British embassy along with his soil samples, the Iraqis probably made him draw the maps again and supplied a new photograph. The Iraqis also published a photograph of a glass vial, taken from a hospital, which Bazoft allegedly used to collect soil samples. But the vial has a plastic cap that would have contaminated the sample; the embassy would have made sure that he had different containers.

At no time did the British admit that Bazoft had been spying, nor did Iraq flesh out its allegations. The reason was clear: if Britain admitted to the spying, the two countries would have had to break off diplomatic relations. For Iraq this would have meant the loss of official British guarantees on credits arranged to fund Iraqi imports, and the further loss of such credits until relations were restored. In Iraq's precarious financial state, this would have been a major blow: British credits for Iraq to buy British goods were running at an average of about $400 million a year. So Iraq contented itself with cries of outrage that Bazoft had been spying and that British denials could not prevail against all the evidence. From the British side, the loss of relations would have meant that British exporters would have demanded payments and London would have had to pay out perhaps over $2 billion.

So the Bazoft incident was left to die down. The soil samples had safely reached Britain and were analyzed. Bazoft's contact at the embassy, his cover blown by Bazoft during interrogation, had already left.

Within weeks of Bazoft's death, Iraq's nuclear weapon program suffered a very public setback. On March 28, the US Customs sting operation involving the nuclear capacitors came to its conclusion. British Customs agents seized the consignment as it was about to be put on an Iraqi airliner at Heathrow, where it had arrived from the United States ten days earlier, labeled as being for use in air-conditioning equipment. Several people were arrested, including an official of Iraqi Airways, whom the British authorities later expelled. For the attempted export to Iraq, the capacitors were listed as being "for the sole use" of a carbon dioxide laser system at a university in Baghdad.

Linked to the Bazoft affair is an Iraqi purchasing attempt more embarrassing to Washington than to Baghdad. About the same time that Iraq made its first inquiry for the capacitors, it also put in a request for high-temperature furnaces, known as skull furnaces, made in New Jersey by the Consarc Corporation. Four furnaces were ordered, two of which were to be made by Consarc's subsidiary in Scotland. Since the order was placed by the Iraqi ministry of industry, there is a good chance that either the CIA or British intelligence spotted this order at an early stage and decided, as in the case of the capacitors, to monitor it. The Iraqis claimed that they wanted the skull furnaces to make artificial limbs for casualties of the Iran-Iraq War. But certain skull furnaces can also be used to make missile nose cones or the nuclear explosive core of an atomic bomb. A problem for the Americans and British was that the particular furnaces ordered were of the wrong specification for military use and might not be stoppable under US law. But the progress of the order was worth watching in order to gather more information about Iraq's nuclear project. And if Iraq bought the wrong equipment and could not make it work properly, well, that would serve the Iraqis right.

Consarc was already a familiar name to those concerned about high-tech exports because it had sold equipment for making missile nose cones to the Soviet Union years before, a sale that should not have been allowed. Decisions on the Iraqi order for skull furnaces, however, were eventually overtaken by events. The order became public knowledge, and their potential export became a political football when the US Defense Department demanded the right to be involved in the debate on whether they should be exported.

The internal debate about the export of the furnaces was at times both vicious and almost childish. The furnaces were so-called dual-use items, that is, they had both a civilian and a potential military use. They therefore needed an export license authorized by the Commerce Department. In deciding whether to grant a license, Commerce works with a list of goods provided by the CIA, with input from the rest of the intelligence community. Among the criteria are whether the goods in question are going to a so-called project of concern, meaning the development of nuclear, chemical, or missile technology, and whether the supply of the goods will make a significant contribution to that project. The Commerce

Department also considers whether the purchasing country could, if refused by the United States, simply turn to another industrialized country for the items: the department is anxious that competing industrial countries do not profit at the expense of the United States.

The State Department and Defense Department are only brought into the license-approval process when the Commerce Department requests an interagency review. In recent years the Defense Department has tried to carve out a greater niche for itself in this procedure, building on the success it had in stopping the export of dual-use items to the Soviet Union and Eastern bloc. A leading light in this grab for bureaucratic turf was Stephen Bryen, until 1988 the deputy under-secretary of defense for trade security policy. A passionate believer in what he was doing at the Pentagon, and a supporter of Israel, Bryen was for several years the object of a potential legal action by the National Association of Arab Americans for allegedly handing over secrets to Israeli diplomats. In the case of the skull furnaces, stopping the proliferation of nuclear and missile technology to the Middle East fell within the gamut of Bryen's work, but to some in the administration his interest was further evidence of partisanship toward Israel.

The Commerce Department viewed the sale of the skull furnaces to Iraq as good for US exports, but at some point the deal became widely known and the row started. (One source says an Iraqi visiting Consarc was identified as a nuclear specialist.) Within bureaucratic Washington, the proposed sale became a cause célèbre, with the Defense Department determined to use it to embarrass Commerce for its previous incompetence. Between 1985 and 1988, according to a Defense Department memo, the Commerce Department had approved "without condition" a dozen sales of American electronics equipment to Saad 16, a site now known to be a missile testing facility outside Mosul, Iraq. At least one sale of missile-related equipment was approved as late as 1990, when there was little doubt about its end use.

The Defense Department, according to one official involved in the discussions, was implacably opposed to the sale of the furnaces, but was extremely weak in its arguments. "They said it was as big as a three-story building," the official said, "but that argument is not good enough. We stop exports because of what they can do, not how big they are."[5]

Opponents of the sale later argued that the Commerce Department had made no effort to ascertain where the furnaces would be installed. But this is not true. As part of the procedure, the US government asked to see the site for the furnaces, and an American embassy staffer paid a visit. "The trouble is that we were not much wiser after the visit," an official said later.

When an interagency review of an export license reaches a stalemate, only the president can be the final arbiter. Yet no bureaucrat likes sending anything less than extremely important to the White House. When the furnaces story became public, however, there was little choice but to refer the issue to President Bush. In the end he ordered the export stopped because of its potential nuclear use. By this time though, the decision was academic. It was July 19, 1990. Iraq was about to invade Kuwait, and there would soon be a complete ban on all exports to Iraq.

★   ★   ★

The saga of Bazoft and the development of Iraq's atomic bomb is not complete without reference to the death of another journalist, although less is known about the circumstances surrounding his demise. Jonathan Moyle, a twenty-eight-year-old British journalist, was found dead in his hotel room in Santiago, Chile, on March 31, 1990. Moyle was the editor of a British specialist journal, *Defence Helicopter World,* and was visiting Chile at the invitation of the Chilean air force to attend the biannual aerospace and arms fair. Trained as a helicopter pilot with the British air force, Moyle was an outgoing personality, and engaged to be married in two months. He was found hanging from a rail in the closet of his hotel bedroom, naked except for a couple of towels wrapped around him like a baby's diaper, held in place by a plastic laundry bag, with two holes in the bottom for his legs. It was made to look like self-inflicted asphyxiation while in some masturbatory act, but the circumstances strongly suggest murder.

In the previous days Moyle had been at the military show and had been in contact with the huge privately owned Chilean arms manufacturer, Cardoen. Founded and owned by Carlos Cardoen, much of the company's prosperity can be traced to business with Iraq. Cardoen had built a factory for the manufacture of cluster bombs in Iraq, and his company was trying to design a military attack version of the Bell 206 helicopter, which it hoped to sell to Iraq, and eventually set up a factory there. In addition, Cardoen owned a license to produce the South African G-5 and G-6 howitzer — the extra-long-range artillery piece designed by the scientist behind Iraq's supergun project, Gerald Bull (who had been assassinated in Brussels a few days before Moyle died). Indeed, US officials say that Cardoen was one of the conduits used by South Africa in sending these guns to Iraq: after the invasion of Kuwait, the United States pressured South Africa into stopping shipment of a $250 million order for the G-5 and the self-propelled G-6.[6] Cardoen had also acquired some of the technical detail behind a British "smart" anti-ship mine, which uses sophisticated electronics to identify the type of ship passing overhead so that it does not blow up a friendly vessel. Western officials believed that this technology, or mines developed with it, had been transferred to Iraq, putting at risk American and European warships in the Gulf.

Given Moyle's helicopter training, the focus of his interest in interviews with officials at Cardoen may well have been the helicopter project, but he might have ranged more widely, into any aspect of Cardoen's relationships with Iraq. Indeed, apart from the trade ties, there was also a personal sympathy between Cardoen and Saddam Hussein. In Cardoen's Santiago office a picture of Saddam Hussein was hung on the wall and remained there until after the invasion of Kuwait. A vignette from the April 1989 Baghdad arms fair is more insinuating. Cardoen, along with representatives of many other nations, attended a dinner for foreign exhibitors, hosted by the newly appointed minister of industry and military industrialization, Hussein Kamel. (As we have seen, Hussein Kamel was also in charge of Iraq's missiles, nuclear weapons, and chemical weapons, as well as conventional arms. He was Saddam Hussein's cousin and son-in-law.) At the end of the meal Hussein Kamel gave a speech welcoming the foreign arms manufacturers to Baghdad and wishing them well in their business relations with Iraq. The minister sat down to a moment of embarrassed silence among the foreign visitors — no one had planned a speech in response. It was Carlos Cardoen who graciously stood up to thank Hussein Kamel for Iraq's hospitality.[7]

The Cardoen company has denied any involvement in Moyle's death. But one other aspect of the company's dealings with Iraq has since come to light. Western intelligence believes that the Cardoen officials provided false end-user certificates so that Iraq could obtain some goods that would otherwise have been prohibited to it.[8] Of particular concern is a consignment of machine tools bought by Cardoen from Matrix Churchill, a British company that was purchased by Iraq in 1987. The machine tools, worth $20 million, can be used for many purposes: to carve out an engine block for a truck or car engine, for example. But the tools could also be used to make driver plates, a component of an atomic bomb.[9] The plates, which are blasted at the nuclear core to increase the pressure on the nuclear explosive, can be incorporated into a design that makes a given-sized bomb produce a more powerful blast. But the driver plates have to be carefully machined, thinner at the edge than in the middle, so that the plates behave predictably when subject to high explosive. Exports to Iraq of such machine tools would be carefully controlled by many Western countries. When it became clear that the machine tools from Britain had been diverted to Iraq while on their way to Chile, suspicions arose that they were for nuclear purposes. Officials of Matrix Churchill are being investigated by British Customs. The switch in destination took place at the German port of Bremen. The freight forwarding agent that handled the transfer was raided by German Customs officers in December 1990.

Afterward a German official said that nineteen different shipments, mostly from Matrix Churchill but also some from a Swiss company, had had their destinations switched in Bremen from Chile to Iraq. The shipments had started in September 1989, but the "most sensitive" ones had occurred in April 1990 — just after Moyle died. All the shipments had been redirected to the Fao State Establishment in Iraq, which, like the Qaqa State Establishment, comes under the Ministry of Industry and Military Industrialization.

★ ★ ★

CHAPTER

19

The Invasion of Kuwait

Western expatriates living in Kuwait in 1990 should not have been surprised when Iraq invaded on August 2, 1990. Iraq's territorial claims to all or parts of Kuwaiti territory were favorite ingredients of dinner-party conversations. The Iraqi trade center, a block away from the Kuwait Sheraton hotel, on the western edge of Kuwait city and fifty miles from the border, was said to mark one frontier of Iraq's claims to Kuwaiti territory. For these expatriates, Iraqi rhetoric and militarism were part of life; as was the threat of subversion by Shia Muslims in Kuwait, encouraged by their religious compatriots in Iran; or brewing beer in their spare bathrooms in contravention of Kuwait's strict ban on alcohol.

Other people who were not surprised by the invasion were the backroom thinkers and analysts in Washington, those with access to diplomatic reporting and secret intelligence reports. In March 1990 one had commented that "Iraqi pressure on Kuwait was continuous."[1] In May, escalating tensions between Iraq and the Gulf states was given as a reason for the US navy maintaining more units than usual on that station. "And the policy is working," an American energy specialist said.[2]

Iraq, though, would not forfeit any chance to undermine Kuwait. At an international football tournament in Kuwait, the emirate used a motif that upset the visiting Saudi team because it alluded to an era before the Al-Saud family had taken over. The Iraqi team could have remained neutral on the issue, but chose to side with the Saudis, and both teams went home before playing all their matches. The Iraqi team's decision was motivated not so much by a desire to show solidarity with the Saudis as to confront the Kuwaitis, and the man who made the decision for the team to depart was the head of the Iraq Football Federation, Udai Saddam Hussein.

Saddam Hussein has himself dated his growing annoyance with Kuwait from May 1990, when Saddam called an Arab summit conference in Baghdad to discuss the emigration of thousands of Soviet Jews to Israel. He says that at the summit he gave the emir of Kuwait, Sheikh Jaber al-Ahmad al-Sabah, the first of three warnings. Kuwait's oil policy, he told the emir, was playing into a US conspiracy to undermine Iraq. Kuwait's policy of exceeding its OPEC oil-production quota was no less than "an act of war."[3]

But the seeds of Saddam's edginess had been sown by the profound changes in Eastern Europe at the end of 1989. History was on the move, and forces that could not be stopped were radically altering the way countries related to each other. The new alignments of power threatened Iraq's diplomatic and trading relations with the Eastern Bloc countries. Close diplomatic ties with many of them had allowed Iraq to barter oil for goods and services, cashless swaps that eased Iraq's financial difficulties. More important, major arms supply relationships were involved. The Soviet Union was Iraq's biggest supplier of weapons, and Poland, Bulgaria, and Czechoslovakia also exported arms to Iraq. Now the Soviet Union, mired in its own economic problems, was starting to ask for payment on earlier shipments and was demanding sharply higher repayment terms on future supplies. To make matters worse, relations with France, Iraq's other most significant arms supplier, were already strained because of unpaid debts.

The historic changes in Eastern Europe coincided with a growing financial mess at home. Oil revenues were stagnant, despite several new pipelines. On the other side of the balance sheet, Iraq's suppliers, after seven years of accepting delayed payments for goods, were being tougher in demanding repayment of old debts, and meaner in offering new credits. The country was desperately short of money: Every two weeks a meeting was held at Iraq's central bank to decide which bills had to be paid and which creditors would be told they had to wait. Estimates in early March 1990, prepared by foreign bankers with access to some of Iraq's tightly held financial secrets, suggested that the country was going to be short $8 billion to $10 billion during the year.[4] This deficit was more than half of what Iraq was expected to earn from oil. The country either had to boost oil production by 40 percent, and hope that the price remained constant, or seek a 40 percent increase in oil prices.

A series of sabotage incidents in Iraq, aimed at targets linked to Saddam personally and to his superweapons projects, were especially worrisome. In July 1989 a bomb had been thrown at a vehicle belonging to the British 600 Group, which was working at Qaqa, at or near the atomic bomb design facility. And in September 1989 a bomb had been found under a car belonging to, and parked outside, the Baghdad office of the Swedish truck manufacturer Saab-Scania. The culprits might have been Kurdish opposition groups, who had threatened in August to attack companies helping Iraq. Or they might have been Iraqis trying to damage the marine house of the US embassy next door. More likely though, certainly in Saddam's mind, was that the bomb was the work of Israeli-backed saboteurs: Saab-Scania trucks are used to tow Iraq's long-range missiles, the ones capable of hitting Israel. Israeli bombs had already terrorized some of Iraq's weapons suppliers in Europe, but for Israel to be able to operate within Iraq was another matter entirely.

One particular event—the overthrow and execution of Nicolae Ceausescu in December 1989—turned international attention to the ominous parallels between Saddam and the Romanian leader. Both had been in power many years, both had tried to radically change their country, both surrounded themselves with relatives in positions of power, and both had erected a brutally efficient state security system. Now Ceausescu had fallen, subverted by economically aggravated popular protest and an army that had sided against its president.

The comparison was made by a number of commentators in December 1989 and January 1990, but what enraged Saddam was an opinion piece on the Voice of America that named Saddam as among the world's remaining dictators. Iraqi officials protested because the comment was prefaced and followed by the remark that the piece described official US policy. Officials in the State Department were both embarrassed and enraged because they had not been consulted before the broadcast. Apologies and clarifications were made, but Saddam remained bitter. He countered by making a speech demanding that US warships be withdrawn from the Gulf.

March 1990 brought further pressure on Saddam. Nuclear capacitors were intercepted by British Customs, and an Iraqi court convicted the Iranian-born journalist Farzad Bazoft for spying and sentenced him to death. Saddam ignored the international calls for clemency because he was convinced—quite rightly—of Bazoft's guilt. In the same speech in which he threatened to scorch half of Israel, broadcast on April 2, Saddam described the hypocrisy of what he called the "big uproar about Bazoft" compared to the silence in the West after the assassination of Gerald Bull. If the question was one of human rights, Saddam insisted, why had the United States not bothered to use its intelligence services to uncover the murderer of Bull? After Bull had left Iraq, Saddam said, "[Someone] killed him. They killed him with a pistol with a silencer. As far as they are concerned, he was not entitled to human rights." And why had the British paid so little attention to human rights when they partitioned Palestine and created the state of

Israel? he asked. "The English have not spared any country on earth from their problems. They charted maps and left things unsettled to create problems."

As the speech continued, it became obvious that Saddam thought the United States, Britain, and Israel were acting in concert: "Bazoft passes intelligence to the Zionist entity [Israel] so that it can accurately hit a plant and kill people . . . they [the United States and Britain] will be deluded if they imagine that they can give Israel the cover to come and strike at some industrial metalworks."

Soon after this speech Saddam's paranoia apparently increased when US intelligence leaked to the media the news that Saddam had transferred some of his long-range missiles to the H-2 airfield in western Iraq. (H-2 is the number of a pumping station on a disused oil pipeline.) From this launching pad, the missiles had more than enough range to hit any target in Israel. In Saddam's eyes this publicity seemed to be preparing US opinion for a preemptive strike against Iraq. The following month parts for Iraq's huge supergun were intercepted at Teesport.

So, as 1990 unfolded, Saddam's anger with the West and with Israel increased. At the same time, he found several reasons to become more annoyed with neighboring Kuwait. Iraq's chief complaint was the fluctuations in the price of oil on the international markets. For most of 1989 the price of Kirkuk crude hovered around $15 to $16 a barrel. In January 1990, however, the price stood at just under $20 per barrel. But this comparatively strong price had encouraged OPEC to increase quotas for production in 1990 by nearly 8 percent. The increase in production was sufficient to tip the supply-and-demand scales, and the price started to weaken. As the weeks passed, the market price fell steadily, dropping below the OPEC benchmark price of $18 a barrel in mid-February. In late March, the rate of decline slowed, but prices again fell sharply in early May, reaching the $14-a-barrel range.

Iraq found itself in the embarrassing position of being able to do little about the fall in oil prices. During periods of weak prices Iraq

Price of oil (US dollars per barrel)

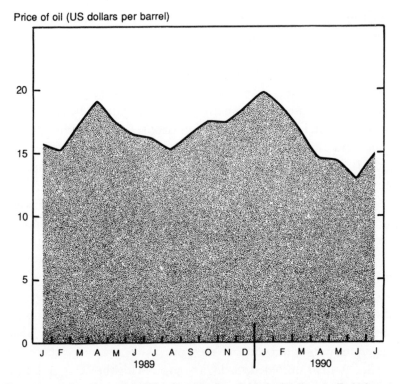

The average price of a barrel of Kirkuk crude oil available for loading at a Turkish port in the months preceding Iraq's invasion of Kuwait shows a precipitous drop from January to July, sharply curtailing Iraq's income. (Figures from issues of *Petroleum Market Intelligence,* a monthly newsletter from New York.)

produced less than its quota, but it had already complained that its quota was too low to support its economy. The leading role in appearing to tackle the oil price problem was left to Saudi Arabia, Kuwait, and the United Arab Emirates. The last two had earned little confidence among oil officials in Iraq: they were the cartel's biggest cheaters, consistently producing more than their quota despite having agreed to abide by the levels set by OPEC ministers. (The United Arab Emirates repeatedly exceeded its quota because member emirate Dubai does not acknowledge that the quota applies to it. Kuwait meanwhile hoped that its overproduction would win it a larger quota. Kuwait was also less concerned about lower oil prices than other OPEC members because its many international investments depended on a low oil price and, anyway, brought in more earnings than oil in any given year.)

Perhaps more annoying still to Iraq was that its regional rival, Iran, was in the happy position of having a healthy production figure, when just a few months previously it had not been able to meet its quota at all. Iran's new vitality disappointed other oil-producing states in the Gulf as well, because they had hoped that low Iranian output would enable each of them to exceed their quota.

In April Saddam initiated direct communication with Iran, trying to find common ground to sort out the two countries' differences concerning border adjustments and the repatriation of prisoners of war. He sent the first of three letters directly to Iran's President Hashemi Rafsanjani, bypassing the United Nations, which had previously been acting as an intermediary. The contact eventually enabled Saddam to settle (at a disadvantage to Iraq) the previously substantial points of contention between the two countries, assuring him a quiet flank at Iran's border while he was engaged at other borders.

In May Saddam used the summit he had called to discuss the emigration of Russian Jews to Israel as an opportunity to speak to the emir of Kuwait about his country's overproduction of oil. Kuwaiti policy did not change after this meeting, although in July oil revenues for Iraq showed a small improvement. But small improvements would not rescue Iraq's desperate economic situation, and so Saddam gave a second, far more serious warning to Kuwait in mid-July. The memorandum sent to Kuwait also demanded compensation of $2.4 billion for oil that Saddam alleged had been stolen from the Rumaila oilfield, part of which straddles the common border. On several counts, the allegation was patent nonsense. First, since the oilfield extends into Kuwait, Kuwait had a right to exploit the field. Disputes over how much oil Kuwait was entitled to could have been resolved by international arbitration

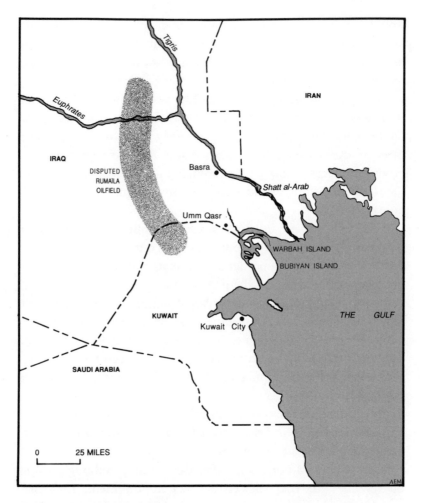

Kuwait and the surrounding territory

using the established formulas for dividing the wealth of resources that cross national boundaries. Second, assuming a price of $18 a barrel, the Kuwaitis would have had to have "stolen" 100,000 barrels a day from the oilfield for the previous three and a half years. In late 1990 the Kuwaitis admitted that they had been taking 30,000 barrels a day from the field, an insignificant amount compared to

Kuwait's oil quota of 1.5 million barrels a day and to Iraq's production from Rumaila, which is estimated at 400,000 barrels a day.

Baghdad had also demanded an immediate cash payment of $10 billion, a figure apparently plucked from the air, perhaps representing Iraq's immediate needs and its perception of how much Kuwait could afford. According to Kuwaiti cabinet minutes of a crucial meeting on July 18, Kuwait had responded by offering $500 million, spread over three years.[5] The Kuwaiti finance minister, Sheikh Ali Khalifa al-Sabah, acknowledged the threat posed by Iraq and suggested Iraq was trying to blame the Gulf states for its own economic failures. "Iraq is going to continue escalating the level of confrontation," he predicted. Bard al-Yacoub, a minister of state, intervened to say that Iraq's objective was to extort money. Sheikh Nawaf al-Sabah, the defense minister, denied that Kuwait had violated the disputed border, claiming instead that Iraq had expanded its military installations and farmland across the border. The foreign minister, Sheikh Sabah al-Ahmed al Sabah, knew the border issue was explosive: "There is a possibility of Iraqi aggression." The crown prince and prime minister, Sheikh Saad al-Abdullah al-Sabah, predicted a limited Iraqi operation to seize land in the border areas close to the Iraqi port of Umm Qasr. Iraq's designs on Bubiyan Island were also mentioned; the minutes say that Iraq wanted to lease Bubiyan, but considered the smaller Warbah Island to be Iraqi territory.

The minutes also reveal some information on Iraq's war debts to Kuwait and Saudi Arabia, details of which had never been officially released. The total amount involved is estimated to be $35 billion, including proceeds of oil sales. The Kuwaitis' contribution is given as $13.5 billion, which, the minutes say, Iraq wanted written off.

After the meeting, Kuwait canceled all military leave and put its armed forces on alert. But the Kuwaiti forces numbered only 20,000, far less than the peacetime complement of Iraqi soldiers based in southern Iraq.

By mid-July statements out of Baghdad were becoming increasingly venomous: Kuwait was labeled an American stooge, and its ministers were traitors. Similar epithets were hurled at the United Arab Emirates, far down the Gulf. The growing crisis prompted King Fahd of Saudi Arabia to offer mediation, while Washington gave a guarded indication that it would support its conservative Arab Gulf allies against possible Iraqi aggression. The US response was muted because of the lack of a treaty obligation toward Kuwait, although Washington was clearly against the use of force by Iraq to enforce its will.

At the regular scheduled OPEC ministerial meeting in Geneva at the end of July, the reference price for oil was raised, and Kuwait and the United Arab Emirates agreed to abide by their production quotas. By this time 100,000 Iraqi troops were reported to have moved up to the border with Kuwait, a maneuver that was generally interpreted as intended to apply pressure on Kuwait at the OPEC meeting.

It now became evident that the Soviet Union had lost its status as a superpower. Although the Soviet Union had had a close diplomatic and military relationship with Iraq, and long established ties with Kuwait (the first Gulf Arab state to recognize Moscow), Soviet officials played no role in the diplomacy and seemed ignorant of Iraqi intentions. (Hours before the Iraqi invasion, US Secretary of State James Baker was meeting his Soviet counterpart, Eduard Shevardnadze, in Siberia. Despite American intelligence predictions, Shevardnadze demurred from believing that Iraq would invade.)

US officials meanwhile were seriously worried and sat through endless meetings trying to come up with plans for promoting mediation and countering aggression. Ironically, a war game, planned well in advance, was being played out at the Pentagon that very week on how to respond to Iraqi moves against either Kuwait or Saudi Arabia.[6] There was no time to learn from it.

At the end of one long meeting, a young representative from one of the intelligence agencies muttered to his colleagues around the table: "Well, I know what I would do if I were stuck in the desert [like the Iraqi army]. After a while I would get up and head for the beach." There was a chuckle of laughter at both the sentiment, common in steamy Washington in the summer, and its pointedness: the nearest beach was in Kuwait.

In Baghdad, the American ambassador, April Glaspie, met one-to-one with Saddam Hussein for the first time in her two years in the post. In a long conversation on July 25, she agreed with Saddam's criticism of the American news media, endorsed his view that oil prices should be higher ("over $25"), and sympathized with his anxiety about low oil prices forcing a huge drop in Iraqi spending. Contrary to some statements from Washington, she declared that "we have no opinion on the Arab-Arab conflicts, like your border disagreement with Kuwait." She was also consoled by Saddam's view that the difficulty with Kuwait would be settled, even though Saddam referred to the necessity of "overcoming Kuwaiti greed." Reassured, Glapsie went to London on leave on July 31.

US officials' main mistake appears to have been putting too much trust not only in Saddam but also in the notion that the inter-Arab dispute would be resolved through mediation. Among the Arab state, the diplomatic initiative was seized by President Mubarak of Egypt. Mubarak managed to persuade the Iraqis to sit down with the Kuwaitis and discuss the issue at a meeting scheduled to start on July 28 in the Saudi port city of Jeddah. But the session did not actually begin until July 31, apparently because Kuwait objected to Iraq's threatening negotiating stance. Iraq was represented by the deputy chairman of the Revolutionary Command Council, Izzat Ibrahim, backed up by the local government minister, Ali Hassan al-Majid, Saddam's cousin. The presence of the latter made two serious points: first, that Iraq considered relations with Kuwait a local government matter: second, that Kuwait should take into account the minister's fearsome reputation in using chemical weapons to punish rebellious Kurdish citizens in northern Iraq in 1988.

By August 1, according to Sheikh Sabah, the Kuwaiti foreign minister, his country had agreed to write off Iraq's war debt and to lease Warbah Island to Iraq as an oil outlet for the Rumaila field. "Iraq asked us to drop the debt and we did not object," he said. "Iraq asked for Bubiyan Island. We agreed to give them Warbah Island instead."[7]

Whether this agreement was final is not clear. Certainly the Kuwaiti team did not have time to report back on the negotiations to their cabinet colleagues or to announce the accord to the nation. At two hours after midnight on the following day, Iraqi forces swept across the border, on tanks and in helicopters. Some were disgorged from ships off Kuwait City. The emir and crown prince fled with other members of the ruling family by car before dawn. As most residents cowered in their apartments, Iraqi forces established themselves at key points throughout the city. (According to subsequent intelligence reports, Iraqi officers pretending to be businessmen and tourists had visited Kuwait regularly for several months to check the lie of the land. One report says that Iraq was helped by Iranian agents from among the Baghdad-based Iranian Mujaheddin-e-Khalq guerrilla group, including Miriam Rajavi, the wife of its leader, Masoud Rajavi.)

By midday on August 2, 1990, Iraqi forces were in full control of Kuwait City, mopping up residual pockets of resistance. The world stood by, shocked.

★ ★ ★

CHAPTER

20

Saddam Versus the World

In the five and a half weeks of air attacks and artillery barrage by US-led coalition forces against Iraq, starting on January 16, 1991, Saddam lost much of the arsenal of sophisticated weapons that he had built up over the previous five years. Apart from damage to military units, his factories for making missiles and chemical weapons were hit, as well as his nuclear facilities. So when the land offensive began in earnest, just before dawn in the Gulf on February 24, the battle seemed likely to be an uneven contest, with the United States and its allies having the technological edge.

But if Saddam felt his chances weakened by the absence of his high-technology arsenal in what he deemed would be "the mother of battles,"[1] he did not show it. In a radio broadcast to the Iraqi nation a few hours after allied tanks rolled into Kuwait, he declared that in the coming fight, "the sophisticated weapons of the enemy will have no meaning." Far from sounding vulnerable, Saddam gave the impression of invincible strength. He had some reason for this.

Although some military experts had predicted that the Iraqi army would crumble within five days under the massive air onslaught, in fact the allies' overwhelming air superiority had failed to dislodge Iraqi forces from Kuwait. While President Bush spoke of "the final phase" of the liberation of Kuwait, which he hoped would come "swiftly and decisively,"[2] in Saddam's mind the battle was going to be a test of the fighting spirit of the Iraqi soldier compared, chiefly, with his American counterpart. And here Saddam Hussein might have thought he had the advantage, for, as he had said to Ambassador Glaspie in the fateful meeting on July 25, 1990, when the American envoy had failed to pick up the signals that Saddam intended to invade Kuwait: "Yours is a society which cannot accept 10,000 dead in one battle."[3] From Saddam's point of view, drawing President Bush into a ground war that could conceivably inflict heavy US casualties was the penultimate step toward a political, if not a military, victory. Indeed, in his broadcast on the first morning of the land battle, Saddam declared, "Victory will be ours."

Such an argument may well have been understood by military planners in Washington and London, and the news blackout declared by the allies after the ground war began may have been intended not only to prevent Iraq from learning details of allied actions but also to insulate the American public from the extent of allied casualties.

Within two days though, Saddam's words were seen to be bluster. From his bunker in Baghdad, possibly the main command center built under a soccer stadium in the mid-1980s, Saddam finally acknowledged a reality. After heavy bombing, he said, Baghdad was as it had been after the sack by Hülegü's Mongol hordes,[4] and in southern Iraq allied armored columns were slicing through Iraqi defenses, not only into Kuwait but also across the great expanse of the deserts and toward the Euphrates River. Saddam quickly decided that it was time to withdraw, and he ordered his army to leave Kuwait within the day.

The military tactics of the US-led coalition, as well as their troops, technology, and equipment, had proved superior to

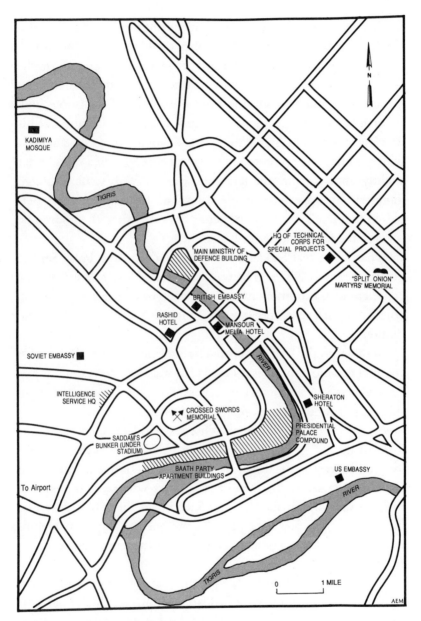

Key structures in central Baghdad

Saddam's war machine. The Iraqi leader's bluff had been called. But if allied commanders thought that they could read Saddam's mind, in most respects the Iraqi leader still seemed to be an enigma: in the face of overwhelming odds, why had he not withdrawn his forces earlier? Why did he continue to risk the lives of his troops and, ultimately, his own position? The almost-hysterical ranting of his wartime speeches in Arabic to the Iraqi people had seemed at odds with the image he presented in newsreel clips, that of a calm leader slightly uneasy before the television camera. With visiting foreign dignitaries he appeared a polite statesman, looking genuinely per-plexed that Iraq's case was not better understood; with children he acted as the fatherly ruler of his country.

What is the real Saddam Hussein like? An Arab Press Service profile of him in 1987 said he was fearless, ruthless, calculating, fair, conscientious, extremely intelligent, analytical, extremely shrewd, efficient, consistent, organized, generous, elegant, polite, and cautious.[5]

Another profile of him, written by a former Western diplomat at about the same time, describes Saddam as unostentatious (apart from a penchant for cigars), merciless, arrogant, often rambling in speech, but at other times sharp and decisive.[6]

A second former diplomat, who saw Saddam in military uni-form in the 1970s, before he became president, says that Saddam looked ill at ease in the tunic, and his disquiet was noted with stifled mirth by the senior Iraqi military officers who were present.[7] A third former diplomat, who met Saddam in the 1980s, describes him as having a powerful physical presence, giving a marvelous example of leadership of the kind that all military officers are taught to emulate.[8]

According to Jerrold Post, a psychiatrist at George Washington University who has analyzed Saddam's actions for the US govern-ment, "Saddam is not crazy. [But] he has the most dangerous personality configuration, which we call malignant narcissism. Such extreme self-absorption. He has no concern for the pain or suffering of others. [He has] a paranoid outlook [with] messianic dreams."[9]

The CIA's assessment of Saddam Hussein has, of course, not been made public. Drawn up by a department called the Office of Leadership Analysis — known in the intelligence community as the bio-people — it would include various studies by specially commissioned analysts. The accuracy and thoroughness of the CIA's biographies of foreign leaders are, however, uneven, according to one intelligence official familiar with the genre.[10]

Israeli intelligence has also made a profile of Saddam, based in part on a handwriting analysis of a letter he wrote to his sons in 1988, which was published in an Iraqi newspaper two years later.[11] Like the CIA, the Israelis have kept quiet about what they have learned, although the Israeli media claimed, probably mischievously, that the handwriting showed that Saddam was dangerous and unpredictable.

But none of these perspectives hints at the essential absurdity of the man illustrated by the personality cult he had developed. Every Iraqi town had a prominent poster of Saddam striking one pose or another — as a soldier or a scholar, in traditional dress or in designer sunglasses. Most Iraqi towns also had a Saddam Hussein Street or Saddam Hussein Square; often the hospital was named after him, as in Baghdad. Wristwatches with Saddam Hussein's picture on the face were de rigueur for loyal officials for several years. Even top ministers dared not question any idea that Saddam suggested. Concerned about food shortages during the war with Iran, and the public perception that leading members of the regime might not be suffering as much as the man on the street, Saddam ordered his cabinet and closest aides to go on a diet. Several months later the weight of each member, along with his height and age, was published in the Baath party newspapers. Three out of thirty-five were deemed to be still overweight.[12]

Saddam's birthday, April 28, has for years been celebrated as a national holiday, with festivities such as competitions for best portraits of the Iraqi leader, or parades of floats depicting an era from Iraq's history. To outsiders, the absurd antics somehow seemed to reduce the growing threat that Saddam was posing to the region.

But even before the invasion of Kuwait in August 1990, it was obvious to many observers that Saddam was going to be a force to be reckoned with. They noted how anxious Saddam was for recognition of his regional importance, and how irritated he seemed by the self-confident assumption of the mantle of Arab leadership by President Mubarak of Egypt and King Fahd of Saudi Arabia. Furthermore, Iraq was a much richer country than, say, Syria, which led Saddam to assert that Baghdad deserved a greater weight in regional forums, and that he should be deferred to by his Baath rival, President Hafez Assad. Saddam could also be expected to simply outlast his regional rivals; at age fifty-three, he was much younger than many other Arab leaders.

Despite all this, after the cease-fire with Iran in August 1988, Saddam felt that he was not receiving the respect he deserved from the other Arab states in the Gulf. After all, he insisted, Iraq had saved Saudi Arabia, Kuwait, Bahrain, Qatar, the United Arab Emirates, and Oman from the revolutionary expansionism of Ayatollah Khomeini's Iran. But in 1981, these conservative and pro-Western states had excluded Iraq from the regional organization they formed — the Gulf Cooperation Council — and they still rejected Saddam's overtures after he drew Iran to a stalemate in 1988. So the following year Saddam formed his own regional block, the Arab Cooperation Council, in which Iraq joined with Egypt, Jordan, and North Yemen. But even in this grouping Saddam was stymied, as Egypt was determined to balance Iraq's power rather than enhance it.

At one point the only countries welcoming Iraqi support were Mauritania, on the Atlantic coast of North Africa, the poorest and most obscure of the Arab states, and the regime of General Aoun, a faction of the Christian enclave in Lebanon. Most other Arab states seemed wary of inviting Iraqi support, even the stateless Palestine

Liberation Organization, which until 1990 preferred to deal with several Arab states rather than be beholden to any particular one.

For Saddam this rejection was more than a matter of hurt pride. It also suggested that Baathism, the political ideology which had dominated his life, had lost its wider appeal. The creed of Arab unity and the notion of a socialist sharing of a nation's wealth no longer appeared to offer any particular promise. If he had been honest with himself, Saddam would have realized that his wing of the Baath party, and Assad's in Syria, each had manipulated the ideology so cynically and for so long as to wholly extinguish the bright hopes of the party's founders in 1940. The fact that Baathism was originally formulated by a Christian Arab, Michel Aflaq, meant also that many Arabs doubted, correctly, its Islamic credentials.

In the region's coolness toward Iraq, Saddam also saw threats to his hopes for his country's future. In his speeches he often referred to these hopes but never fleshed them out with much detail. Yet the outlines were clear: Iraq had once been a great country and should be so again. The nation's vast oil wealth should benefit the people, and Iraq's two huge rivers, the Tigris and the Euphrates, should again be a source of great agricultural wealth. The nation was also blessed by the presence of a great leader, himself.

The principal problem was that oil exports were not providing the revenues that he thought Iraq deserved. The price, he said, should be $25 a barrel, certainly not bouncing around below $20.[13] Moreover, the Turks were building dams on the headwaters of the Euphrates, which threatened the river's free flow through Iraq. In any direction Saddam looked, he saw conspiracies against him, and the hands of clients of the United States, or Britain, or Israel, or all three, somehow at work.

Even at home, the permanence of his rule had yet to be guaranteed. Although Saddam could credit himself with having built Iraq into more of a cohesive state during the eight years of the Iran-Iraq War, there was no hiding the social tensions caused by the mutual antipathy between the regime and the Kurds, a full fourth of Iraq's population, nor the effects of centuries of hostility between the

Sunni minority and the Shia majority, which was gravely under-represented in Saddam's government.

To meet these challenges Saddam employed the same sort of mixture of long-term vision and short-term initiative that has always characterized his rule. In order to strengthen his domestic power base, he initiated a program of political reform, holding elections for the national assembly and for the Kurdish assembly, and drafting major revisions of the interim constitution by which the Baath had ruled for more than twenty years. None of these moves loosened the tightness of his rule or diminished the domi-nant role played by his cult of personality. But they allowed for a certain political and social mobility designed to appeal to a new generation of Iraqis seeking their own role in the nation. The elections and reforms also enabled Saddam to weed out some underperforming politicians. Under the new constitution, the political structure was to change and the Revolutionary Command Council would cease to exist. These transformations would have completed Saddam's process of pensioning off the political old guard and replacing them with relatively young technocrats.

In terms of innovation on the domestic political front, there seemed no limit to what Saddam would try. Such tactics were probably intended to keep his rivals and opponents wrong-footed. One example was his order, in 1988, for the renovation of the graves housing the remains of King Faisal I and his grandson, King Faisal II. Although Iraqi nationalists despised these men for collaborating in the foreign domination of Iraq, Saddam's gesture was probably intended to suggest that the period of revolution was over, that Iraq was now embarking on a new era of stability and tradition. One political prize from this rehabilitation of the Faisals was the cement-ing of friendship with King Hussein of Jordan, who in 1958 had watched from the sidelines while his relative, King Faisal II, was murdered and then dragged through the streets. After Saddam and King Hussein visited the cemetery together, the Jordanian monarch developed into a steady supporter of the Iraqi leader.

Saddam followed up on this alliance by establishing military links with Jordan (a joint training squadron of aircraft) and offering Jordan access to intelligence about Israel gained by Iraqi reconnaissance flights near the border. When Israel expressed disquiet in early 1990, the people in many Arab states praised Saddam's adventurous stance, while some Arab governments were quietly relieved that his military ambitions seemed directed at the Arab world's traditional enemy, rather than themselves. And when Saddam expressed concern about the influx of Soviet Jews to Israel in 1989 and 1990, he caught the imagination of the Arab world. Open threats to Israel, in response to imagined challenges to Iraq, elevated him to a regional hero, particularly among the Palestinians under Israeli rule in the West Bank and Gaza Strip. Yasir Arafat threw his traditional caution to the wind and accepted Saddam's friendship and patronage.

Saddam's confidence and prestige appeared to grow, at least among his fellow Arabs. Elsewhere he appeared hopelessly unworldly. In June 1990 he told an American television interviewer, in response to a question criticizing his treatment of the Kurds, that North American Indians had no political rights and had to live on a reservation unless they had a certificate saying they were fit to live in US society. And when asked why his regime harshly punished anyone who criticized the president, he replied, "In your country, the law does not punish whoever tries to insult the president?" (The reporter responded by telling Saddam that those critical of President Bush are given their own TV shows.)[14]

From such encounters emerges the image of a man curiously unsure of himself in a world of which he had little experience. (Saddam rarely traveled outside the Arab world and during his trips to France, Cuba, Yugoslavia, the Soviet Union, and India he always remained within the cocoon of the protocol of state visits.) His desperate quest for recognition of his status as the victor in the war with Iran led him at one time to seek a meeting with British Prime Minister Margaret Thatcher.[15] This was denied him, as were high-level meetings with American officials. The series of snubs compounded his paranoid fear that the world was against him, and he responded by issuing his own threats. Instead of a long-term political vision, as he claimed, he strove for short-term political advantage and, in so doing, made the mistake of invading Kuwait.

Colonel Qaddafi had a similar perspective on regional politics, though he was brought up short by the US bombing of his compound in 1987. Saddam, however, was not the same kind of person as the Libyan leader, whose erratic behavior and flamboyant clothes made him the laughingstock even of other Arabs. Saddam was prepared to play a tougher game, and his long-range missiles, battle-hardened army, chemical weapons, and sponsorship of international terrorist groups convinced him that he had more cards.

Some of these cards will remain in the hands of Saddam or his successor. For any Iraqi leader it will be a point of national honor to resent the countries that joined or supported the US-led coalition in pushing Iraqi troops out of Kuwait and destroying the main units of the Republican Guard within the borders of Iraq. Though the United States will continue to be The Great Satan, the complicity of Syria, Saudi Arabia, Egypt, Turkey, and Kuwait will be remembered, and future demands for vengeance are likely to garner some political support.

Some Western and pro-Western Arab leaders have announced their expectations of a more stable Middle East after the liberation of Kuwait, especially once a settlement is reached in the Arab-Israeli dispute. But the reality will probably be bleaker, with the region locked in a new series of bitter arguments, claims, and counterclaims, each with its own self-justifying logic. A particular danger is that President Assad of Syria expects a reward for joining the coalition, a move many considered ironic in light of Syria's support for international terrorism over the years. The memory of the bombing of Pan Am flight 103 over Lockerbie, Scotland, by terrorists with Syrian links is still fresh.

One danger for the immediate future is that the conflict will reignite and spread. Another danger is that Iraq's neighbors, particularly the Iranians, will press for the dismantling of Iraq, perhaps into Kurdish, Sunni Arab, and Shia Arab zones. The Islamic regime in Tehran could even demand a degree of control over the Shia area, which would include the holy cities of Najaf and Kerbala. At this point Turkey would almost certainly intervene to secure the northern area of Iraq for itself and thereby impede the development of an independent Kurdish state, lest such a state attract Turkey's substantial Kurdish population to split off and join it. Whatever their agendas for the region, both Syria and Iran are likely to make use of Moscow's disquiet at the course of events in February 1991, when the Soviet Union's diplomatic efforts to avoid a land battle were rejected by the allies.

Apart from Saddam and his immediate coterie, the other main losers in the postwar readjustment in the Middle East are Yasir Arafat and the Palestinians. The PLO chairman has supported Saddam so closely, incurring the resentment of other crucial Arab states by doing so, that his status, if not his survival, would be at risk were he to lose Saddam's patronage. From an Arab point of view, the imposition by force of United Nations sanctions against Iraq, while earlier resolutions against Israel just gathered dust, was a sign of world hypocrisy. The resentment of more than 1.5 million Palestinians living unwillingly under Israeli rule seems to ensure that the issue will remain on the international agenda.

For the Israelis, the invasion of Kuwait again demonstrated their nation's need to depend on military strength to guarantee its security. And the rain of Scud missiles that hit Tel Aviv and other cities only reinforced the impression that Arab states would always be difficult to deal with.

For American policymakers, there were risks to every option in dealing with Saddam. But there was a particular risk in doing nothing: the status of the United States as a superpower would have been diminished, limiting Washington's effectiveness the next time it might want to act. The routing of Saddam Hussein's military forces has removed one threat to the region, but the experience of the confrontation with Iraq is unlikely to be rewarding. In retrospect, Saddam's continuing, albeit weakened, leadership might come to be seen as the most stabilizing alternative among the range of possibilities for the governance of Iraq. In the sweep of history, the months of Saddam's efforts to achieve an instant empire by invading Kuwait might be as nothing compared with continuing turmoil in the Middle East.

★ ★ ★

Saddam's Multiple Layers of Government

(as of February 1, 1991)

Council of Ministers

President, prime minister, secretary-general of the Baath Party Regional Command, chairman of the Revolutionary Command Council, commander-in-chief of the armed forces: Saddam Hussein

Vice president: Taha Moeddin Marouf

First deputy prime minister: Taha Yassin Ramadan

Deputy prime minister: Saadoun Hammadi

Deputy prime minister, foreign affairs: Tariq Aziz

Culture and information: Latif Nassif Jassem

Industry and military industrialization, acting oil minister: Hussein Kamil Hassan

Defense: Saadi Tuma Abbas al-Jabburi

Trade, acting minister of finance: Mohammed Mehdi Saleh

Transport and communications: Mohammed Hamza al-Zubaidi

Agriculture and irrigation: Abdul-Wahab Mahmoud Abdullah

Interior: Samir Mohammed Abdul-Wahab

Planning: Samal Majid Faraj

Housing and construction: Taher Mohammed Hassoun al-Marzouk

Education: Abdul-Qader Izzadin

Higher education and scientific research: Mundhir Ibrahim

Justice: Akram Abdul-Qader Ali

Labor and social affairs: Umeed Madhat Mubarak

Local government: Ali Hassan al-Majid

Health: Abdul-Salem Mohammed Saeed

Religious endowments: Abdullah Fadel Abbas

Head of presidential diwan: Ahmed Hussein al-Samarrai

Deputy head of presidential diwan: Adnan Daoud Salman

Chairman of national assembly: Saadi Mehdi Saleh

Chairman of Kurdish legislative council: Ahmed Abdul-Qader Naqshabandi

Informal High Command

Ad hoc decision-making body established and headed by Saddam Hussein since the invasion of Kuwait; a similar body was constituted during the war with Iran. Membership seems to include the Revolutionary Command Council, senior generals, Hussein Kamil Hassan (the industry and military industrialization minister, and acting oil minister), and Latif Nassif Jassem (the information and cultural minister).

Baath Party Revolutionary Command Council

Chairman: Saddam Hussein

Vice-chairman: Izzat Ibrahim

Secretary-general: Khaled Abdul-Moneim Rashid

Taha Yassin Ramadan
Tariq Aziz
Hassan Ali
Taha Mohieddin Maarouf
Saadoun Hammadi

Baath Party Regional Command

Secretary-general: Saddam Hussein

Deputy secretary-general: Izzat Ibrahim

Taha Yassin Ramadan
Tariq Aziz
Hassan Ali
Saadoun Shaker
Latif Nassif Jassem
Saadoun Hammadi
Samir Mohammed Abdul-Wahab
Mohammed Hamza al-Zubaidi
Saadi Mehdi Saleh
Abdul-Hassan Rahi Faroun
Mizban Khader Hadi
Ali Hassan al-Majid
Kamil Yassin Rashid
Abdul-Ghani Abdul-Ghafour

Reserve members
Fadel Barrak Hussein
Adnan Daoud Salman
Radhi Hassan Salman

Intelligence and Security

Intelligence: Sabawi Ibrahim

Military intelligence: Sabir Abdul-Aziz Hussein al-Duri

Public security: Ahmed Abdul Rahman al-Duri

Special security organization: Hussein Kamil Hassan

Police: Samir Mohammed Abdul-Wahab

Baath Regional Offices

Northern region: Hassan Ali

Central region: Kamil Yassin Rashid

Euphrates region: Abdul-Hassan Rahi Faroun

Southern region: Abdul-Ghani Abdul-Ghafour

Provinces, and Mayors/Governors

1 Dohuk (Kurdish autonomous area), Mohammed Ferouz Rostam

2 Irbil (Kurdish autonomous area), Mohammed Yahya al-Jaff

3 Sulaimaniyah (Kurdish autonomous area), Kaka Hamad Maalloud

4 Nineveh (in northwest, along Syrian border), Taher Tawfiq

5 Tamin (in north, center), Mundhir Musayyif Jassim

6 Saladin (north of Baghdad), Khaled Abdul-Moneim Rashid

7 Anbar (west of Baghdad), Adan Ghaiden

8 Diyala (east of Baghdad), Abdul-Rahim Abdul-Hamid

9 Baghdad (center), Khaled Abdul-Moneim Rashid

10 Wasit (east of Baghdad), unknown

11 Babil (south of Baghdad), Hisham Hassan al-Majid

12 Qadisiyya (south of Babil province), Zeki Faida al-Ali

13 Kerbala (southwest to Saudi border), Ghazi Mohammed Ali

14 Najaf (southwest to Saudi border), Thabit Fahd Ali

15 Misan (southeast, along Iranian border), Abdullah Mahmoud al-Mashadani

16 Dhiqar (in south, center), Taha Yassin Hussain

17 Muthanna (in south, along Saudi border), Khadhim Nima Salman

18 Basra (extreme southeast), Abdullah Tilib Azjan

19 Kuwait (after November 1990), Aziz Saleh al-Nouman

★ ★ ★

Brief Biographies

(as of February 1, 1991)

Principal Iraqi Political Figures

ABBAS, Abdullah Fadel, born 1941 in Samarra. Arab, Sunni. Dismissed from Revolutionary Command Council and Regional Command in June 1982; since then minister of religious endowments.

ABDUL-GHAFOUR, Abdul-Ghani, born 1944 in Baghdad. Arab, Sunni. Minister of religious endowments in 1982, since then member of Regional Command.

ABDUL-WAHAB, Samir Mohammed, born 1945 in Baghdad. Arab, Sunni. Mayor of Baghdad 1980–85. Minister of higher education 1985–87. Head of police and minister of interior since 1987.

ABDULLAH, Abdul-Wahab Mahmoud, born 1934 in Mosul. Arab, Sunni. Minister of agriculture and irrigation since April 1990.

ALI, Akram Abdul-Qader, born 1928 in Samarra. Arab, Sunni. Minister of justice since 1988.

ALI, Hassan, born 1938 in Baghdad. Arab, Shia. Member of Revolutionary Command Council and Regional Command from 1974. Lost job as minister of trade in 1987. Since 1989 head of Baath party in northern region. Head of National Progressive Front, the ruling coalition of the Baath party, the Kurdistan Democratic party, and the Kurdistan Revolutionary party.

AZIZ, Tariq, born 1936 in Mosul. Arab, Christian. Member of the Revolutionary Command Council since 1978 and of the Regional Command from 1977. Foreign minister since 1983.

FARAJ, Samal Majid, born 1936 in Sulaimaniya. Kurd. Minister of planning since 1982.

FAROUN, Abdul-Hassan Rahi, born 1942 near Najaf. Arab, Shia. Member of Regional Command since 1982. In charge of Baath party in Euphrates district since 1982.

HADI, Mizban Qader, born 1938 in Mandali. Arab, Shia. Member of Regional Command since 1982.

HAMMADI, Saadoun, born 1930 in Kerbala. Arab, Shia. Educated at University of Wisconsin. Member of Revolutionary Command Council and Regional Command. Deputy prime minister since 1989.

HASSAN, Hussein Kamil, born 1954 in Takrit. Arab, Sunni. Cousin and son-in-law of Saddam Hussein. In charge of expansion of Republican Guard in 1982. In charge of military industries in 1987. Minister of industry and military industrialization since 1988. Acting minister of oil since November 1990. Head of Al Amn Al Khas (Special Security Organization) since 1987. Holds military rank of lieutenant-general.

HUSSEIN, Fadel Barrak, born 1942 in Saladin province. Arab, Sunni. Related to Saddam Hussein by marriage. Graduate of military academy; doctoral degree in oriental studies from Soviet Science Academy. Reserve candidate to Regional Command since 1986. Head of intelligence from 1984 to 1988.

HUSSEIN, Qusai Saddam, born 1967 in Baghdad. Arab, Sunni. Son of Saddam Hussein. Believed to work in security services.

HUSSEIN, Saddam, born 1937 near Takrit. Arab, Sunni. President, prime minister, chairman of Revolutionary Command Council, secretary-general of Baath Regional Command, and commander-in-chief since 1979.

HUSSEIN, Udai Saddam, born 1964 in Baghdad. Arab, Sunni. Son of Saddam Hussein. Head of Iraq Football Federation and Olympic Committee since February 1990.

IBRAHIM, Barzan. Arab, Sunni. Half-brother of Saddam Hussein. Former head of intelligence. Ambassador to United Nations organizations in Geneva since 1988.

IBRAHIM, Izzat, born 1942 in Samarra. Arab, Sunni. Vice-chairman of Revolutionary Command Council since 1979.

IBRAHIM, Mundhir, born 1929 in Takrit. Arab, Sunni. Minister of higher education and scientific research since 1988.

IBRAHIM, Sabawi. Arab, Sunni. Half-brother to Saddam Hussein. Head of intelligence service since 1989.

IBRAHIM, Watban. Arab, Sunni. Half-brother to Saddam Hussein. Adviser in presidential palace since 1989.

IZZADIN, Abdul-Qader, born 1932. Arab. Minister of education since 1981.

JASSEM, Latif Nassif, born 1941 in Baghdad. Arab, Sunni. Member of Regional Command since 1986. Minister of information and culture since 1979.

MAROUF, Taha Moeddin, born 1924 in Sulaimaniya. Kurd, Sunni. Vice-president of Iraq since 1974.

AL-MAJID, Ali Hassan, born in 1941 in Takrit. Arab, Sunni. Cousin of Saddam Hussein. Member of Regional Command since

1986. Minister of local government since 1989. Governor of Kuwait from August to November 1990.

AL-MAJID, Hisham Hassan, born 1942 in Takrit. Arab, Sunni. Cousin of Saddam Hussein and brother of Ali Hassan al-Majid. Governor of Babil province.

AL-MARZOUK, Taher Mohammed Hassoun, born 1946 in Babil. Arab. Minister of housing and construction since 1988.

MUBARAK, Umeed Madhat, born 1939 in Sulaimaniya. Arab. Minister of labor and social affairs since 1988.

NAQSHABANDI, Ahmed Abdul-Qader, born 1929. Kurd. Chairman of Kurdish legislative council since 1977.

AL-NOUMAN, Aziz Saleh, born 1945 in Dhiqar province. Arab, possibly Shia. Former governor of Kerbala province and Najaf province, former minister of agriculture. Presidential adviser since 1987. Named governor of Kuwait in November 1990.

RAMADAN, Taha Yassin, born 1939 in Mosul. Arab, Sunni. First deputy prime minister since 1979. Member of Regional Command since 1968 and Revolutionary Command Council since 1969. Commander of Popular Army.

RASHID, Kamil Yassin, born 1931 near Takrit. Arab, Sunni. A former local government minister. Appointed director-general of Baath party regional leadership 1983. Member of Regional Command since 1986.

RASHID, Khaled Abdul-Moneim, born 1944 in Baghdad. Arab, Sunni. Secretary-general of the Revolutionary Command Council since 1982. Mayor of Baghdad since 1986.

SAEED, Abdul-Salem Mohammed. Arab. Minister of health since 1988.

SALEH, Mohammed Mehdi, born 1947 in Rawa, Anbar province. Arab, Shia. In presidential office 1981–87. Minister of trade since 1987, acting minister of finance since 1989. Chairman of national assembly.

SALEH, Saadi Mehdi, born 1940 in Takrit. Arab, Sunni. Member of Regional Command since 1982.

SALMAN, Adnan Daoud, born 1945 in Diyala province. Arab. Minister of local government 1983–89. Elected reserve member of Regional Command in 1986. Acting head of presidential office since October 1990.

SALMAN, Radhi Hassan, born 1939 in Kerbala. Arab. Elected member of Regional Command in 1986.

AL-SAMARRAI, Ahmed Hussein, born in Samarra. Arab, Sunni. Head of presidential office.

SHAKER, Saadoun, born 1939 in Baghdad. Arab, Shia. Minister of interior until 1987. Member of Revolutionary Command Council and Regional Command since 1977, but lost position on Revolutionary Command Council in August 1990.

SHANSHAL, Abdul-Jabbar Khalil, born 1920 in Mosul. Arab, Sunni. Former chief of staff. Minister of defense from 1989 until December 1990, when made minister of state.

AL-ZUBAIDI, Mohammed Hamza, born 1938 in Babil province. Arab, Shia. Member of Regional Command since 1982. Minister of transport and communications since 1987.

Principal Iraqi Military Leaders

No names of Iraqi corps commanders have appeared in the Iraqi press since the end of the war with Iran in mid-1988; recent appointments are cited where known.

ADIL, Yaljin Umar. In 1988, commander of sixth army corps.

AHMAD, Sultan Hashim. In 1988, commander of first army corps.

AZIZ, Kamil Sajit. In 1988, commander of second army corps.

AL-DHIRIB, Yunis Mohammed. In 1988, commander of fifth army corps.

AL-DURI, Sabir Abdul-Aziz Hussein. In 1988, head of military intelligence.

AL-JABBURI, Saadi Tuma Abbas. Shia. In 1988, commander of first special army corps, since disbanded; then inspector-general. Appointed defense minister in December 1990.

MAHMOUD, Salah Abboud. In 1988, commander of third army corps.

AL-MAINI, Abdul-Satter. Shia. In 1988, assistant chief of staff for administration and supplies.

MIRZA, Sabah. Kurd. In 1988, head of president's bodyguard. Reported pensioned off in June 1990, although opposition claims he was killed in a car accident.

MOHSIN, Abdul-Jabber. In 1988, head of political guidance in defense ministry.

RAIB, Raib Hassun. In 1988, commander of navy.

RASHID, Hussain. Kurd. Until 1987, commander of Republican Guard. Assistant chief of staff for operations in 1988. Made chief of staff in October 1990.

AL-RAWI, Iyad Ftayh Khalifa. Commander of Republican Guard since 1987.

SHAABAN, Hamid, born 1930s in Takrit. In 1988, head of air force. Stepped down in 1989 and made presidential adviser.

TAWFIQ, Arshad. Head of president's bodyguard since June 1990.

ZAKI, Iyad Khalil. In 1988, commander of fourth army corps.

Chronology

★ ★ ★

3000 BC	Earliest settlements in Mesopotamia.
1792–1750 BC	Hammurabi, founder of first legal system, rules in Babylon.
587 BC	Conquest of Jerusalem by Nebuchadnezzar (reigned 605–562).
AD 632	Mohammed, founder of Islam, dies; his supporters conquer Babylonia.
637	Arabs of Babylon victorious over Persians at battle of Qadisiyya.
749–1258	Abbasid caliphs rule from Babylon and Baghdad.
1258	Baghdad pillaged by Mongol invaders.
1634	Start of Ottoman Turkish rule over Baghdad.
1899	Ruler of Kuwait enters into agreement of protection with British.
1914	Kuwait declared an independent state under British protection. British troops occupy the Fao peninsula and Basra.
1920	League of Nations grants Britain a mandate to govern Iraq. Popular uprising against British rule quelled.
1921	King Faisal installed by the British as king of Iraq.
1922	Anglo-Iraqi treaty defining British powers.
1925	Oil discovered in Iraq.

1932   Iraq declared independent.

1933   Assyrian community in northeastern Iraq suppressed by central government. King Faisal I dies, succeeded by son, Ghazi.

1936   Bakr Sidqi takes political control of Iraq — the first military coup in the modern Arab world.

1937   Birth of Saddam Hussein in a village near Takrit.

1939   King Ghazi dies in car accident; infant son, Faisal, named as king, and father's cousin Abdul Illah appointed to act as regent.

1941   Pro-Nazi rebellion in Baghdad put down by British; several hundred Jews murdered in Baghdad (the Farhoud).

1947   Michel Aflaq forms the Baath party.

1948   Riots in Iraq against the Portsmouth Treaty, the new pact with Britain. The state of Israel founded.

1956   Egypt nationalizes Suez Canal.

1957   Saddam joins the Baath party.

1958   Iraqi monarchy overthrown by a military coup; General Qassem becomes prime minister and commander-in-chief.

1959   Saddam, as part of a hit squad, fails to assassinate Qassem.

1960   OPEC founded.

1961   Qassem threatens to invade Kuwait. Iraqi offensive against Kurds.

1963   Qassem overthrown by army and Baathists; Baathists pushed out by army nine months later.

1967   Israel defeats Eygpt, Syria, and Jordan in Six-Day War. Small Iraqi contingent also defeated.

1968   Baath party again seizes power in Iraq from military regime.

1969   Public hangings in Baghdad, including eleven Jews.

1972   Iraq-Soviet Friendship Treaty; Iraq nationalizes oil industry.

1973   October war between Israel, and Egypt and Syria. Iraqi contingent fights in support of Syria.

1974   Open rebellion by Kurds.

1975   Algiers agreement between Iraq and Iran: Iran cuts off support for Kurds, and Iraq gives up half the Shatt al-Arab waterway.

1978   Ayatollah Khomeini expelled from his exile in Iraq. Baghdad summit condemns Egypt for signing Camp David accords with Israel.

1979   Iranian revolution overthrows the shah. Saddam Hussein takes over from al-Bakr; Saddam purges Baath party and top leadership.

1980   Iraq invades Iran.

1981   Israeli jets destroy Iraq's Tuwaitha nuclear reactor.

1982   Iraqi army withdraws from Iranian territory.

1984   Iraq and US reestablish diplomatic relations after a break of seventeen years.

1987   Iraqi jet seriously damages USS *Stark* with Exocet missiles.

1988   Cease-fire in the Iran-Iraq War.

1990   Iraq invades Kuwait and declares it to be a province of Iraq.

1991   US-led forces attack Iraq; Iraq fires missiles at Israel and Saudi Arabia; US-led coalition defeats Iraqi army in Kuwait and southern Iraq.

★ ★ ★
Notes

CHAPTER 2

1. Ofra Bengio in the *Jerusalem Post*, September 26, 1990.

CHAPTER 3

1. At least two classic books describe their existence: one, *The Marsh Arabs* (Penguin Books, 1967), is by the famous explorer Wilfred Thesiger, who lived among the Madan for much of the 1950s. Another, *A Reed Shaken by the Wind* (Penguin Books, 1983), is by the celebrated writer Gavin Maxwell, who joined Thesiger on one of his tours and, to the evident annoyance of Thesiger, produced an excellent book.

CHAPTER 4

1. All energy statistics in this chapter are taken from the *BP Statistical Review of World Energy*, June 1990, which draws much of its data from the *Oil and Gas Journal*.

2. Judgment of the author, who met Chalabi in Baghdad in 1986, before he became minister, and again in Washington, DC, in 1988.

3. "Saddam Hussein on Peace, Weapons and War," *Wall Street Journal* [European edition], June 29, 1990.

4. View of events by a foreign oil executive who is a frequent visitor to Baghdad.

CHAPTER 5

1. Interview of Saddam Hussein by Majid Khadduri of Johns Hopkins University.

CHAPTER 6

1. This account of the assassination attempt is taken from Uriel Dann's *Iraq under Qassem*. Dann, an Israeli academic, made extensive use of contemporary newspaper reports.

2. This account of the assassination attempt comes from Fuad Matar, *Saddam Hussein: The Man, the Cause, and the Future*.

3. See Matar, *Saddam Hussein*.

4. Much of the description of the coup is taken from an account given to the author by an English resident in Baghdad at the time.

5. See Matar, *Saddam Hussein*.

6. See Matar, *Saddam Hussein*.

CHAPTER 7

1. Fuad Matar, *Saddam Hussein: The Man, the Cause, and the Future*.

2. Remark made by a former diplomat to the author in 1988.

3. Told to the author in December 1990.

4. Interviewed by the author, July 1989.

5. The seven stages are: his birth; the attempt to assassinate Qassem; the July 17, 1968, revolution; the consolidation of Baathist power on July 30, 1968; his assumption of the presidency in 1979; the start of the war with Iran in 1979; and the end of the war in 1988.

CHAPTER 8

1. US official, speaking on condition of not being identified, December 1988.

2. *Al Thawra*, April 23, 1988.

CHAPTER 9

1. Much of the information in this chapter comes from a number of prominent Israelis who discussed their country's links to Iraq on the condition that they not be identified.

2. US Department of State, *Country Reports on Human Rights Practices, 1989*.

3. Phebe Marr, *The Modern History of Iraq*, p. 10.

4. *Mideast Markets*, February 8, 1988.

5. Interview with the author in London, 1988.

6. *Middle East Contemporary Survey*, 1988, p. 639.

7. Radio Baghdad, January 6, 1988.

CHAPTER 10

1. The author interviewed some of these refugees at Qasr-e-Shirin in early 1980.

2. Seen by the author in 1980.

3. Described to the author by a British foreign office official in 1989.

4. The author, covering the southern Gulf for the *Financial Times* [London] from the vantage point of Bahrain, reported this version of events at the time. The Iraqi aircraft refueled at Bahrain airport on their way south. *Financial Times,* September 29, 1980.

5. Robert Graham, *Iran: The Illusion of Power* (London: Croom Helm, 1979).

6. The author visited Baghdad at this time.

7. Told to the author in 1990 by a former diplomat based in Baghdad.

8. Described to the author by a former Western diplomat who had analyzed the raw intelligence data.

9. This interpretation of events at Halabja is compatible with the official US government view. The author's source, a diplomat who investigated the Halabja incident soon after it happened, quoted the thirteenth-century Persian poet Saadi, as a way of explaining the callousness of the act: "Expediency mixed with a falsehood is better than the truth which stirs up trouble."

10. The marriage took place in 1986. The couple were said to have separated after the ouster of General Rashid in 1988.

CHAPTER 11

1. "Iraqis 'Oust' Saddam and Make Peace Offer to Iranians," *Financial Times* [London], June 10, 1982.

2. Section on Iraq in *Middle East Contemporary Survey,* 1982.

3. *Official Report of Baath Party Ninth Regional Congress.*

CHAPTER 12

1. Conversation with a Western intelligence official in December 1990.

2. Interview in May 1989 with an Austrian engineer who had worked on the Condor project.

3. Interview by the author with an intelligence officer in November 1990.

4. Interview with an Austrian engineer in May 1989.

5. *Flight International,* October 1990.

6. Briefing by officials in London, March 1990.

7. Conversation with an intelligence official, November 1990.

8. Conversation with a Western official, May 1990.

9. Conversation with an intelligence official, November 1990.

10. Briefing given to author by Western officials in November 1990.

11. Conversation with a Western intelligence official, February 1985.

12. Interview with a Pakistani official, September 1990.

13. Interview with a British foreign office official, November 1990.

14. Interview with US official, December 1989.

CHAPTER 13

1. The incident was described to the author in May 1990 by one of the British Customs team involved in the interception.

2. Conversation with a British official in November 1990.

3. Interview with a British official in May 1990.

4. Interview with a British official in May 1990.

5. The official, who was asked by the author for a public comment, gave it on the basis that he not be identified. There was a delay of twenty-four hours before the comment was ready.

6. Conversation with a British official in March 1990.

7. Conversation with a British official in April 1990.

8. *Financial Times* [London], May 26, 1990.

9. Conversation with a Western intelligence official in July 1990.

10. Conversation with a Western intelligence official in November 1990.

11. These photographs were shown to the author in May 1990.

12. Speech by Saddam Hussein to Iraqi army commanders on April 1, 1990, broadcast on Radio Baghdad on April 2, 1990.

CHAPTER 14

1. Interview with the author, May 1989.

2. Interview by the author with Smith, April 1989.

3. The author, along with colleagues at the *Financial Times,* broke the story of the BNL's role in the funding of suspicious Iraqi purchases, in "U.K. Link Alleged on Unauthorised Lending by BNL," *Financial Times* [London], September 8, 1989.

4. Comments by bankers to the author during 1989 and 1990.

5. Interview with a British banker, August 1990.

6. Interviewed with Fadel Khaddoum in London, July 1989.

7. Report in possession of the author.

8. I am grateful to the German investigative journalist Egmont R. Koch for this information.

9. First reported in the German magazine *Der Spiegel* in December 1989.

CHAPTER 15

1. Conversation with Soviet diplomat in London in 1989.

2. Publisher's note: Information about exports of US technology to Iraq was obtained by Mercury House from the Natural Resources Defense Council, a non-profit organization in Washington, which had filed a request under the Freedom of Information Act on January 15, 1991. In March the Secretary of Commerce released summaries of 771 export permits. As a result, Mercury House was able to make this previously classified information available to the author.

CHAPTER 16

1. In possession of the author.

2. *Report of the Congressional Committees Investigating the Iran-Contra Affair* (November 1987), page 255.

3. Much of the information and opinion in this chapter comes from conversations with American officials over a number of years. The officials spoke on condition that they not be identified.

4. Told to the author by diplomats in Baghdad, July 1986.

5. Conversation with Peter Galbraith, staff member of the US Senate Foreign Relations Committee, in December 1990.

6. The author spoke at a conference organized by the US-Iraq Business Forum in May 1988, at the request of the Washington-based Middle East Institute. The author's paper discussed Iraq's economic liberalization, restructuring, and privatization policies.

7. "War in the Persian Gulf: The US Takes Sides," staff report to the Committee on Foreign Relations, United States Senate, November 1987.

8. *Mideast Markets,* October 30, 1989.

9. *Mideast Markets,* June 26, 1989.

10. Baghdad *Observer,* April 18 and 19, 1990.

11. Based on interviews with diplomats, US officials, and visitors to the embassy. All spoke on the condition that they not be identified.

12. *Mideast Markets,* February 8, 1988.

13. Transcript of meeting obtained by ABC News and published in the *New York Times,* September 23, 1990. The authenticity of the transcript is not disputed by the State Department.

CHAPTER 17

1. Printed sources for incidents mentioned in this chapter include Middle East Watch, *Human Rights in Iraq* (New Haven: Yale University Press, 1990), and

Walid al-Hilli, *Human Rights in Iraq, 1968–1988,* a booklet published privately in London in 1990.

2. Told to the author by a frequent visitor to Iraq who had learned of the practice from the foreign representative of a medical supplies company. One of the company's products, for giving blood transfusions, had been altered so that it sucked rather than pumped blood, the businessman alleged.

3. The scale of the destruction of the villages was witnessed by Peter Galbraith, a staff member of the US Senate Foreign Relations Committee, who wrote a report on the subject.

4. The first use of such camps dates back at least to 1973, when the main Kurdish rebellion failed. A diplomat, then resident in Baghdad and living on the outskirts of the city, recalled to the author how he had been awakened at night by the sound of heavy trucks. He walked to the main road and saw hundreds of vehicles, each crammed with Kurds under armed guard, driving southward. The convoys went on for several nights.

CHAPTER 18

1. Details of the nuclear capacitors case are taken from indictments issued on March 23, 1990. The indictments were against five individuals and two companies in Britain, alleging conspiracy to export without a license, to transfer funds for unlawful activity, and related offenses. The cases were taken up by the British authorities because none of the people were in the United States.

2. *Sunday Times,* London, December 16, 1990.

3. Information given to the author by a former British official on condition that he not be identified.

4. At the time of Bazoft's arrest, the British foreign secretary had been John Major, who became prime minister after Margaret Thatcher in November 1990.

5. US official, speaking with the author on the condition that he not be identified, December 1990.

6. US official, who spoke on the condition of not being identified, in conversation with author, August 1990.

7. Told to the author by a person at the dinner.

8. Western intelligence official, in conversation with author, April 1990.

9. Western official, in conversation with author, December 1990.

CHAPTER 19

1. Comment made to the author, March 1990.

2. Comment made to the author in a discussion of the Gulf situation.

3. Interview with ITN, a British television news program, November 1990.

4. Told in confidence to the author, so that he could use the figures when addressing a conference on Iraq at the Royal Institution for International Affairs, London, in March 1990.

5. *Financial Times,* August 18, 1990.

6. Told to the author by a US official who spoke on the condition that he not be identified.

7. Interview in *al-Mussawar,* an Egyptian magazine, quoted in *Financial Times,* August 18, 1990.

CHAPTER 20

1. Radio Baghdad, February 24, 1991.

2. Address to the nation after the ground fighting began, February 23, 1991.

3. From a transcript of the meeting, published in the *New York Times,* September 23, 1991.

4. Phrase used by Saddam Hussein in broadcast on Radio Baghdad on February 22, 1991.

5. Arab Press Service profile, April 13, 1987.

6. Taken from an unpublished consultancy document.

7. In conversation with the author, October 1990, the former diplomat spoke on condition that he not be identified.

8. Conversation with a former diplomat, who spoke on condition that he not be identified, November 1990.

9. "The Mind of Saddam," BBC Television Panorama program, February 11, 1991.

10. US intelligence official, who spoke with author in Washington in December 1990 on condition that he not be identified.

11. *Al Thawra,* April 17, 1990. Saddam was writing to his sons as Iraq was pushing Iranian forces out of the Fao peninsula.

12. *Al Thawra,* May 17, 1988. Saddam's height was given as 5 feet 10 inches, and his weight was 170 pounds.

13. Interview, "Saddam Hussein on Peace, Weapons, and War," *Wall Street Journal* [European edition], June 29, 1990.

14. Interview with Diane Sawyer, "PrimeTime Live," June 28, 1990. The two-hour interview was edited to a few minutes on US television. It was broadcast in its entirety on Iraqi television, except for the remarks about criticizing the US president and about American Indians, according to a US official familiar with the situation who spoke on condition that he not be identified.

15. According to a former British diplomat, who spoke on condition that he not be identified.

★ ★ ★
Bibliography

Among the many books on Iraq and Saddam Hussein, the following are the more useful:

Armstrong, Scott, ed. *The Chronology: The Documented Day-by-Day
Account of the Secret Military Assistance to Iran and the Contras.* New
York, Warner Books, 1987.
   Vital to understanding the way Iraq was affected by the Iran-Contra
affair.

Axelgard, Frederick W. *A New Iraq? The Gulf War and Implications for
US Policy.* New York: Praeger, 1988.
   One of the series of Washington Papers from The Center for Strategic
and International Studies. The author of this sympathetic account is now a
Bush appointee as director of the Office of Weapons Proliferation Policy at
the State Department.

Batatu, Hanna. *The Old Social Classes and the Revolutionary Movements
of Iraq.* Princeton: Princeton University Press, 1978.
   The classic academic study of the political background of Saddam and
the Baath party.

Bull, Gerald, and Charles Murphy. *Paris Kanonen — the Paris Guns
(Wilhelmgeschütze) and Project HARP.* Bonn: Mittler, 1988.
   The book that gives the technical explanation of Iraq's supergun,
Project Babylon. Author Gerald Bull was assassinated, probably by the
Israeli Mossad, in March 1990.

Dann, Uriel. *Iraq Under Qassem: A Political History, 1958–1963*. New York: Praeger, 1969.

An account, based on contemporary newspapers, by a scrupulous Israeli academic.

Farouk-Sluglett, Marion, and Peter Sluglett. *Iraq since 1958.* London: I. B. Tauris, 1987, 1990.

Academic and highly critical.

Fromkin, David. *A Peace to End All Peace.* New York: Holt, 1989.

Excellent book for understanding the breakup of the Ottoman empire and the establishment of Iraq.

Gazit, Shlomo, and Zeev Eytan. *The Middle East Military Balance, 1988–1989.* Jaffee Center for Strategic Studies, The Jerusalem Post. [annual]. Boulder, Colorado: Westview Press, 1989.

An Israeli publication that provides much basic core detail on Iraq's infrastructure and its military arsenal.

Gilbert, Martin. *The Arab-Israeli Conflict, Its History in Maps.* Jerusalem: Steimatzky, 1984.

Good maps to show Iraq's involvement in wars with Israel.

Gilbert, Martin. *Jewish History Atlas.* London: Weidenfeld and Nicholson, 1976.

Good maps on history of Iraq's Jewish community.

Helms, Christine Moss. *Iraq: Eastern Flank of the Arab World.* Washington, DC: The Brookings Institution, 1984.

Analysis and description by American expert on Baath party who has interviewed many top Iraqis, including Saddam.

Hillel, Shlomo. *Operation Babylon.* New York: Bantam, Doubleday, 1987.

Description of emigration of Iraqi Jewish community after 1948.

Holden, David, and Richard Johns. *The House of Saud.* London: Sidgwick and Jackson, 1981.

Strong reporting on the earliest relations between Saudi Arabia and Iraq, and the agreement on the border between them.

Ismail, Tareq Y. *Iraq and Iran: Roots of Conflict.* Syracuse, New York: Syracuse University Press, 1982.

Good history of the border disputes between the two countries.

Izzard, Molly. *The Gulf, Arabia's Western Approaches.* London: John Murray, 1979.

Detailed descriptions of the Gulf states as they were being set up and their borders drawn.

Khadduri, Majid. *Independent Iraq, 1932–1958, a Study in Iraqi Politics.* London: Oxford University Press, 1960.

Khadduri, Majid. *Republican Iraq, a Study in Iraqi Politics since the Revolution in 1958.* London: Oxford University Press, 1969.

Khadduri, Majid. *Socialist Iraq, A Study in Iraqi Politics since 1968.* Washington, DC: Middle East Institute, 1978.

Close examination of all three of Khadduri's books is worthwhile for anyone interested in the history of Iraq during the last sixty years.

al-Khalil, Samir. *Republic of Fear.* Berkeley: University of California Press, 1989.

Written by an Iraqi exile using a pseudonym, this book presents a devastating critique of Saddam's regime, although much of the analysis may be impenetrable to all but academic experts.

Lacey, Robert. *The Kingdom.* London: Hutchinson, 1981.

Traces the history of Iraq's tensions with Saudi Arabia.

Lewis, Bernard. *Semites and Anti-Semites.* London: Weidenfeld and Nicholson, 1986.

Scholarly examination of anti-Semitism among Arab Semites.

Marr, Phebe. *The Modern History of Iraq.* Boulder, Colorado: Westview, 1985.

A standard work; the author is now adviser to the Pentagon.

Matar, Fuad. *Saddam Hussein: The Man, the Cause, and the Future.* London: Third World Center, 1981.

An uncritical biography; copies were given out to the press by Iraqi officials in Baghdad.

Middle East. Paris: Hachette World Guides, 1966.

Travel guide with otherwise hard-to-find, though dated, descriptions of many places in Iraq.

Middle East Contemporary Survey. Dayan Center, Tel Aviv University [annual].

Standard work by team of mostly Israeli experts using Arabic newspapers as the core source material.

Middle East and North Africa Yearbook. London: Europa [annual].

Standard work, regularly updated, with background detail.

Middle East Watch. *Human Rights in Iraq.* New Haven and London: Yale University Press, 1990.

Critique of Saddam's record and policies, and Washington's mistakes, produced after the invasion of Kuwait.

Miller, Judith, and Laurie Mylroie. *Saddam Hussein and the Crisis in the Gulf.* New York: Random House, 1990.

First "instant" book to emerge after the invasion of Kuwait. No sources given.

Nyrop, Richard F., ed. *Iraq, a Country Study.* Washington, DC: The American University, 1979.

Standard work, part of a series produced for American officials.

Pelletiere, Stephen C., Douglas V. Johnson II, Leif R. Rosenberger. *Iraqi Power and US Security in the Middle East.* US Army War College. Washington, DC: Government Printing Office, 1990.

This booklet praises Iraq for winning the war with Iran and emphasizes that the US should recognize this achievement, without saying how.

Report of the Congressional Committees Investigating the Iran-Contra Affair. Washington, DC: Government Printing Office, 1987.

The expurgated version of what Congress learned, often in closed session.

Roosevelt, Archie. *For Lust of Knowing: Memoirs of an Intelligence Officer.* London: Weidenfeld and Nicholson, 1988.

Marvelous descriptions of life in Iraq in the 1940s, of Baghdad, the Marsh Arabs, and the Kurds.

Spector, Leonard S., with Jacqueline R. Smith. *Nuclear Ambitions: The Spread of Nuclear Weapons, 1989–1990.* Boulder, Colorado: Westview Press, 1990.

Standard work of carefully checked information on nuclear weapons development in third world countries, including Iraq.

Woolfson, Marion, *Prophets in Babylon: Jews in the Arab World.* London: Faber and Faber, 1980.

Written by an anti-Zionist Jew; an Iraqi official handed out copies free of charge at a conference at Exeter University, England, in July 1982.

World Factbook, 1990. Central Intelligence Agency: Washington, DC, 1990.

Available publicly, this volume is produced annually and gives basic data for all countries in the world, including the Iraq–Saudi Arabia Neutral Zone.

World Military Expenditures and Arms Transfers, 1989. US Arms Control and Disarmament Agency: Washington, DC, 1990.

Analysis of weapons transfers and essays, produced annually. A source of basic information.

The Economist Intelligence Unit (EIU) in London has published several detailed reports on Iraq in the last ten years, all of which provide excellent basic material and analysis: *Iraq, a New Market in a Region of Turmoil* (1980); Keith McLachlan and George Joffee, *The Gulf War: A Survey of Political Issues and Economic Consequences* (1984); and *Iran and Iraq, the Next Five Years* (1987).

After Iraq's invasion of Kuwait, the EIU printed a briefing by Mehran Nakhjavani, *Iraq: What If Sanctions Fail?* The parent organization of the EIU, Business International, has published a research report, *Iraq: Postwar Opportunities* (1989).

★ ★ ★
Index

Members of Iraq's political leadership as of early 1991 are listed in the index only where their names appear in the text. For positions in the government and brief biographies, please refer to the appendices.

★ ★ ★
About the Author

Photo: Cresswell Studios Ltd.

Simon Henderson was the London *Financial Times* correspondent in Iran from 1978 to 1980, covering the revolution and the hostage crisis. He received a US government travel award to study the Middle East and arms control as well as a Dayan Fellowship at Tel Aviv University to research Saddam Hussein. Henderson has lectured around the world on the Middle East and was one of the Middle East advisers for the BBC during the war over Kuwait. He is editor of the *Financial Times East European Markets* newsletter.